# Introducing Multimodality

This accessible introduction to multimodality illuminates the potential of multimodal research for understanding the ways in which people communicate. Readers will become familiar with the key concepts and methods in various domains while learning how to engage critically with the notion of multimodality.

The book challenges widely held assumptions about language and presents the practical steps involved in setting up a multimodal study, including:

- formulating research questions;
- collecting research materials;
- assessing and developing methods of transcription;
- considering the ethical dimensions of multimodal research.

A self-study guide is also included, designed as an optional stand-alone resource or as the basis for a short course. With a wide range of examples, clear practical support and a glossary of terms, *Introducing Multimodality* is an ideal reference for undergraduate and postgraduate students in multimodality, semiotics, applied linguistics and media and communication studies. Online materials, including colour images and more links to relevant resources, are available on the companion website at www.routledge.com/cw/jewitt and the Routledge Language and Communication Portal.

Carey Jewitt is Professor of Technology and Learning at University College London, Institute of Education. She has authored/edited a number of books on multimodality, including *The Routledge Handbook of Multimodal Analysis* (2009/2014), *Technology, Literacy and Learning: A Multimodal Approach* (2008), *Urban English Classrooms: Multimodal Teaching and Learning* (2005), with Gunther Kress and colleagues, and *The Rhetorics of the Science Classroom: A Multimodal Approach* (2001), with Gunther Kress and colleagues.

Jeff Bezemer is Reader in Learning and Communication and Co-Director of the Centre for Multimodal Research at University College London, Institute of Education. He is co-author of *Multimodality, Learning and Communication* (with Gunther Kress, 2015).

Kay O'Halloran is Associate Professor of Communication Studies at Curtin University, Western Australia. Her publications include *Multimodal Analysis Image* (2012), *Multimodal Studies: Exploring Issues and Domains* (2011), *Mathematical Discourse: Language, Symbolism and Visual Images* (2005) and *Multimodal Discourse Analysis* (2004).

# Introducing Multimodality

**CAREY JEWITT, JEFF BEZEMER
and KAY O'HALLORAN**

Routledge
Taylor & Francis Group

LONDON AND NEW YORK

First published 2016
by Routledge
2 Park Square, Milton Park, Abingdon, Oxon OX14 4RN

and by Routledge
711 Third Avenue, New York, NY 10017

*Routledge is an imprint of the Taylor & Francis Group, an informa business*

*British Library Cataloguing-in-Publication Data*
A catalogue record for this book is available from the British Library

*Library of Congress Cataloging-in-Publication Data*
Names: Bezemer, Josephus Johannes, 1976– | Jewitt, Carey, editor. | O'Halloran, Kay L., editor
Title: Introducing multimodality / by Jeff Bezemer, Carey Jewitt and Kay O'Halloran.
Description: Milton Park, Abingdon, Oxon ; New York, NY : Routledge, [2016] | Includes bibliographical references and index.
Identifiers: LCCN 2015039260 | ISBN 9780415639231 (hbk) | ISBN 9780415639262 (pbk) | ISBN 9781315638027 (ebk)
Subjects: LCSH: Modality (Linguistics) | Cognitive grammar. | Discourse analysis. | Psycholinguistics.
Classification: LCC P299.M6 B44 2016 | DDC 415—dc23
LC record available at http://lccn.loc.gov/2015039260

ISBN: 978-0-415-63923-1 (hbk)
ISBN: 978-0-415-63926-2 (pbk)
ISBN: 978-1-315-63802-7 (ebk)

Typeset in Akzidenz Grotesk
by Apex CoVantage, LLC

MIX
Paper from
responsible sources
FSC® C013056
www.fsc.org

Printed and bound in Great Britain by
TJ International Ltd, Padstow, Cornwall

# Contents

# Illustrations

## Figures

## Tables

# About this book

This book is about multimodality. Taking stock of two decades of theorizing and researching, we sketch the history and current state of affairs in a fast growing academic field. Our focus is on three distinct traditions in which multimodality has been taken up: systemic functional linguistics, social semiotics and conversation analysis. We outline the history, key concepts and methods of each; point to seminal studies and critiques; and reflect on their synergies and differences. We also identify ways in which these focal approaches have been transformed through amalgamation with or incorporation into other research traditions. Throughout the book, we illustrate concepts and methods with examples from a variety of different studies, reflecting the breadth of domains that have now been explored from a multimodal perspective.

The book is written for anyone who is interested in language, communication and meaning, including undergraduate and postgraduate students in applied and sociolinguistics. No prior specialist knowledge in linguistics or semiotics is required or assumed.

The aim of the book is to help you to:

- Engage critically with the notion of multimodality, with reference to seminal studies on multimodality
- Recognize similarities and differences in theoretical and methodological positions
- Identify and describe how multimodality has been taken up in systemic functional linguistics, social semiotics and conversation analysis
- Assess the quality of multimodal research, notably aptness of fit between research questions, theories and methods
- Reflect on the potentialities, challenges and future directions of multimodal research
- Understand how to go about designing a multimodal study

The book consists of seven chapters.

In Chapter 1, 'Navigating a diverse field', we discuss the history of the notion of multimodality and formulate key premises that can be used to differentiate between different types of multimodal studies and consider one's own position in the diverse field of multimodality.

In Chapter 2, 'Why engage with multimodality?', we provide a rationale for doing multimodal research. We challenge widely held assumptions about language and review the arguments for taking a multimodal approach.

In Chapters 3 to 5, we set out three distinct approaches to multimodality. Chapter 3 introduces *systemic functional linguistics*, Chapter 4 introduces *social semiotics*, and Chapter 5 *conversation analysis*. In each of these chapters, we outline the key principles, concepts and methods of the respective approaches. We also illustrate their areas of application, as well as their limitations.

In Chapter 6, 'Five more approaches to multimodality', we explore the ways in which the three focal approaches discussed in Chapters 3 to 5 have been taken forward by combining them with other traditions. Thus we present five more approaches to multimodality: geo-semiotics; multimodal (inter)actional analysis; multimodal ethnography; a corpus-based approach to multimodality; and multimodal reception analysis. We introduce each of these approaches with attention to their origins, methods used and their distinct contribution to multimodality.

In Chapter 7, 'Designing a multimodal study', we present the steps involved in setting up a multimodal study. This includes deciding on a theoretical frame for your study, formulating research focus and questions, collecting research materials, assessing methods of transcription and considering the ethical dimensions of multimodal research.

In addition to these seven chapters, the book includes a *self-study guide*, designed as an optional stand-alone resource or basis for a short course. You can use this resource as a guide to reading the book and engaging with the issues raised by it. It consists of seven comprehensive study units: one for each chapter. Each unit provides the following set of resources: a chapter overview, with chapter topics and a summary; a set of study questions; a series of 'hands-on' exercises; tips; and suggested resources, including readings and online resources. If you consider using the self-study guide, we suggest you first read the book, and then work through the self-study guide units in the order that they are presented, rereading the accompanying chapter as you tackle each study unit.

The book also includes a glossary of terms.

# Acknowledgements

We would like to acknowledge the following copyright holders for permission to reprint the following material:

- The World Health Organization for the reproduction of three images from *WHO / Ebola* [Internet] in Figures 3.1b, 3.2a and 3.3a. Available from http://apps.who.int/ebola/ [cited 19 June 2015]. The WHO website operated during a certain period of Ebola outbreak, but it is no longer operational. For up-to-date WHO information on Ebola, please refer to the following website: http://www.who.int/csr/disease/ebola/
- Diane Mavers and SAGE Publications for the transcript in Figure 4.1.
- Heinemann Educational Publishers for the reproduction of an image from *Salters GCSE Science: Y11* student book in Figure 4.2a.
- Gunther Kress for the reproduction of his reorganized images of the digestive system in Figure 4.2b. and 4.2c. Reprinted from Gunther Kress (2014).
- Christian Heath and colleagues for the reproduction of a transcript in Figure 5.3
- Sigrid Norris for the reproduction of a transcript in Figure 6.1.

Every effort has been made to contact copyright holders. Please advise the publisher of any errors or omissions, and these will be corrected in subsequent editions.

# CHAPTER 1

# Navigating a diverse field

## What is multimodality?

'Multimodality' is a term that is now widely used in the academic world. The number of publication titles featuring the term has grown exponentially since it was first coined in the mid-1990s. Since then, a myriad of conferences, monographs, edited volumes and other academic discussion forums have been produced that are dedicated to multimodality. Signs of its becoming a shorthand term for a distinct field include the publication of the first edition of the *Handbook of Multimodal Analysis* (Jewitt, 2009), now a revised second edition (Jewitt, 2014), the launch of the Routledge *Series in Multimodality Studies* (2011) and the launch of a journal titled *Multimodal Communication* (2012). These and many other outlets inviting contributions in the area of multimodality provide platforms for scholars working in different disciplines, including semiotics, linguistics, media studies, new literacy studies, education, sociology and psychology, addressing a wide range of different research questions.

With the term being used so frequently and widely, it may seem as though a shared phenomenon of interest has been recognized and a common object of study identified. Indeed, we can, in relatively generic terms, describe that phenomenon, or object of interest, as something like, 'We *make meaning* in a variety of ways', or, 'We *communicate* in a variety of ways'. Yet we must immediately add that 'multimodality' (and related concepts, including 'mode'/'modality', '[semiotic] resource') is differently construed. Exactly how the concept is articulated and 'operationalized' varies widely, both across and within the different disciplines and research traditions in which the term is now commonly used. Therefore, it is very difficult and potentially problematic to talk about multimodality without making explicit one's theoretical and methodological stance.

Before going any further, we turn to those who first used the term and explore what it was that they were trying to draw attention to. As far as we can reconstruct, the term first appeared in the middle to late 1990s in different parts of the world. It is used, for instance, by Charles Goodwin, in a seminal article that he submitted to the *Journal of Pragmatics* in 1998 (Goodwin, 2000). It also features in Gunther Kress and Theo van Leeuwen's *Multimodal Discourse: The Modes and Media of Contemporary Communication* (2001), the manuscript of which had been 'in the making' for a number of years. These scholars started using the term more or less independently of each other, with Goodwin in the US working in the tradition of ethnomethodology and conversation analysis, and Kress and van Leeuwen (then) in the UK in the tradition of social semiotics. Around this same time, O'Halloran, working (then) in Australia and drawing on earlier work by O'Toole (1994) and Kress and van Leeuwen (1996), began to use the term 'multisemiotic' to describe the multimodal character of mathematics texts (see, for instance, O'Halloran [1999b], published in *Semiotica*).

If a 'means for making meaning' is a 'modality', or 'mode', as it is usually called, then we might say that the term 'multimodality' was used to highlight that people use multiple means of meaning making. But that formulation alone does not accurately describe the conceptual shift these scholars were trying to mark and promote. After all, disciplines such as linguistics, semiotics and sociology have studied different forms of meaning making since well before the term 'multimodality' was introduced. Indeed, Ferdinand de Saussure (1857–1913), writing in the early 20th century, already suggested that 'linguistics' was a 'branch' of a more general science he called semiology. Yet the branches of that imaginary science have continued to *specialize* in the study of one or a small set of means for making meaning: linguistics on speech and writing, semiotics on image and film, musicology on music; and new subdisciplines have emerged: visual sociology, which is concerned with, for example, photography; visual anthropology, which is concerned with, for example, dress. These (sub)disciplines focus on the means of meaning making that fall within their 'remit'; they do not systematically investigate synergies between the modes that fall inside and outside that remit.

Multimodality questions that a strict 'division of labour' among the disciplines traditionally focused on meaning making, on the grounds that in the world we're trying to account for, *different means of meaning making* are not separated but almost *always appear together*: image with writing, speech with gesture, math symbolism with writing and so forth. It is that recognition of the need for studying how different kinds of meaning making are combined into an *integrated, multimodal whole* that scholars attempted to highlight when they started using the term 'multimodality'. It was a recognition of the need to move beyond the empirical boundaries of existing disciplines and develop theories and methods that can account for the ways in which we use gesture, inscription, speech and other means together in order to produce meanings that cannot be accounted for by any of the existing disciplines. This fact only became more noticeable with the introduction of digital technologies, which enable people to combine means of making meaning that were more difficult or impossible to disseminate before – for the majority of people anyway (moving image being one pertinent example). So that is how the introduction of the notion of multimodality marks a significant turn in theorizing and analysing meaning.

What the early adopters of the term recognized was not only the need to look at the co-occurrence and interplay of different means of making meaning but also that each 'mode' offers *distinct possibilities and constraints*. It had often been argued (e.g. by Saussure and Vygotsky) that language has, ultimately, the highest 'reach', that it can serve the widest range of communicative functions or that it enables the highest, most complex forms of thinking and is therefore the 'most important'. Others, including Goodwin, Kress, van Leeuwen and others who first introduced the notion of multimodality, have pointed out that there are *differences* between semiotic resources in terms of the possibilities they offer for making meaning but that it is not the case that one resource has *more or less* potential than the other. The same point was made by O'Halloran, who in her definition of 'multisemiotic' emphasized the significance of the combination of different resources, each with their own potential. Thus multimodality marks a departure from the traditional opposition of 'verbal' and 'non-verbal' communication, which presumes that the verbal is primary and that all other means of making meaning can be dealt with by one and the same term.

We can now formulate three *key premises* of multimodality:

1   Meaning is made with different semiotic resources, each offering distinct potentialities and limitations.
2   Meaning making involves the production of multimodal wholes.
3   If we want to study meaning, we need to attend to all semiotic resources being used to make a complete whole.

We should add four important footnotes to this. First, not everyone working in multimodality uses the notion of meaning making. Depending on their disciplinary background and focus, they might say that they are interested in 'multimodal *communication*', 'multimodal *discourse*', or 'multimodal *interaction*'. We will use the term 'meaning making' unless we are writing about a specific approach to multimodality. Nor does everyone working in multimodality use the term 'mode': some prefer to talk about 'resource', or 'semiotic resource', and generally avoid drawing strong boundaries between different resources, highlighting instead the significance of the multimodal whole ('gestalt'). Indeed, for that very reason, some scholars whose work we subsume under the heading of 'multimodality' do not use that term themselves, while otherwise committing to the three key premises we just presented.

Second, scholarly interest in the connections between different means of making meaning predates the notion of multimodality. For instance, the study of gesture and its relation to speech, gaze and the built environment has a long history in linguistic anthropology, interactional sociology and other disciplines (see e.g. Goffman, 1981; Kendon, 2004a; Mehan, 1980); the relation between image and writing has been studied in semiotics (e.g. Barthes, 1977 [1964]) and so on. These early contributions have produced important insights in what we now call multimodality. At the same time, we should note that the potential empirical scope of multimodality goes further still. We can see a development from an exclusive interest in language to an interest in language and its relations to other means of making meaning, to an interest in making meaning more generally, without a clear base point, whether language or any other mode.

Third, while those using the term 'multimodality' generally aim to develop a framework that accounts for the ways in which people combine distinctly different kinds of meaning making, their *epistemological perspectives* (i.e. their perspective on how we can know the world) are different. As we shall see later on in this chapter, in some approaches to multimodality the assumption is that it is possible and indeed necessary to develop an integrated theoretical and methodological framework for *some* kinds of meaning making, for instance for the study of speech, gesture, gaze and the material environment. In other approaches, the assumption is that it is possible and necessary to develop an encompassing theoretical and methodological framework to account for *all* kinds of meaning making – whether in image or in gesture or in writing or in any other mode. So researchers who adopt the notion of multimodality (or whose work is treated by others as being part of the field of multimodality) still draw different boundaries around what it is in the empirical world that they aim to account for. This is not a matter of ambition but a matter of epistemology: some argue that the differences between, say, image and speech are too great to handle within one and the same framework; others argue that, notwithstanding the differences, it is still possible, at a more general level, to establish common principles of meaning making.

Fourth, when exploring how the notion of multimodality has been and is being developed along diverse lines and schools of thought, it is important to keep an eye on the 'original' premises we just outlined. Fundamental to all those premises is a concern with the *cultural* and *social* resources for making meaning, not with the *senses.* While there are, of course, important relations to be explored between the senses and the means for making meaning, it is important not to conflate the two. The focus on the cultural and the social shaping of resources used for making meaning also sets the approaches apart from the popular notion that observation of 'non-verbal behaviour' offers a 'way in' to what an individual 'really' thinks (as suggested in e.g. best-selling guidebooks on 'successful business communication').

## What makes a study 'multimodal'?

When reviewing literature or when planning your own study, it is important to clarify what makes a study multimodal. The following sets of questions about aims, theory and method can help you assess the centrality (or marginality) of multimodality in a study:

1 *Aims and research questions:* Does it address research questions about meaning, communication, discourse or interaction? Is one aim of the study to contribute to the development of a theory of multimodality? For instance, you might find questions such as, 'What is the semiotic relation between objects displayed in museums and their captions? What is the role of gaze in turn taking?'
2 *Theory:* What is the place of multimodality in the theoretical framework of the study? Is it a central concept, or is it referenced but not expanded on? It may also be that a theory is presented that could be described as multimodal even though it is not described as such by the authors/researchers themselves.
3 *Method:* What empirical materials are collected and analysed, and how? Do the collected materials include documentation of human artefacts and social interactions? Do the researchers attend to all (or at least a number of different) means of meaning making that can be reconstructed from the collected materials? Do they give equally systematic attention to all?

Considering the place of multimodality on these dimensions, we can distinguish between:

- *Doing multimodality:* Designing a study in which multimodality is central to aims/research questions, theory and method;
- *Adopting multimodal concepts:* Designing a study in which multimodality concepts (such as mode, semiotic resource) are used selectively.

When *adopting multimodal concepts*, you can draw selectively from approaches to multimodality such as the ones we discuss in the book. But picking and mixing can be a tricky approach. When selecting concepts from the frameworks and connecting them to concepts derived from other frameworks, it is important to reflect on their 'compatibility'. Drawing on a theory raises expectations about methods used. For example, claiming to 'use' a theory from one of the approaches discussed in this book raises the expectation (among others, as we shall see in the next section) that you will analyse human artefacts or social interactions. So if you choose to combine that theory with the method of the interview, you are likely to be seen as having produced an incoherent framework. If you believe there are good reasons to use the interview as a method, you need to make a case for it (alternatively, you could treat the interview not as a method but as an object of study and analyse it multimodally).

Making explicit what the place of multimodality is in one's study along these lines can be a way of setting appropriate expectations about the coherence of the research design. When you submit a research paper to a journal and suggest that the study you present is multimodal, some reviewers will expect multimodality to be central throughout the paper. When you explain that you adopt selected multimodal concepts, reviewers are more likely to assess the 'fit' between those concepts and the theoretical and methodological frame within which you integrate it. We will elaborate on the issue of mixing approaches in Chapter 6.

## Three approaches to multimodal research

In Chapters 3, 4 and 5 of this book we discuss three approaches to doing multimodality. We will elaborate on how elements of the three approaches have been incorporated into other approaches in Chapter 6. Each is grounded in a distinct discipline, with a distinct theoretical and methodological outlook: conversation analysis, systemic functional linguistics and social semiotics. Not all scholars working in these originating disciplines are interested in multimodality. For instance, many conversation analysts or systemic functional linguists continue to focus on the study of 'talk' or 'speech'. Yet within each of the three disciplines, we can identify a substantial and growing body of literature and a community of scholars engaging with multimodal research. It is these bodies of work that we will focus on.

While there are significant differences between them, they share a number of important features:

- They draw on disciplines that originally focused on *language in use*, that is disciplines concerned with what people do with language in their everyday life, notably how they construe the social world through language.
- They have a preference for collecting and analysing observable traces of meaning making, notably those found on human *artefacts* and video recordings of *social interaction*.
- They aim to describe, transcribe, annotate and analyse materials at a *micro level*, that is with attention to the fine-grained detail of form and meaning.
- Through micro analysis, they have produced rich, detailed *metalanguages* for theorizing about the social world.
- They have all in recent decades *branched out*, maintaining the focus on the social and incorporating means of meaning making beyond speech and writing in their theoretical and methodological frameworks.

As the last bullet point suggests, the approaches that we focus on in this book have developed a more encompassing multimodal frame, largely by expanding their original frame: all had developed sophisticated toolkits to investigate language in use and then *branched out*, as it were, to explore meaning made with other means – gesture, for instance, or image. We should point out from the outset that the risk of branching out is that the new territory is described in the terms of the originating discipline. Indeed, this is a common critique of all three approaches, and one that we will attend to throughout the book. When expanding the traditional scope, it is important to keep a close eye on what is typical of a mode or semiotic resource and what may count as a more general principle of meaning making, making sure that linguistic categories are not imposed onto other modes. Every time the frame is expanded, old terms and categories need to be revisited and re-evaluated, in the light of the wider range of empirical cases being considered. So we might ask, 'What would the counterpart be of a verb in image?' But we can ask that only if we then immediately add, 'Maybe image doesn't have anything like the verb. Maybe it has categories unlike anything language has'.

The same can be said about the names of the originating disciplines. The terms 'conversation analysis' or 'systemic functional linguistics' no longer match the scope of the disciplines they describe. A number of new terms are now being used to mark the changing scopes of these disciplines. We will, for the moment, continue to use some of the old names and use new names if they are widely used within the community they represent. Thus we use the term 'systemic functional multimodal discourse analysis' (SF-MDA) but not, for instance, 'multimodal conversation analysis'.

We will discuss the three approaches at length in Chapters 3, 4 and 5, respectively. Here we summarize them by briefly introducing their aims, history, theory of meaning, concept of mode, empirical focus and methodology. We also present a typical research question for each approach. If you have problems understanding some of the bullet points at this point, rest assured that we will come back to all of them.

## Systemic functional linguistics

- *Aim:* To understand the ways in which language is organized and used to fulfil a range of social functions.
- *History:* Originally developed by Michael Halliday in the 1960s in the UK, influenced by European functionalism. O'Toole, van Leeuwen, Martin and O'Halloran and others have taken SFL procedures to explore what is now often called multimodal discourse, resulting in systemic functional multimodal discourse analysis (SF-MDA). The approach aims to understand and describe the functions of different semiotic resources as systems of meaning and to analyse the meanings that arise when semiotic choices combine in multimodal phenomena over space and time.
- *Theory of meaning:* Language is conceptualized as a social semiotic resource for creating meaning. The meaning potential of language is reflected in its underlying organization, which is modelled as interrelated systems of meaning. The systems are 'networks of interlocking options' (i.e. choice between different forms), and 'text' is a process and product of selection (and materialization) from that potential (e.g. Halliday, 2008).
- *Concept of mode:* The notion of semiotic resource is central to multimodal studies grounded in SFL. Semiotic resources are seen to fulfil four main social functions: (1) to construct our experience of the word, (2) to make logical connections in that world, (3) to enact social relations and (4) to organize the message.
- *Empirical focus:* 'Artefacts' of all kinds, including print and digital texts, videos and three-dimensional objects and sites. Usually these artefacts are

readily available as popular media (advertisements, TV programmes, websites, social media), educational media (e.g. textbooks and other education materials) and art and crafts (e.g. sculptures, buildings).

- *Methodology:* Detailed transcription and analysis of selected fragments of the texts, as well as the analysis of larger corpora and 'multimodal analytics' (e.g. Bateman, 2008, 2014c; O'Halloran, Tan & E, 2014; O'Toole, 2011).
- *Typical research question:* Unsworth (2007), building on Martinec and Salway (2005), explored the nature of text–image relations in school textbooks and other educational materials by developing a classification system that documents the types of logical relations established between the text and images. In this SF approach, the questions that are asked include, 'What is the nature of the text-image relations? Are these compatible with the communicative purpose of the educational materials? What, if any, challenges do they represent for young learners?'

## Social semiotics

- *Aim:* To recognize the agency of social actors and social/power relations between them.
- *History:* Pioneered by Gunther Kress and Bob Hodge in the early 1980s in Australia, building on critical linguistics, SFL, semiotics and social theory. Van Leeuwen brought inspiration from music and film studies.
- *Theory of meaning:* Based on the notion of the motivated sign (Kress, 1993), which holds that the relation between signifier and signified is always motivated and never 'arbitrary', as Saussure suggested.
- *Concept of mode:* Central to social semiotic theory. Indeed most theorizing on what counts as mode comes from social semiotics. A short definition would be 'a set of socially and culturally shaped resources for making meaning' that has distinct 'affordances' (cf. Kress, 2014).
- *Empirical focus:* Initially focused on 'artefacts' (especially print media, film and games – both 'professional', e.g. an advert in a magazine, and 'vernacular', e.g. a child's drawing), it then also began to account for social interaction recorded on video through fieldwork.
- *Methodology:* Typically detailed analysis of selected small fragments (e.g. a drawing or a small set of them), sometimes involving historical comparisons; is often combined with ethnography.

- Typical *research question*: Mavers (2011) looked at a teacher's instructions and the drawings that children made subsequently in a science classroom. As in any social semiotic study, questions she addressed included, 'How did the sign makers use the modes available to them (in this case, drawing and writing) to re-present the world? What did they attend to? What did they highlight? What was gained and lost in the process of 'translating' from one mode to another?'

## Conversation analysis

- *Aim:* To recognize 'order' in the ways in which people *organize* themselves in and through interaction.
- *History:* Originally developed in the US in the early 1960s by Schegloff, Sacks and Jefferson, influenced by interactionism and ethnomethodology. Goodwin, Heath, Mondada and others have taken CA procedures to explore what is now often called multimodal interaction.
- *Theory of meaning*: Based on the notion of *sequentiality*: Action unfolds in time, one action after another. Each social action is understood in relation to the action that preceded and followed. That principle provides a basis for making claims about the meanings that people make.
- *Concept of mode:* While it is recognized that people use a range of different ('semiotic') 'resources' and that these resources are 'mutually elaborating', the term 'mode' is rarely used.
- *Empirical focus:* Video recordings of 'naturally occurring' social encounters (i.e. encounters that were not initiated by the researcher), obtained through fieldwork, showing all participants involved in an activity. Activities include those in which speech is only used occasionally, such as when two people assemble a piece of furniture.
- *Methodology:* Typically involves detailed transcription and analysis of (collections of) small fragments or strips of interaction (say, 30 seconds) illustrating a phenomenon of interest.
- *Typical research question*: Goodwin and Tulbert (2011) looked at toothbrushing in family houses. In 'plain English', their question can be formulated as, 'How do parents get their children to brush their teeth?' In a CA framework, such formulations get translated into questions, such as, 'How do members of a community (in this case, families) organize their routine activities? How

do they use their bodies, objects and the built environment as resources for the accomplishment of these activities? How do they achieve a joint focus of attention? How do they jointly 'build' the activity up? How are the activities related?'

Throughout the book, we will cross-reference and point out differences and similarities among these three focal approaches. The main differences are summarized in Table 1.1.

We want to highlight two significant differences here: one theoretical and one methodological.

The theoretical point is, first of all, an issue of naming. The three approaches have different terminological preferences, coupled with different conceptualizations of what we have described so far as 'means for making meaning'. In SS and SFL, the terms 'mode' and 'semiotic resource' are both used, and definitions

Table 1.1   Mapping three approaches to multimodality: SFL, social semiotics and conversation analysis

|  | SFL | Social semiotics | CA |
|---|---|---|---|
| Aims | Recognition of social functions of forms | Recognition of power and agency | Recognition of social order in interaction |
| Theory of meaning | Meaning as choice | Motivated sign | Sequentiality |
| History | European functionalism | SFL, critical linguistics, semiotics | American interactionism, ethnomethodology |
| Conceptualization of 'means for making meaning' | Semiotic resource, mode | Mode, semiotic resource | (Semiotic) resource |
| Example representatives | O'Toole, Martin, Unsworth, O'Halloran | Kress, van Leeuwen | Goodwin, Heath, Mondada |
| Empirical focus | Artefacts, including texts and objects | Artefacts, mostly texts | Researcher-generated video recordings of interaction |
| Method of analysis | Micro analysis of selected short fragments, corpus analysis, multimodal analytics | Micro analysis of selected short fragments, historical analysis | Micro analysis of (collections of) selected short fragments |

have been proposed that make a distinction between the two. In CA, '(semiotic) resource' is used, but 'mode' is not, or very rarely, and some attempts at defining '(semiotic) resource' have been made. Yet none of these definitions is (as yet) widely and consistently used beyond those who proposed them.

There is, put simply, much variation in the meanings ascribed to mode and (semiotic) resource. Gesture and gaze, image and writing seem plausible candidates, but what about colour or layout? And is photography a separate mode? What about facial expression and body posture? Are action and movement modes? You will find different answers to these questions not only between different research publications but also within. To avoid potential confusion, it is important to make a deliberate decision on what categories and terms to use when engaging with multimodal research. It will be helpful to formulate some 'working definitions', drawing on the ones already put forward by the approach you adopt. Even though the working definition is unlikely to be entirely satisfactory, it is important to strive for maximum conceptual clarity and consistency. We will discuss the definitions proposed within our focal approaches in the respective chapters.

The methodological point is this. CA is primarily interested in meanings made in situ, in dynamic, face-to-face interactions. It looks at artefacts only insofar as these artefacts are being oriented to in observed interactions. So, for instance, Charles Goodwin (2000) looked at the Munsell chart, a tool used to determine the colour of soil by the archaeologists participating in the interactions he had video-recorded. In social semiotics, artefacts have been explored in situ – for instance the use of 3D models in the science classroom (Kress and van Leeuwen 2001) – but in other social semiotic work, artefacts have also been studied away from specific situated interactions. For instance, Bezemer and Kress (2008) studied textbooks. Their focus was on meanings made by the makers of textbooks (including authors and graphic designers), not on the meanings of those who engage with textbooks, such as teachers and students. In SFL, a similar position is usually taken, recognizing that it is possible to reconstruct meanings from (collections of) artefacts. Thus SS and SFL generally cover a wider empirical scope than CA. For instance, the architectural design of a building would normally fall outside the scope of CA.

There is, of course, significant variation in the degree to which scholars stay close (some might say 'faithful') to the principles put forward by the founders of the originating disciplines. Indeed there is a tension between staying faithful to concepts as they were originally defined and the need to revise old concepts in the light of the changing world. After all, the world we live in now looks very different from what it looked like when the originating disciplines appeared. Social, cultural and technological changes constantly challenge old notions.

There are close connections between scholars working with the different frameworks, and indeed some are active members in both communities. The closest links are between SFL and SS; there is far less interaction between representatives of CA, on the one hand, and SFL and SS, on the other. For instance, at the International Conference on Multimodality, CA has to date been underrepresented, while SS and SFL were hardly represented at the tenth edition of the International Conference on Conversation Analysis (2010), which was dedicated to 'multimodal interaction'. CA is closely linked with interactional (socio) linguistics and linguistic anthropology, and this connection is reflected in early work on the role of, for example, gaze in classroom interaction (see the work of Ray McDermott and Frederick Erickson). Social semiotics is closely linked with critical discourse analysis, which developed as a separate branch of critical linguistics. That is visible, for instance, in the joint work of David Machin and Theo van Leeuwen on media discourse (e.g. 2007).

In many studies, selected elements of one of the three approaches have been adopted and brought into connection with concepts and methods derived from other disciplines, such as psychology. For instance, you could use eye-tracking technology to 'test' certain concepts proposed in social semiotics (Holsanova, 2012). Other work has attempted to bring together concepts from social semiotics with ethnography. We will elaborate on how elements of the three approaches have been incorporated into other approaches in Chapter 6.

# CHAPTER 2

# Why engage with multimodality?

## Introduction

In the previous chapter, we formulated three key premises of multimodality. We highlighted that multimodality does not just mean that recognition is given to the fact that people use a number of different semiotic resources. Multimodality also means recognition of the differences among different semiotic resources and of the ways in which they are combined in actual instances of meaning making. We then also pointed to the methodological implication of these premises, namely the need to attend to multimodal wholes.

In this chapter, we will elaborate on these key premises by engaging with and challenging assumptions about language widely held among those studying language and the general public. We assume that few people will disagree with the view that language is one among a number of quite different sets of resources that humans have developed to make meaning. What we will focus on instead are the following two more contentious issues:

- Language is the most resourceful, important and widely used of all modes.
- Language can be studied in isolation.

The counterarguments we will present are derived from the approaches to studying multimodality that are central to this book. That means that you will not find arguments here that come from psychological and ethnological studies, suggesting, for example, that '50 per cent of communication is body language'. The focus is on the detailed study of empirical traces of meaning making using analytical procedures from disciplines that originally focused on the study of language in use. Our arguments have both theoretical and methodological ramifications: they challenge claims about the place of language in the social world as well as claims about how insight can be gained in language.

Before we present these arguments, we need to clarify what we mean by language and mode or semiotic resource. By 'language' we mean speech and writing. By 'mode' and 'semiotic resource', we mean, for the moment, a set of resources, shaped over time by socially and culturally organized communities, for making meaning. That means that we break with the practice of naming all means of making meaning 'language', prefixed with such terms as 'body' or 'sign' or 'non-verbal' or 'visual'. We argue that language is language and that the range of resources subsumed under 'body language' – gesture, gaze – are in fact distinctly different modes, each significantly different from language, and therefore demand separate terms. Indeed, some multimodality scholars have proposed to treat speech and writing as separate modes, for they constitute sets of resources that are only partially overlapping. (Others conceptualize language differently. For instance, in systemic functional linguistics, language is conceptualized as a semiotic resource, and spoken and written language is seen as variations in language use.) It is important to reiterate here that we use this terminology as a means of synthesizing different approaches to multimodality; it has not (yet) been universally adopted!

## Is language really the most resourceful, important and widely used of all modes?

Early 20th-century semioticians are often given credit for having been among the first to propose studying language alongside other modes, or 'sign systems', as they often called them. For instance, Saussure suggested that linguistics is a 'branch' of a more general science he called semiology and that:

> [i]f one wishes to discover the true nature of language systems, one must first consider what they have in common with all other systems of the same kind.
> (Saussure, 1983: 19)

Interestingly, the very same theorists have suggested that language stands out as the most important, central and powerful of all sign systems. Daniel Chandler summarizes their views as follows:

> Saussure referred to language (his model being speech) as 'the most important' of all the systems of signs (Saussure, 1983, 15). Many other theorists have regarded language as fundamental. Roman Jakobson insisted that

'language is the central and most important among all human semiotic sys-tems' (Jakobson, 1970, 455). Émile Benveniste observed that 'language is the interpreting system of all other systems, linguistic and non-linguistics' (Benveniste, 1969, 239), while Claude Lévi-Strauss noted that 'language is the semiotic system par excellence; it cannot but signify, and exists only through signification' (Lévi-Strauss, 1972, 48). Language is almost invariably regarded as the most powerful communication system by far.

(Chandler, 2007: 5–6)

This conception of language as being somehow more important to other modes is often used to justify the privileging of language as the single most important object of study, as well as the practice of studying language with little or no ref-erence to other modes. It is a stance that is still widely held today in linguistics and beyond. To give one example, take the following quote from an introduction to applied linguistics:

Language is at the heart of human life. Without it, many of our most impor-tant activities are inconceivable. Try to imagine relating to your family, making friends, learning, falling in love, forming a relationship, being a parent, holding – or rejecting – a religious faith, having political ideals, or taking political action, without using words. There are other important activities, of course, which do seem to exist without language. Sexual relations, preparing and eating food, manual labour and crafts, the visual arts, playing and listening to music, wondering at the natural world, or grieving at its destruction. Yet even these are often developed or enhanced through language. We would perceive them quite differently had we never read about them or discussed them.

(Cook, 2003: 3)

A brief answer to this would be to say that it is just as inconceivable to participate in the activities Cook lists using language alone. A slightly longer answer would need to include the following considerations:

- The status of language varies across communities and contexts of use.
- Many 'linguistic' principles are actually general semiotic principles.
- Each mode offers distinct possibilities and limitations.

We will discuss each of these in some detail.

## The status of language varies across communities and contexts of use

The first response is that it is impossible to make general claims about what people do with language. We need to ask, for *whom* is language the most resourceful, widely used and important mode of all, and in what *contexts of use*?

The commentators just quoted all focus on a very specific community of meaning makers: the hearing community. If we consider signing communities, we can see that gesture can be just as important in a community as speech can be, in that it can be used to serve all social and communicational needs. If we based our account of the significance of language on an inquiry of communication between babies and their parents, or between blind people, or between people who do not share a language, we would get an entirely different picture. We could go further: we could observe the language use of people with aphasia or of people with autism; in each case, language plays a different, particular role.

And, of course, even when considering the hearing and speaking majority, we would find significant variation. People spending a lot of time taking pictures, making music, dancing, painting, pottering – whatever – may well ascribe the highest expressive potential to modes other than language.

Put simply, language has a different status in different *communities* and in the *repertoires* of different people.

Language also has differing status in different *contexts of use*. Much, if not most, communication happens without the use of speech (or writing). We only need to walk out into the public space to realize just how much is being communicated without the use of speech and writing. There are, of course, signs (in the everyday sense of the word) placed everywhere, often not featuring any written language, which we may or may not attend to and interpret; and there are signs made (in a semiotic sense) by other users of the public space. When we cross a street, we might momentarily communicate with the driver of a car that is approaching. Drivers might use facial expressions and gestures to communicate that they give way for you to cross the street. But before that happens, you will have anticipated what the driver is likely to do next on the basis of your recognition and interpretation of changes in speed and direction of the car. On these occasions, gesture, facial expression and other modes fulfil all the social needs of a situation.

Resources other than language are used in all kinds of interactions in seemingly routine and mundane, everyday situations. For instance, Norris (2004), analysing video recordings of a school crossing guard helping children cross a street, noted that:

> [W]hile the crossing guard shifts her focal attention from directing the cars to directing the children and back again, she simultaneously engages in two higher-level actions on different levels of attention/awareness. In other words, when the traffic guard is directing traffic, she is engaged in focused interaction with the drivers, while she is simulatenously engaged in interaction with the children at the corner: making sure that they are safe. Her engagement in the interaction with the children at this time is not as focused as her interaction with the drivers, but is clearly ongoing.
>
> (Norris 2004: 96)

In many circumstances, speech and writing are not available or indeed suitable for what needs to be communicated, and yet those who find themselves in those situations are perfectly capable of jointly achieving quite complex tasks that heavily rely on communication. Football players, surgeons, friends assembling an IKEA bookcase all communicate primarily and often entirely in modes other than speech. We could also point to images posted on social media, or picture books, or IKEA assembly instructions, or any other artefact, in which complex matters are often communicated in the absence of language.

What these examples show is that even when language is occasionally used in a situation, it does not provide the 'key' to understanding that situation. Goffman has already noted that, in many activities, talk is used only intermittently:

> [T]ake the open state of talk that is commonly found in connection with an extended joint task, as when two mechanics, separately located around a car, exchange the words required to diagnose, repair, and check the repairing of an engine fault. An audio transcription of twenty minutes of such talk might be very little interpretable even if we know about cars; we would have to watch what was being done to the car in question. The tape would contain long stretches with no words, verbal directives answered only by mechanical sounds, and mechanical sounds answered by verbal responses.
>
> (Goffman, 1981: 143)

We can illustrate this with an example from Bezemer et al. (in press) of an interaction between a surgical trainee, who is operating on a patient, and his supervisor, who is giving him instructions (Transcript 2.1).

Transcript 2.1

| | |
|---|---|
| Chief Surgeon: | I think you're fine there now M. I'd jus I'd just take it all |
| Surgical Trainee: | Clip em? |
| Chief Surgeon: | Yeah. Because you can see if you just push up on the gall bladder – with your hook just push up on the gall bladder – go through there – and then you can see you've got a nice big window there |

Clearly, we'd need to see what the surgeons are doing before we can begin to analyse what they say. Only if we have access to a visual record of the operative field – that is the focus of attention of the surgeons – can we recognize the referents of deictic elements such as 'there' and 'here' in the pointing gestures of the trainee. What's more, only if we have visual record can we account for all those exchanges between the trainee and the surgeon where no speech was used at all: for instance, when the surgeon gently repositioned the hand of the trainee or when he drew attention to a different tissue plane by pushing structures to one side.

The point is that language, like any other mode, is used differently in different activities and artefacts. Of course, if you are drawn to those activities in which speech and/or writing appear to play a central role, you are likely to be left thinking that language is, overall, the dominant mode in the lives of everybody, always and everywhere.

Another point is that if you are interested in social practices and you use language as a 'way in' to those practices, you need to be aware of what will remain inaccessible to you. Tony Hak made the following observations about conversation and discourse analysis of health care work:

[They] tend not to study in detail activities that are considered menial (such as preparing hospital meals), not 'discursive' enough (such as physical examination), not interactive enough (such as copying laboratory results into a log), or activities that are difficult to audio – or videorecord (such as ad hoc encounters in the corridor). The result is that we have a lot of studies on consultations, meetings and ward rounds. If we would not know what goes on in hospitals by other means than through conversation and discourse analysis we would think that almost all work done in hospitals is done by doctors (or doctors in training) and that their work mainly consists of talking to patients or to each other.

(Hak, 1999: 440–441)

He then went to say that:

> [They] tend to concentrate on doctors who either talk a lot (general practitioners, psychiatrists) or who are studied in situations in which they talk (oral history taking, teaching) and, further, on only such other professionals whose work consists mainly or entirely of talk (counsellors, therapists, health visitors, takers of calls to an information service).
>
> (Hak, 1999: 441)

Perhaps it is no surprise that that point is often overlooked by academic *writers* with a special interest in *language*: it is that preconceived interest that draws their attention to everything linguistic, just like a particular interest in, say, image draws one's attention to the ubiquity of image in people's lives. A multimodal orientation puts the significance of certain modes in perspective, that is in relation to other modes, and enables us to see that the status of and functions served by language relative to other modes vary significantly.

## Many 'linguistic' principles are actually general semiotic principles

The second response to the claim that language is the most resourceful, important and widely used mode of all is that that claim is, at the very least, premature. There is a relatively long history of the study of language, and much progress has been made in developing means of characterizing language in a highly detailed manner. As long as such sophisticated toolkits do not exist for the description of, say, the resources of gesture, colour, dress, or scent, we have no means of 'evidencing' the resourcefulness of such modes. In the meantime, it would be premature to conclude that language has, overall, more meaning potential than other modes.

Indeed, recent work in multimodality does suggest that some of the principles and properties traditionally attributed to language can also be found in other modes. For instance, in their study of *image*, Kress and van Leeuwen (2006) showed that image not only has the equivalent of what linguists call lexis, it also has a 'grammar':

> Just as grammars of language describe how words combine in clauses, sentences and texts, so our visual 'grammar' will describe the way in which

depicted elements – people, places and things – combine in visual 'statements' of greater or lesser complexity and extension.

(Kress and van Leeuwen, 2006: 1)

Adopting a similar approach, Michael O'Toole showed that a *building* – in his case, the Sydney Opera House – can be described using concepts that have been derived from 'linguistic' terms:

> Like a clause in language, a building incorporates Types of Process and their Participants; its specific functions are Modified in terms of material, size, colour and texture; and its component elements are organized taxonomically like lexical items in the vocabulary of our language.
>
> (O'Toole, 2004: 15)

What these scholars – who took inspiration from systemic functional linguistics – showed was that, just like language, modes such as image and object design are made up of elements and rules for combining them, which can be used to serve four main social functions: (1) to construct our experience of the word, (2) to make logical connections in that world, (3) to enact social relations, and (4) to organize the message. These are the 'metafunctions' of semiotic resources, a concept we explore in Chapter 3.

Similarly, in conversation analysis, it has been shown that speech is not unique in its so-called sequential organization. For instance, the *adjacency pair* – two-part structures such as question-answer, greeting-greeting, offer-acceptance – has been described as a fundamental unit of conversational organization (Levinson, 1983) and is almost always illustrated with examples in which both the first and second parts are realized linguistically. Take the following example (Transcript 2.2):

## Transcript 2.2

John:   Hi Peter
Peter:  Hi John

Multimodal research does not reject the notion that the adjacency pair is a fundamental unit of conversational organization; it shows that it is a fundamental unit of interaction more generally. Mondada (2014) illustrates this with examples from interactions between surgeons and their assistants. Looking at instructions given by surgeons and the responses they elicit from the trainees being addressed, she shows that the actions of the instructor and the instructed form 'a complex multimodal gestalt temporally arranged in a finely tuned way, presenting the fundamental characteristics of the *adjacency pair*' (Schegloff 2007: 147). She found that '[f]irst pair parts can be formatted in a variety of ways, by verbal directives only – which is a rare case in my subset – and most frequently either by a verbal and a gestural instruction or a silent embodied instruction. The second pair part is always silently achieved' (157).

In other words, a multimodal perspective reminds us that many of the principles for making meaning described by those studying language can be realized in a variety of different modes: they are *semiotic* principles.

## Each mode offers distinct possibilities and limitations

The third response to the claim that language stands above other modes is to say that while language has unique possibilities, it also has unique limitations, like any other mode. Although this may seem obvious, linguists such as Jerrold Katz have, not so long ago, suggested that one unique property of language is its 'principle of effability': 'there is nothing to indicate that there is any type of information that cannot be communicated by the sentences of a natural language' (Katz, 1972: 19). Let's take a moment to reflect on the implications of this statement. It means that someone being 'lost for words' points to a limitation on the side of the language user. It is never a reflection of the limitations of the meaning potential of language. Katz's claim also means that any meaning made in any mode can be *transcribed*, without any significant 'gains' or 'losses' in meaning.

Observation of meaning making suggests otherwise. To give one brief example: surgeons have developed a specialist language for describing the human body. And yet when you listen to what surgeons say when they operate, you will often hear them referring to 'that stuff' or 'that bit over there' (Bezemer et al., 2014). In spite of a history of anatomical study that began in 1600 BCE, language provides only a fraction of the resources required to communicate the information needed in this situation. The pointing gesture cannot, in fact, be transcribed without losing some of its precision. Indeed, social semioticians have argued that any attempt to translate something into words always involves a kind of 'transformation' or 'transduction' (see Chapter 4).

If we want to map the potentialities and limitations of different modes, we need to attend to what modes have in common as much as to what is distinct about them. A linguistic toolkit is therefore of limited use: linguistic categories will not draw attention to those properties not shared with language. The point is that we should not assume that all categories have equivalents in other modes. On the contrary, the aim of doing multimodality is precisely to identify what is particular and what is general in each mode.

When studying meaning making across different modes, we can identify which semiotic principles are shared and how these principles are realized differently in each mode. This goes back to an ambition formulated by Jakobson, who proposed that semiotics 'deals with those general principles which underlie the structure of all signs whatever and with the character of their utilization within messages, as well as with the specifics of the various sign systems' (1968: 698).

An example of how this ambition is approached in present-day social semiotics is given by Bezemer and Kress (2016):

> All communities need means for expressing/realizing (the general semiotic feature) *intensity*. In the mode of *speech* that is realized by the intensity of sound, 'loudness'; it is also realized lexically, e.g. as 'very'. *Lexis* is available in the mode of *writing* as well; here intensity can also be indicated by visual prominence, as in the use of a **bold font**, or by CAPITALIZING. In the mode of *gesture* intensity might be realized by the *speed of movement* of the hand, or by the *extent* of the movement. In the mode of *colour* it might be done through degrees of saturation.
>
> (Bezemer and Kress, 2016: 17)

In other words, a multimodal perspective draws attention to the *general* and the *particular* in language, recognizing both what language has in common with other modes and how it is distinctly different. From a multimodal perspective, therefore, language is not 'more' resourceful, but 'differently' resourceful; it does not have more potential but different potential for making meaning – just like any other mode.

## Can language really be studied in isolation?

As you are reading this, you might be thinking, 'Well, that's all very exciting, but I'd define my interest more narrowly; if no or hardly any language is involved, it falls outside my area of interest. I'm a linguist, after all.' To this we would say that the meaningful units that people produce are almost always multimodal. In some ways the argument is not unlike that put to medical specialists who lose sight of the whole body when dealing with only a part of it. It is the 'body' that constitutes the meaningful whole; organs are merely constituent, interacting parts of it. In the same way, multimodality encourages us to establish what the contribution is of each to the construction of a meaningful whole – a 'text'.

Take a look at the following YouTube video (Figure 2.1), which has been viewed more than 60 million times (https://www.youtube.com/watch?v=J4-GRH2nDvw). It is one of Michelle Phan's make-up tutorials. In the video, Phan uses both speech and writing. Yet they are only two of a range of different modes. Phan uses gesture, gaze, postures and objects as she demonstrates how to transform into Barbie. She also uses the resources of film, such as camera angle, lighting, set design, as well as the resources made available in post-production to edit the film and add music, voice-over and so on.

The point is that language is almost always part of a bigger whole, namely a 'text' that is made with a number of different modes. If we wanted to analyse what the meaning maker constructed as a meaningful, coherent whole, we would need to treat the entire video as our object of inquiry, not just extract and examine a part (such as the spoken or the written) of that whole. If you want to understand how language is used within that text, you will have to attend to those other

Figure 2.1    Screen capture image of Michelle Phan's YouTube Barbie Transformation Tutorial

modes in the text as well: you can't interpret or analyse what was said or written in isolation.

The example here is an instance of digital media. It is the case that the texts we find on the Internet are almost always multimodal – in fact, the challenge is to find one that is not! Multimodal texts such as these do, of course, predate the Internet era, but digital technologies have given a majority access to the resources needed to produce and disseminate multimodal texts at relatively low cost. The new technologies now draw our attention to what had previously been possible to overlook. As we shall see later in the book, both SFL and SS have developed ways of analysing texts such as these in a systematic manner.

With a multimodal whole identified, the question that immediately arises is how to understand the relations between its constituent elements across different modes – what we might describe as a multimodal grammar. This has been an important area of theorizing and inquiry.

For instance, working in the tradition of systemic functional linguistics, Martinec and Salway (2005) have described the relations between image and writing in terms of Halliday's analysis of clause relations. One distinction he makes is between 'equal' and unequal clause relations. An example of an equal relation would be the relation between the two clauses in, 'He picked up the box and left'. An example of an unequal relation would be the relation between the two clauses in, 'The man picked up the box that laid on the table'. Drawing on online news stories, art gallery catalogues and science texts, Martinec and Salway present examples of similar relations between image and writing in multimodal texts. In some instances, image and writing are 'on equal footing'; for example, when image and writing complement each other, such as in a science textbook, you will find diagrams complementing the written text. In other instances, the relation between image and writing can be shown to be unequal; for example, in an art catalogue you will find photographs of artworks that are in an unequal relation to their captions.

Martinec and Salway (2005) looked at image-writing relations. In conversation analysis, and to some degree also in social semiotics, the relations between speech, gaze and gesture have been explored, albeit in different terms. How such intermodal relations are accounted for in these approaches will be discussed in Chapters 5 and 4, respectively. Right now it suffices to say that all our focal approaches show that elements in a multimodal whole are *mutually modifying*, making it highly problematic to attend to language or any other mode in isolation.

## Understanding language when it appears to be the 'dominant' mode in a text: a job interview

You might at this point say, 'Well, okay. In Phan's YouTube video, speech and writing are clearly not the dominant modes of representation, but if I audio-recorded an interview, then I can get pretty far with my analysis just by transcribing and analysing what the interviewer and interviewee say. After all, in the interview, participants may use gesture, say, but clearly speech is the dominant mode. Attention to the gesture is not going to substantially change my interpretation of the interview.'

So let's look at a job interview. We will use an example from a study by Sarah Campbell and Celia Roberts (2007), who video-recorded job interviews to analyse the effect of discourse practices on the success or failure of candidates. A larger segment of the recording from which the example was drawn is discussed from a linguistic ethnographic perspective in Rampton and colleagues (2007).

In the example, an interviewee, Pippa, is applying for a position as a delivery driver, in a company where she has previously worked (placed there through a job agency). Pippa is being interviewed by Daniel, the delivery manager, and Roger, the HR (human resources [personnel]) manager. She has just been asked to say something about the organizational changes that the company is implementing, involving moving from two deliveries per day to one. In her response, she mentions some of the implications of the change for delivery staff. Transcript 2.3 gives a brief excerpt.

## Transcript 2.3

Pippa:   the walks have doubled
Daniel:   some

Some linguists might say that Pippa has produced a 'statement' – 'the walks have doubled' – that highlights one effect of the change. It does so without identifying the *agent* of this action (i.e. the leadership of the company that has introduced the new policy) or indeed the *affected* participants (i.e. the members of staff who now need to walk twice as much). Agency of two kinds (who has done the doubling and who does the walking) is not mentioned through the use of the agentless form: rain has fallen/walks have doubled.

Other linguists might say that more details could be added to the transcript, for example about the production of speech. For instance, we could point out that the vowel in 'have' is lengthened. Vowel lengthening is, literally, an elongation, producing a momentary slowdown, a hesitation perhaps, certainly drawing attention to it, as if Pippa is taking her time carefully formulating the contentious part of the statement. Attention might also be drawn to the rising intonation used at the end of 'doubled', which keeps the 'information flow' open, suggesting that there is more to come, or that a completion/response is requested from one of the interviewers.

Adopting a multimodal perspective, we could add the following observations to this (admittedly selective) linguistic commentary.

First, a note on *gaze*. Attention to this mode helps us explain why Pippa is looking at Daniel. Roger, by making notes, has made himself unavailable for eye contact, despite having asked Pippa the question she is now answering. Daniel, on the other hand, is looking at Pippa when she makes the statement, and Pippa looks at Daniel while making her statement. They use *gaze* to display what and whom they are 'attending to', as well as whom the speaker is addressing. These gaze patterns are also shaped by the placement of objects in the built environment, notably the triangular seating arrangement.

Second is *facial expression*. When Pippa says 'doubled' (with a final rising intonation), she raises her eyebrows and keeps them raised for about a second. As with the intonation she uses, this expression can be used to signify uncertainty, provisionality, noncompletion: a deferring of judgement, indeed a 'hedging' or a modulation of the truth (value) of the contentious part of the statement (a gestural 'maybe') about the implications of a major policy change vis-à-vis official representatives of the company. The effect of the raised eyebrows is to invite a 'completion', probably in the form of a 'justification', though without having to use *speech*.

Third, there are *hand gestures* to attend to. While Pippa says 'doubled' – with its specific intonation and raising of eyebrows – she also makes a hand gesture. She prepares for this gesture by placing her hands flat against each other. She then moves them outward, about a foot apart, 'landing' them on the edge of the table, just before she comes to the end of 'doubled'. Pippa uses her hand movement to 'map out': she 'shows' the doubling of the walking distance (the signified). Figure 2.2 is a line drawing of a video still of that moment.

Fourth, in a multimodal account, attention is also drawn to the one-second silence between Pippa's and Daniel's taking turns at talk. In that time, she maintains the gesture and the raised eyebrows momentarily. Eventually she drops her

Daniel

Pippa

Roger

Figure 2.2    Impression of a job interview

eyebrows and starts *smiling*, 'producing' an ameliorating affect in the midst of her potentially provocative 'sensitive statement'. As she smiles, she keeps her hands in the position in which they 'arrived' at the end of the 'stroke' and maintains her gaze at Daniel. This 'post-stroke hold' (Kendon, 2004b), that is momentarily 'frozen' gesture, and *gaze* constitute a rather forceful *request* to respond, that is to offer *confirmation* of the statement she has just made before moving on to other implications of the organizational change. In response, Daniel says 'some', while *smiling* 'minimally' and making a little *head nod*. The head nod and spoken item together appear to signify 'partial' agreement/confirmation, while the 'minimal' smile adds specific affective-ameliorative meaning.

We can summarize: Pippa and Daniel do not just produce one spoken utterance each, as Transcript 2.3 suggests. Their spoken utterances coincide with gaze directions, facial expressions and gestures, and their 'silences' are filled with more meanings made in those modes. Looking at speech alone, we might have taken Daniel's 'some' to be a response to Pippa's 'the walks have doubled'. Running with the transcript alone, readers would be inclined to interpret Daniel's response as an *intervention* of Pippa's statement. That interpretation becomes questionable as soon as we draw attention to the raised intonation at the end of 'doubled' and the one-second silence between the two spoken utterances, which would suggest that Pippa is awaiting a response from Daniel before continuing to list what has changed; that is, rather than Daniel having to step in at his own initiative, Pippa was *inviting* him to respond. Yet if we attended to Pippa's facial expression and gesture during the silence, we would have to revise our interpretation again: by keeping her raised eyebrows and gesture stroke frozen momentarily before putting on a smile, she is *forcing* Daniel to respond to her statement. And to understand how Daniel responds to this, we need to look at all parts of the multimodal whole he subsequently produces: the spoken item ('some'), as much as the head nod and the little smile.

In short, analysis of more and different modes used in the same fragment can be used to aggregate sources of evidence and build a much more plausible account of what is happening during the job interview. It shows that even in an activity that is seemingly dominated by speech, there are significant limits on what a linguistic analysis can offer.

We could, of course, add more examples to make the same point, namely that when studying texts that appear to be dominated by writing or speech alone, other modes cannot be ignored without significant implications for the account of the text. Whether you study a political 'speech' or a 'written' post on a blog, the other parts of the whole of which language is a part are worthy of as detailed an analysis as language itself.

In the following chapters of the book, we will give many more examples, demonstrating the potential of multimodal analysis in different ways and in relation to different domains.

# CHAPTER 3

# Systemic functional linguistics

## Introduction to the approach

### Origins, background and early developments

Michael Halliday developed systemic functional linguistics (SFL) based on the view that language is a social semiotic system, that is a resource for making meaning. Halliday proposes that the functions that language has evolved to serve in society are reflected in its underlying organization. From this perspective, a major goal of SFL is to develop a functional grammar to account for the meaning-making potential of language:

> Language has evolved to satisfy human needs; and the way it is organized is functional with respect to those needs – it is not arbitrary. A functional grammar is essentially a 'natural grammar', in the sense that it can be explained, ultimately, by reference to how language is used.
>
> (Halliday, 1994: viii)

Similarly, systemic functional approaches to multimodal discourse analysis (SF-MDA) are concerned with the 'grammatics' of semiotic resources, with the aim of understanding the functions of different semiotic resources and the meanings that arise when semiotic choices combine in multimodal phenomena over space and time (O'Halloran and Lim, 2014).

Halliday's SFL was originally conceived for teaching Mandarin (Halliday, 1976 [1956]), but it was fully developed for the study of English (e.g. Martin and Rose, 2007; Halliday and Matthiessen, 2014). Halliday's approach to language was built upon the foundations established by his teacher J. R. Firth, who was concerned with (a) the way language was used in different contexts, regardless of the perceived value of the form of language use, and (b) linguistics as a form of social action that aimed to understand the relations between the individual and culture (Hasan, 2015). Halliday and Firth's views of language are entirely compatible with Marxist forms of linguistics, which study 'the underlying relationship between language and society – the interaction between linguistic and social processes and systems' (Halliday, 2015: 96). Halliday (1978) introduced the term 'language as social semiotic', a broad umbrella term that provided the basis for the subsequent development of the specific subfield of social semiotics developed by Gunther Kress, Robert Hodge and Theo van Leeuwen (see Chapter 4). SF-MDA is a different subfield within Halliday's broad conception of social semiotics; SF-MDA is concerned with the systematic organization of semiotic resources as tools for creating meaning in society. In this book, we use 'social semiotics' to refer specifically to the approach developed by Kress, Hodge and van Leeuwen.

As Matthiessen (2015) explains, theories of language depend on how language is conceived by the scholars who develop those theories. In the case of SFL, Halliday's view of 'language as a resource' means that the underlying theoretical principles are very different from those found in formal linguistics, where language is conceived as 'a set of rules'. For example, formalists believe that the ability to learn language is hardwired into the human brain in the form of a universal grammar, whereas Halliday believes that language is learned and mastered according to experience. Formalists see language as existing in the mind, separate from the external world, but Halliday sees language as an integral part of the human experience. The examples generated by formal linguists are constructed in order to see whether they are acceptable according to grammatical criteria, which stands in stark contrast to Halliday's scientific account of language as verifiable through actual language use. In this regard, Halliday's SFL is in all respects a social view of language.

The conflict between Halliday's view of language as a resource and the formalist view of language as a set of rules presents a problem for students. For example, when children begin to learn language, they see it as a resource for making meaning, but when they enter the school system, they are confronted with the 'folk linguistics of the classroom, with its categories and classes, its rules and regulations, its do's and, above all, its don'ts' (Halliday, 2003 [1977]: 94). As such, students learn to view language as a set of rules rather than seeing it as a versatile tool that is capable of creating a range of different meanings according to context. For example, as Halliday has shown, there are different strategies for encoding meaning in spoken and written language, resulting in the fluidity and intricacy of spoken interactions, compared to the static and dense nature of writing (Halliday, 1985b). In particular, information is packed into long noun groups in order to effectively develop a logical argument in scientific writing (Halliday, 2006). This form of writing, which students need to master for success in school, is found in most domains of human life today (e.g. economics, politics, research and so forth).

Halliday views linguistic theory as something that should be applied to real problems to improve the human condition. Therefore, Halliday developed SFL as an 'appliable linguistics', achieving the daunting task of describing the grammatical systems through which language achieves its various functionalities (see 'Function' and 'System' subsections later in this chapter). The resulting grammatical description is called systemic functional grammar (SFG). The first account of SFG was published in 1985 (Halliday, 1985a), later followed by the second edition (with an index) in 1994. Christian Matthiessen worked with Michael Halliday to revise and extend this book, resulting in the third and fourth editions in 2004 and 2014. Simultaneously, Ruqaiya Hasan (Halliday's wife and long-term collaborator) extended SFL in the field of cohesion, semantics and context, and Jim Martin (Halliday's former PhD student) and colleagues in the Sydney School developed discourse systems, appraisal theory and genre theory, which extended the SFL model beyond the grammatical descriptions found in SFG. Other systemicists have made countless contributions to SFL, including Len Unsworth, Geoff Williams, Frances Christie, David Butt, Michael O'Toole, Mick O'Donnell, Eija Ventola, Erich Steiner and Robin Fawcett, to name but a few.

## SFL and multimodality

Halliday studied language as a semiotic resource, resulting in SFL. However, Halliday always understood that language was one semiotic resource amongst many constituting society and culture:

> There are many other modes of meaning, in any culture, which are outside the realm of language. These will include both art forms such as painting, sculpture, music, the dance, and so forth, and other modes of cultural behaviour that are not classified under the heading of forms of art, such as modes of exchange, modes of dress, structures of the family, and so forth. These are all bearers of meaning in the culture. Indeed we can define a

culture as a set of semiotic systems, as a set of systems of meaning, all of which interrelate.

(Halliday and Hasan, 1985: 4)

Although Halliday developed SFL for the study of language, systemic functional theory is a theory of meaning, and, as such, the fundamental principles of the approach are applicable for the study of other semiotic resources. For this reason, the term 'systemic functional theory' (SFT) is used to refer to the higher-order principles of the theory that apply to SF-MDA, and SFL is used to refer to the application of SFT for the study of language.

SFT has been used, modified and extended to explore the ways in which spoken and written language and non-linguistic resources (e.g. image, gesture, space, 3D objects, sound, music and so forth) create meaning, both as individual resources and as interrelated systems of meaning. Kress and van Leeuwen (2006) and O'Toole (2011) pioneered the use of SFT for multimodal studies by developing systemic frameworks for analysing images and displayed art, respectively. Following O'Toole, O'Halloran (1999b, 2000) developed SFT approaches to study the integration of language, images and mathematical symbolism in mathematical texts and classroom discourse. From these early beginnings of SF-MDA and in parallel with developments in social semiotics, SF-inspired approaches to multimodality rapidly emerged over the next few decades. This work includes the study of 3D space, museum exhibitions, buildings, websites, online news, body language, children's picture books, disciplinary knowledge (e.g. mathematics, science and history) and so forth (e.g. O'Halloran, 2004; Ventola, Charles, & Kaltenbacher, 2004; Jones & Ventola, 2008; Unsworth, 2008; Ventola & Moya, 2009; Dreyfus, Hood, & Stenglin, 2011). There are close connections between SF-MDA and social semiotic approaches (see Chapter 4), given the common theoretical foundations that are based on Halliday's work. The major difference is the degree of adherence to the major principles of SFT, as described in the next section.

## Key principles and concepts

SFT is well suited to the study of multimodality because the underlying premise that semiotic resources are tools for creating meaning applies equally well to the multitude of sign systems in society: for example, language, images, gesture, music, dress, architecture and so forth. The view of semiotic resources as forms of social practice, where recognizable configurations of semiotic choices combine to constitute society and culture, provide the basic foundations of the approach. The key principles of SFT are now described.

## Function

A fundamental principle of SFT is that language and other semiotic resources are (multi)functional tools for creating meaning and structuring thought and reality. Following SFT, semiotic resources are seen to create four strands of meaning, called metafunctions:

| | |
|---|---|
| Experiential meaning: | To construct our experience of the world |
| Logical meaning: | To logically connect happenings in that world |
| Interpersonal meaning: | To enact social relations and create a stance to the world |
| Textual meaning: | To organize messages |

Experiential and logical meaning together constitute ideational meaning (i.e. ideas about the world). The capacity of semiotic resources to fulfil the metafunctions is not evenly distributed, however; that is, some semiotic resources are better equipped to make certain types of meanings compared to others. For example, language is specifically designed to order the world as sequences of logically connected happenings. As Halliday (2004, xvii) explains:

> The grammar of every language contains a theory of human experience; it categorizes the elements of our experience into basic phenomenal types, construing these into configurations of various kinds, and these configurations in turn into logical sequences.

Images, however, do not structure and order the world in the same way as language does. On the contrary, images order human experience by situating happenings in relation to other happenings, as parts of a whole. For example, in a photograph, painting or scientific diagram, many happenings and actions are taking place in relation to each other simultaneously. However, certain aspects of the image are made salient through semiotic choices such as gaze, light and framing and immediate features of the context of the situation (e.g. instructions to view parts of the image or captions); that is, although we see everything in relation to the whole in images, we also 'read' images in particular ways, depending on the semiotic choices made within the image and the context. Similarly, music unfolds in a serial fashion over time like language, but the world constructed through this semiotic resource does not consist of easily identifiable actions and happenings that are logically connected, as in language. As van Leeuwen (1999: 190) explains, 'The resources of sound simply did not seem as specialized as those of language and vision, and the mode of sound simply did not seem so clearly structured along metafunctional lines as language and visual communication'. From this perspective, as van Leeuwen (1999) explains, semiotic resources have different 'metafunctional configurations' that are not universal or a function of their intrinsic nature, but rather they are the result of their uses in society and the values attached to them. In this regard, the power of multimodal semiosis is derived from the integration of different metafunctional capabilities that are accessed to create meanings that would not be possible if one resource were used alone.

The metafunctional principle thus plays an important role in SF-MDA for understanding the functionalities and underlying organization of semiotic resources and investigating the ways in which semiotic choices combine and interact to create meaning in multimodal phenomena. As O'Halloran and Lim explain, the metafunctional organization of meanings is particularly useful for SF-MDA 'because it provides a common set of fundamental principles to compare semiotic resources and the meanings which arise when semiotic choices integrate in multimodal texts. That is, the organization of metafunctional meanings offers a unifying platform for studying semiotic resources and their inter-semiotic relations' (O'Halloran and Lim, 2014: 140).

## System

Halliday specifies the systems of meaning through which the metafunctions are realized using the concept of system formulated and defined by J. R. Firth (Halliday, 2008). Halliday's main innovation was to formulate these systems of meaning in terms of systemic choices (the paradigm), which are mapped onto the structure of language (the syntagm or chain). These two different dimensions of language are called the paradigmatic and syntagmatic axes respectively, following Swiss linguist and semiotician, Ferdinand de Saussure. Halliday identified the 'clause' (which has one major process, as opposed to a sentence, which may have many processes) as the smallest unit in which the four metafunctions are realized in language. Jim Martin and colleagues (e.g. Martin and Rose, 2007) developed discourse systems (including appraisal systems) that operate across stretches of text to complement Halliday's clause-based grammar.

The systems that realize the four metafunctions in language involve:

| | |
|---|---|
| *Experiential meaning:* | Happenings, in the form of processes, participants and circumstance |
| *Logical meaning:* | Semantic relations between clauses (i.e. expand or report) and the nature of the relationship (i.e. dependent or independent) |
| *Interpersonal meaning:* | The exchange of information or goods and services and the expression of modality in terms of truth-value and likelihood of happenings |
| *Textual meaning:* | The information that is foregrounded in the message |

The systems are represented as system networks of options (e.g. see Figure 3.1a on page 45), organized according to ranks. For example, systems operate at the rank of words, word groups, clauses, clause complexes and larger stretches of text in language and of figures, episodes and work in images (see O'Toole, 2011). The SFL model also has different strata (i.e. the material sign, grammar, meaning and context) to account for how meaning is organized and realized contextually.

In SF-MDA, the SFT principle of describing semiotic resources as the sets of system choices that realize the four metafunctions is adopted, although the systems and structures for language are not applicable for other semiotic resources (apart from text-based semiotic systems such as mathematical symbolism which has evolved from language). That is, the metafunctional principle for organizing systems of meaning applies in SF-MDA, but each semiotic resource has its own systems of meaning, units of analysis, and structure. For example, Kress and van Leeuwen (2006) and O'Toole (2011) describe visual systems for images and displayed art according to metafunction. Examples of these systems (see also Figure 3.1a) are:

| | |
|---|---|
| *Experiential meaning:* | Visual happenings in terms of processes, participants and circumstances |
| *Interpersonal meaning:* | Gaze, framing, light and perspective |
| *Textual meaning:* | Proportion and alignment |

Bateman and Schmidt (2012) and Bateman (2014a) identify systems of meaning for film from the perspective of sets of system choices and syntagmatic structures, cohesive devices and layout structure, but, again, the systems are different from those found in language. From this perspective, key challenges for SF-MDA are (1) describing the systems of meanings for different semiotic resources (as sets of options), (2) specifying the units of analysis and (3) analysing the meanings that arise through semiotic interactions according to context. (See Example 3.1.)

*Example 3.1*   Language and images in art forms

Michael O'Toole (2011) develops an SF-MDA approach to investigate how different forms of art are organized to create meaning. For this purpose, O'Toole develops systemic frameworks for paintings, sculptures and architecture, where the systems of meaning are organized according to metafunction. For example, O'Toole uses SFL for language and his SF framework for paintings to explore how poetry and paintings construct reality. As part of this exploration, O'Toole analyses W. H. Auden's poem 'Musee des Beaux Art' (1939) and Pieter Bruegel the Elder's painting *Landscape with the Fall of Icarus*. Both the poem and the painting deal with the Greek tragedy of Icarus, the son of the master craftsman Daedalus, who escapes from Crete using wings that his father has constructed from feathers and wax. Icarus does not follow his father's instructions, however, and flies too close to the sun, after which the wax in his wings melts, and he falls into the sea and drowns. As O'Toole explains, in Auden's poem, the main point of the drama about Icarus's failure to stay in flight and his drowning is conveyed by weak grammatical structures (e.g. dependent clauses and circumstances), which frame the tragedy in terms of everyday events, such as the passing of a ship, and aspects of the landscape, such as the sun shining. Similarly, in Bruegel's painting, Icarus's splashing white legs in the sea are framed in the lower right-hand eighth part of the canvas using visual framing devices – for example, the horizontal formed by the ship's yardarm, which continues with a brightly lit coastal headland, the vertical formed by the ship's foremast and the rocky corner of the coastline and the lower right and bottom edges of the canvas. In comparison, about one-third of the painting is devoted to a ploughman and a shepherd who are engaged in routine activities, and the remainder is a depiction of the sea and the sky. In comparing the verbal and visual accounts of the story of Icarus, O'Toole demonstrates how both artists make semiotic selections (e.g. framing devices) that situate the tragedy as inconsequential to people who are engaged in everyday life. As O'Toole (2011) explains, we can see 'how skillfully Auden frames the central tragedy of Icarus's fall to make it as peripheral to the everyday lives of the workers and sailors as it is in Bruegel's painting' (111). O'Toole does not stop at observing the similarities between the poem and the painting, however. Rather, he also describes a crucial difference in the linguistic and visual depictions of the Icarus myth: '[t]he individual tragedy is framed and marginalized by both artists as just one more event in the busy lives of ordinary people. Auden, however, generalized the fall of Icarus as just one more mythical disaster . . . framing each event in the unsentimental viewpoint of the 'The Old Masters' (114), the skilled painters who were commissioned by rich and powerful people to depict such scenes. In doing so, Auden gives a colloquial touch to the recurrent theme that he reads in Bruegel's painting: '[h]owever tragic for the individual, and however fraught with the consequences for mankind, for you and me and the ploughman the great disasters are outside our routine frames of reference and are "not an important failure"' (O'Toole, 2011: 115).

## Register and genre

In SF-MDA, the focus on the metafunctional organization of semiotic resources is critical, but the actual choices in multimodal texts and processes are interpreted in relation to the context using the concepts of register and genre (e.g. Eggins, 2005; Martin, 1992, 2002; Martin and Rose, 2008). Register theory is concerned with configurations of ideational (experiential and logical meanings), interpersonal and textual meanings, which correspond to three key register variables of field, tenor and mode. Field is concerned with the nature of the activity, tenor is concerned with social relations in terms of the dimensions of power and solidarity, and mode is concerned with the composition and information flow of the message. Genre is derived from the registerial configurations of tenor, field and mode, which unfold as social processes in a given culture; that is, genre is defined as 'the system of staged goal-oriented social processes through which social subjects in a given culture live their lives' (Martin, 2002: 56).

Register and genre are useful concepts for situating multimodal phenomena (i.e. any instance of meaning making in the form of semiotic artefacts, interactions and processes) in the larger socio-cultural context that functions to constrain semiotic choices and, by default, the nature of the social practices in any given culture. This is a significant aspect of SF-MDA because the various linguistic, visual and multimodal combinations in multimodal phenomena need to be inter-preted in relation to existing social practices that have a major impact on the types of multimodal choices made; that is, multimodal patterns are built up cul-turally over time, so that any instance of multimodal semiosis is conditioned by previous configurations of choices.

## Multimodal systems, processes and texts

Halliday (2008: ii) sees 'language as system' (the potential) and 'language as text' (the selection of choices), highlighting the fact that system and text are two aspects of a single phenomenon. The SFT principle of system and text is significant in SF-MDA because it encapsulates the two major aims of the approach: namely (1) to model the meaning potential of semiotic resources as interrelated sets of systems and (2) to analyse the meaning arising from the semiotic interactions in multimodal processes and texts according to context. However, the whole is seen to be *other than* the sum of the parts, following gestalt theory (Koffka, 1935); that is, multimodal semiosis results in an expanded meaning potential that is not the same as the sum of the individual resources, and multimodal choices combine to create meanings that are not the same as the sum of individual choices. From this perspective, SF-MDA involves formulating the systems of meaning for semiotic resources, defining the units of analysis and analysing the meanings that arise from semiotic interactions in multimodal phenomena. Thus, although it is possible to set up system networks for each semiotic resource as metafunctional configu-rations, the actual meaning is the result of the integration of semiotic choices in multimodal semiotic processes and artefacts, as explored in the next section.

## Intersemiosis and resemiotisation

SF-MDA involves so-called multimodal grammatics, where interacting systems of meaning are a key motif. In this regard, the processes of intersemiosis, where semiotic choices interact and combine, and resemiotisation, where semiotic choices are re-construed within and across multimodal phenomena, is central to the approach. As Iedema (2003: 29) explains, resemiotisation provides the 'analytical means for (1) tracing how semiotics are translated from one into the other as social processes unfold, as well as for (2) asking why these semiotics (rather than others) are mobilized to do certain things at certain times' (Iedema, 2003: 9).

However, as Lemke (2009) explains, while the use of multimodal resources multiplies the potential meanings that can be made, those choices are constrained at any given time, given the context of the situation and the context of culture that condition the sorts of combinations that do actually occur in social practices, as discussed earlier (e.g. van Leeuwen, 2008). In this light, SF-MDA explores how semiotic resources are organized to create meaning and the actual options that are selected to create meaning in any given instance. For example, SF and wider semiotic perspectives have been used to study intersemiotic relations between text and image (Bateman, 2014b) (see Example 3.2). Similarly, SF-MDA has been used to study the expansions of meaning in mathematics (O'Halloran, 2008, 2015a, 2015b) (see Example 3.3).

## Example 3.2  Text–image relations

Bateman (2014b) provides an overview of SF-MDA–inspired (and other) approaches to text–image relations. For example, Bateman reviews Martinec and Salway's (2005) grammatical descriptions developed from the logical relations (i.e. expanding and reporting relations) for language in SFL. In doing so, Bateman raises issues concerning the units of analysis for text–image relations in multimodal texts and the types of relations found in different image types (e.g. pictorial representations versus scientific diagrams). Bateman discusses Unsworth's (2007) extension of Martinec and Salway's (2005) approach, which is used to analyse how text and images work together in educational materials. Unsworth and colleagues are concerned with text–image relations that are either incompatible with the purpose of the text or not comprehensible to young learners who lack the necessary semiotic experience to understand the text. Following this, Bateman makes the point that it is insufficient to just copy across the logical relations from SFL that are based on clear linguistic structures (i.e. in this case, relations between clauses). This same point is recognized by Unsworth and Cleirigh (2009), who use the term 'intermodal identification' to identify text–image relations, rather than use terms from SFL. Bateman moves beyond approaches that use grammatical concepts from language to discuss discourse levels of representation for mapping text–image relations. As Bateman explains, the approach involves analysing multimodal discourse moves of various kinds that function in human communication (e.g. a nod, gesture and action) but that apply to text–image relations. For this purpose, Bateman discusses Jim Martin's (1992) conjunctive relations that describe logical relations across stretches of text. SF-MDA approaches use Martin's model of cohesive relations for analysing film and television documentaries (van Leeuwen, 1991, 2005) and text–image relations in print media (Liu and O'Halloran, 2009). However, as Bateman (2014b: 206) claims, while such frameworks provide templates for multimodal relations, 'it then remains a challenging and exciting research question to find out more precisely just whether there are further relations that are supported in other semiotic modes and to determine which particular subset of linguistic conjunctive relations may be employed and which not'.

## Example 3.3   The integration of language, image and symbolism in mathematics

O'Halloran (2015a, 2015b) develops a SF-MDA approach to mathematics to explore how the integration of language, images and mathematical symbolism gave rise to new views of the physical world. O'Halloran first examines the linguistic features and grammatical difficulties of mathematical language using Halliday's (2006) formulations of scientific writing. O'Halloran analyses a written mathematical text, showing how technical terms, semantic discontinuities and metaphorical expressions result in multiple layers of grammatical complexity. As O'Halloran (2015a: 66) explains, 'the grammatical difficulties . . . combine in various ways in scientific language, rendering mathematical texts largely inaccessible to a general audience, including novice learners unfamiliar with these sophisticated grammatical strategies'. O'Halloran then discusses the grammatical features of mathematical symbolic notation and associated difficulties of understanding these texts arising from, for example, the use of special symbols, new grammatical strategies for encoding meaning (e.g. spatial notation, rule of order, intentional omission of symbols for multiplication, use of brackets etc.), new process types and extended chains of reasoning based on established results that are often not explicitly stated. As O'Halloran explains, mathematical symbolism evolved from language in order to provide an even more specialized tool for reasoning, where meaning is precisely and unambiguously encoded. O'Halloran also explores mathematical images, which also have precise grammars for encoding meaning. O'Halloran then examines the integration of language, images and mathematical symbolism, showing that each resource has a particular functionality in mathematics. That is, language is used to introduce and reason about the mathematical results, giving rise to a discourse of argumentation. Mathematical symbolism captures the relations between mathematical entities and processes and is used to derive results through a grammatical organization that permits mathematical relations to be easily rearranged to solve problems. Lastly, mathematical relations are visualized, opening up the vast potential of the visual semiotic where patterns of patterns can be viewed and reasoned about. In this regard, visual reasoning is becoming even more significant with advances in digital technology, which permit complex, dynamic and interactive visualizations of mathematical phenomena.

Mathematics involves a semantic circuit, where the meaning potentials of each resource are accessed, but beyond that, the resemiotisation of key elements across the resources results in meaning expansions that extend beyond those possible with each individual resource. Indeed, mathematics is the classic case where the whole is other than the sum of the parts. O'Halloran also discusses the nature of spoken language in mathematics classrooms and associated difficulties that children have learning mathematics, given the new systems of meaning that differ from those found in language. O'Halloran develops the concept of multimodal register for mathematics to highlight the significance of multiple semiotic resources where mathematics resulted in a new reordering of reality. Mathematics is the ultimate tool for reasoning that has basically changed the nature of life on Earth, through science and technological innovation.

## Methods and analysis

SF-MDA involves developing systemic descriptions of semiotic resources, organized according to metafunctions: ideational meaning (i.e. experiential and logical meaning), interpersonal meaning and textual meaning. Intersemiotic systems have also been developed to analyse the types of meaning expansions that occur (see Example 3.2). Following this, the multimodal text is annotated according to the system choices that have been selected, so that elements of the text are coded multiple times. The combinations of semiotic choices are interpreted according to context. The theoretical and analytical procedures work together, so the theory is developed from multimodal text analysis and vice versa.

In summary, then, the SF-MDA approach involves:

1    Developing metafunctionally organized systems;
2    Analysing the text according to the system choices that are selected;
3    Interpreting combinations of choices according to register and genre.

For example, O'Halloran, Tan and Wignell (in press) adopt this approach to analyse the World Health Organization (WHO) Ebola website using Multimodal Analysis Image software (O'Halloran, Tan and E, 2015), which is purpose-built software, specifically designed for SF-MDA. The software comes with a catalogue of systems, but these systems can be edited and new ones added according to the user's requirements. O'Halloran and her colleagues use SFL systems, visual systems derived from O'Toole (2011) and register and genre theory to analyse the WHO Ebola home page. Examples of the SF-MDA systems are provided in Table 3.1, and a screenshot of the visual systems entered into the software are displayed in Figure 3.1a.

Table 3.1    SF-MDA text and image systems

| Semiotic resource metafunction | System | Explanation |
|---|---|---|
| **Text** | | |
| EXPERIENTIAL | | |
| Clause | Processes, Participant Roles and Circumstance | Happenings and actions |
| INTERPERSONAL | | |
| Clause | Speech Function | Exchange of information (e.g. statements and questions) and goods and services (e.g. commands and offers) |

*(Continued)*

Table 3.1 (Continued)

| Semiotic resource metafunction | System | Explanation |
|---|---|---|
| **TEXTUAL** | | |
| Clause | Information Focus | Organization of information, with points of departure for what follows |
| **Image** | | |
| **EXPERIENTIAL** | | |
| Work | Narrative Theme, Representation, Setting | Nature of the scene |
| Episode | Processes, Participant Roles and Circumstance | Visual happenings and actions |
| Figure | Posture, Dress | Characteristics of the participants |
| **INTERPERSONAL** | | |
| Work | Angle, Shot Distance, Lighting | Visual effects |
| Episode | Proportion in Relation to the Whole Image | Happenings in relation to the whole image |
| Figure | Gaze-visual Address | Direction of participant's gaze as internal to image or external to viewer |
| **TEXTUAL** | | |
| Work | Compositional Vectors, Framing | How the parts of the image are organized as a whole, with the visual marking of certain parts |
| Episode | Relative Placement of Episode, Framing | Position of the happenings in relation to the whole image and the visual marking of certain aspects within the happening |
| Figure | Relative Placement of Figure within the Episode; Framing | Position of the figures in relation to the happening and the visual marking of certain aspects of the figure |

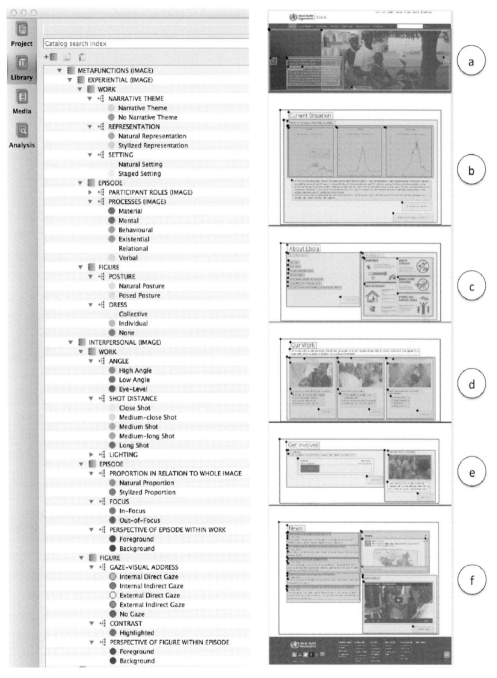

(a) Visual systems

(b) Sections of the WHO Ebola website

Figure 3.1    SF-MDA approach to the WHO Ebola website (O'Halloran, Tan and Wignell, in press)

The WHO Ebola website is composed of various subsections, with discourse types that are (a) Reporting; (b), (c) and (d) Information; (e) Promotional; and (f) News, as displayed in Figure 3.1b, where the various sections and the components of each section are marked using the overlay facilities in Multimodal Analysis Image software.

The Reporting section (a) has seven text–image complexes, which unfold to form a moving banner of reports, arranged in chronological order. The large images contrast with the other sections in the home page and thus function interpersonally to engage the viewer with the home page. Two of the text–image complexes (the first and fourth), displayed in Figures 3.2a and 3.3a, were analysed according to the systems discussed earlier. The choices were annotated using overlays, to which system choices were attached. A screenshot of the whole analysis for the first text–image complex is displayed in Figure 3.2b, and a close-up of the visual analysis for the second text–image complex is displayed in Figure 3.3b.

In the first image–text complex in Figure 3.2, the viewer conceptualizes the image as a photograph of a family, due to the characteristics of each figure (e.g. age and gender) and the various combination of semiotic choices in terms of (a) experiential meaning: process types (smiling and sitting on a motorbike with the man holding the child) and posture (posed); (b) interpersonal meaning: the gaze of each figure, which is directed towards the viewer; and (c) textual meaning: the relative placement of the episode in the centre of the photograph, framed by the tree on the right. Visually, the combinations of semiotic choices construe the image of a happy family. The text sets up an expectancy of success through the heading 'Despite Ebola, vigilance and hope prevail in Forecariah' and then specifically identifies the group as a family, naming the father and mother and describing how they overcame Ebola, 'providing a message of survival and hope'. The bright and colourful image of the smiling family group is co-contextualized with the hopeful message in the linguistic text, where participants are identified and logical sequences of events are constructed to provide further information about the Ebola situation in this location. In this case, the combinations of semiotic choices function within and across the image and the text construct a positive message with regard to the Ebola epidemic.

The image complex in Figure 3.3a is analysed using the same SF-MDA framework for text and images, and the overlays for the photograph are displayed in

(a) Text–image complex in WHO Ebola Website

Figure 3.2   Reporting section of the WHO Ebola website

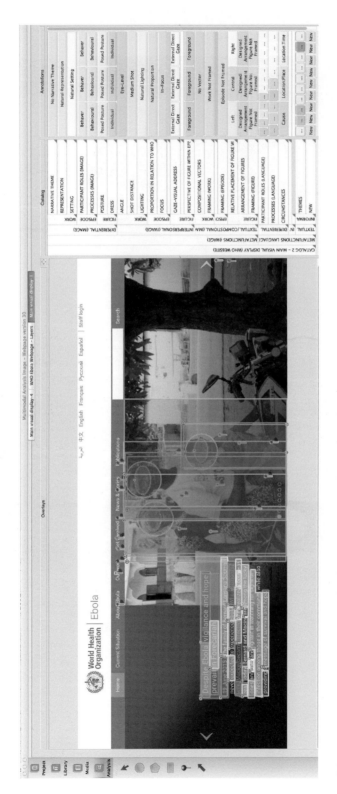

(b) SF-MDA analysis: Overlays (left) with system choices (right)

Figure 3.2 (Continued)

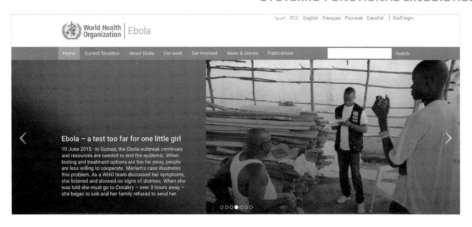

(a)  Text–image complex in the WHO Ebola home page

(b)  SF-MDA analysis of the photograph

Figure 3.3    Reporting section of the WHO Ebola home page

Figure 3.3b. In this case, the image consists of three people, with two figures in the foreground and one figure in the background. One would expect the figures in the foreground to be the most salient figures in the photograph, but the semiotic choices for (a) experiential meaning: process types (sitting, standing and looking);

(b) interpersonal meaning: the gaze of the foregrounded figures, which are directed towards the middle figure in the background; and (c) textual meaning: the framing of the middle figure by the two other figures and the poles in the background, creates a perspective where attention focuses on the middle figure who is looking down writing. This demonstrates how semiotic combinations function to create meaning: in this case, the significant figure in this image is the smaller middle figure in the background, which runs counter to expectations. In this photograph, the viewer is free to observe the scene (like a participant in the scene) rather than engage with it, given that gaze of the three participants are internal to the scene itself, rather than being directed to the viewer. The colours in the image (the colours are not shown but can be seen on the companion website) are sombre, matching the experiential meaning in heading in the text: 'Ebola – a test too far for one little girl', in which the distressing situation facing families affected by Ebola is described. In the text, the visually significant figure in the middle is identified as the WHO worker, who is discussing the case of the girl, advising the family that she must travel to another place for treatment, after which the girl breaks down and cries. The image and text relations co-contextualize each other, but in this case, the semiotic choices function to describe the desperate situation facing families affected by the Ebola crisis, in a report that predates the happier report just discussed. In this regard, we can see how combinations of semiotic choices function to order and structure the world, in this case with respect to controlling the Ebola crisis.

SF-MDA involves formulating a theoretical framework with descriptions of the semiotic choices that realize experiential, logical, interpersonal and textual meaning and then annotating the text according to the choices that have been made in order to analyse the meaning arising from semiotic interactions in the text. SF-MDA can also involve analysing the nature of the intersemiotic relations that are established and identifying the expansions of meaning that take place as semiotic choices are resemiotised. The SF-MDA approach allows the multimodal analyst to understand how semiotic choices combine to create meaning, with a view to identify 'hotspots' (O'Toole, 2011) of significant semiotic combinations. For example, the semiotic repetitions in Figure 3.2 (i.e. smiling faces, direct gaze, posture and the parallel alignment of the right arms, along with the angle at which their bodies are positioned) permit the viewer to identify the group as a happy family. Similarly, the viewer is drawn to the middle person in the background who is responsible for the fate of the little girl through semiotic combinations such as gaze, stance, perspective and framing in Figure 3.3b. (The little girl is almost entirely obscured by the figure on the left, with only the top of her head visible.) In each case, language functions to organize key participants in logically connected events so we learn more about the Ebola crisis, as constructed by the World Health Organization.

---

*Example 3.4*   SF-MDA for video analysis

SF-MDA analyses of dynamic media are particularly complex, time-consuming and difficult, given the multitude of systems for language, image, gesture, film editing techniques and so forth, which combine over time. However, digital tools such as Multimodal Analysis Video software (O'Halloran and Lim, 2014; O'Halloran, Tan and E, 2015) offer a solution to this problem. The software has graphical user interfaces for importing and organizing media files; creating and editing catalogues of systems and system choices for video annotation; storing projects; annotating and analysing media files; visualizing combinations of multimodal choices; and exporting data from the analyses to Excel spreadsheets for further data processing and visualization.

O'Halloran, Tan and E (2015) use the software to analyse the advocacy advertisement 'Tigers Are Running Out of Time' by the World Wildlife Fund (WWF), which aims to present a compelling argument about the urgent need to protect tigers. A catalogue of metafunctionally organized systems were entered into the software for analysing experiential content (e.g. participants, processes and circumstances), the social relations between participants (e.g. power and social distance), the orientation towards the content presented (modality and truth values), and the composition resources for different effects (e.g. cinematographic and editing techniques).

The user interface for annotating and analysing the video (see Figure 3.4a) is designed for quick and efficient annotation of system choices with time stamps. As such, there are functionalities for viewing the video in the player window, and inserting time-stamped annotation nodes (2) in system strips (3). The annotation nodes are synchronized with the video, the filmstrip (4), the sound strip (5), and the verbal transcription (6). To make an

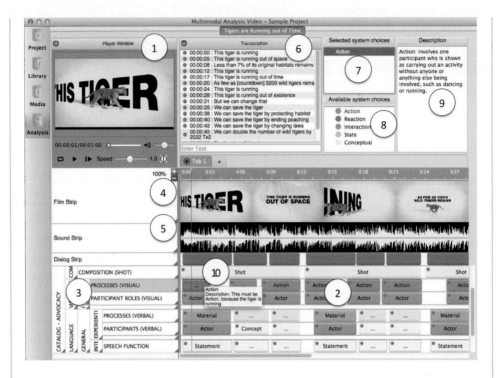

(a)  Player window (1), time-stamped annotations (2), system strips (3), filmstrip
     (4), sound strip (5), transcription of verbal text (6), selected system choice
     (7), list of available system choices (8), system choice definition (9), free-text
     annotation (10) (O'Halloran, Tan and E, 2015)

Figure 3.4(a)    Screenshot of sample analysis in Multimodal Analysis Video

annotation, a system choice (7) is selected from a list of available system
choices (8) based on the descriptions (9), and the choice is assigned to the
annotation node in the systems strip. Free-text descriptions on an annotation node in the system strips can also be added, as shown in (10).

The 'Tigers Are Running Out of Time' video was annotated for processes (e.g. material processes that describe actions and relational processes that describe the qualities and characteristics of persons, animals
and things), participants (e.g. actors and concepts) for both visual and
verbal modes, and the speech functions (e.g. statements and questions)
that were used to present information. While the colour-coding of system choices helps the analyst to see semiotic patterns, the combinations

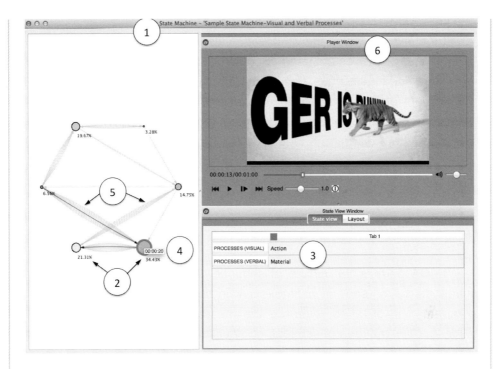

(b) Visualization window (1), state(s) (2), selected systems in the analysis (3), percentage/time in terms of total video duration (4), transitions (5), player window (6) (O'Halloran, Tan and E, 2015)

Figure 3.4(b)    Screenshot of state transition diagram in Multimodal Analysis Video

of semiotic choices are typically so complex that further data processing methods are required. For this reason, the annotations are stored in the database so that they can be later visualized as state transition diagrams, as displayed in Figure 3.4b. In these diagrams, a 'state' (2) is the combination of system choices that have been selected (3) in terms of total video time/duration (4). The state transition diagram also displays the shifts between the individual states (5), which can be viewed dynamically as the video unfolds in the player window (6).

The state transition diagram in Figure 3.4b reveals different aspects of the multimodal construction of the 'Tigers Are Running Out of Time' video. For example, there is considerable time (34.4 per cent, or 20 seconds in terms of total movie time) when the material and action processes in visual and linguistic semiotic resources combine in the video, reinforcing the image of tigers physically running, which is accompanied by music for greater effect. However, the visualization also reveals that language (rather than image) resources are used to construct the conceptual argument that tigers are endangered (i.e. 'tigers are running out of space' and 'tigers are running out of time') through relational processes (19.6 per cent, or 11 seconds in terms of total video duration), as indicated by the top left circle in the state diagram in Figure 3.4b. The visualization of the SF-MDA analysis reveals how combinations of semiotic choices 'combine in real time to contribute to the video's symmetry, consistency and innovation in terms of its communicative functions and hence its perceived effectiveness' (O'Halloran, Tan and E, 2015).

SF-MDA permits the nature of semiotic combinations to be analysed in dynamic media, as seen in Example 3.4. In this case, semiotic combinations are repeated in order to reinforce the message that is conveyed. In other instances, combinations of semiotic choices may function to provide contrasting choices, as for example, in the final phases of the television advertisement, which aims to end with a memorable climax (O'Halloran, Tan and E, 2013; O'Halloran and Lim, 2014). Significantly then, SF-MDA permits the multimodal analyst to see how key combinations of semiotic choices construct the registerial configurations of field, tenor and mode in order to identify key phases in the multimodal text. For example, the analysis of language choices, intonation, gesture and body posture in a multiparty government debate reveals how the semiotic choices of one participant, initiated by a change of intonation, function to reorientate the field of discourse in order to criticize and undermine the government (O'Halloran, 2011). In this case and others (e.g. Bateman 2008, 2014a; O'Halloran, E and Tan, 2014), the use of digital technology provides new opportunities for handling the complexity of multimodal semiosis, with a view to developing the theory and practice of SF-MDA research (see Chapter 6).

## Fields of application

Halliday views language as a social phenomenon to 'fully understand the relationship between observed instances of language behaviour and the underlying system of language' (Halliday, 2002: 8). As Halliday explains, 'if you don't know the system, then you cannot understand the text' (Halliday, 2002: 10). Halliday's view of language means that SFL has been applied to fields that include discourse analysis, education, language development, second language development, computational linguistics, clinical linguistics, translation, language typology and the study of language in various domains, such as science, medicine, literature and the law (e.g. Thompson et al., in press).

SF-MDA is derived from Halliday's SFT, and so the approach is being applied to the same fields as those previously listed for SFL: for example, multimodal discourse analysis, educational semiotics, computational multimodal studies, multimodal translation and multimodal literacy. Moreover, as SF-MDA offers the means to explore language in operation with other semiotic resources, new fields of research are being opened up, such as brand semiotics, design semiotics and multimodal approaches to new media. In fact, SF-MDA can be applied to any field of activity that involves human communication.

## Critique of SFL and SF-MDA

The most common critique of SFL is that it is difficult and complex to learn, given the large number of technical terms that are specific to the approach. The expansion of the field has resulted in an increasing number of technical terms, for example, for modelling discourse systems and context. As a result, SFL is a hierarchical knowledge structure (like mathematics and science), which initially appears daunting to newcomers. However, there are introductory texts that explain the principles of SFL in accessible language for beginners (Thompson, 2004; Eggins, 2005; Bloor and Bloor, 2013), in addition to the earlier versions of SFG (Halliday, 1985a, 1994).

More generally, however, there has been a surprising lack of critique of Halliday's SFL, from both within and outside SFL circles. Within the systemic community, there is enormous respect for Halliday's work, which has been variously extended, developed and improved in many directions. Also, there is a tendency to avoid confrontational attacks in the SFL community, as is common in some schools of formal linguistics (Halliday and Fawcett, 1987). More generally, however, it appears that the grammar that Halliday developed actually works, as demonstrated by text analysis. Outside of SFL circles, Halliday's SFG has been compared with other functional approaches (Butler, 2003a, 2003b), but for the large part, a large part of Halliday's work has not been subject to much critique, particularly in the US, perhaps largely in part because formalists ask different questions, given their different conceptions of language.

A criticism of SF-MDA is that SFL grammar is taken as a model for constructing the meaning of systemic choices, and this has included the importation of linguistic concepts (Bateman, 2014b). While some of these concepts are sufficiently abstract as to apply to different levels and scales in linguistic and multimodal texts (e.g. logical relations, processes and participants), other approaches in the form of discourse levels of representation are promising. Moreover, meaning is seen to arise from semiotic combinations rather than from individual choices: that is, the choice of camera angle by itself does not have meaning; rather, it is the semiotic combination of the camera angle with other system choices (e.g. shot distance, lighting, framing and the nature of the participants and processes) that realize meaning.

Within multimodal studies, SF-MDA has been criticized as having a focus on the text without reference to context, but largely this is the result of grappling with the main problem of developing systemic descriptions that can then be applied to multimodal text analysis. At the same time, however, SF-MDA should not be too prescriptive in terms of the meanings assigned to individual system choices, given that meaning is the result of systemic combinations.

## New directions

A major problem for SF-MDA is the complexity and time-consuming nature of SF-MDA analysis, particularly for dynamic texts such as videos and websites. As a result, SF-MDA approaches have tended to focus on the close analysis of a small number of multimodal texts, from which generalizations are made. In response, Bateman and colleagues have called for empirical approaches to be developed in multimodal studies (Bateman, Delin and Henschel, 2004; Bateman, 2014c) (see Chapter 6), basically following the computational approach that has always been part of SFL (O'Donnell and Bateman, 2005; Bateman and O'Donnell, 2015). As part of this movement, digital approaches to SF-MDA have been developed in the form of purpose-built software, such as Multimodal Analysis Image and Multimodal Analysis Video. Such applications permit the multimodal annotations to be stored in a database for further data processing, such as mathematical modelling techniques and visualizations (O'Halloran, Tan and E, 2013, 2014). This approach, termed multimodal analytics (O'Halloran, Tan and

E, 2014), offers an exciting path forward for SF-MDA because it is designed to handle the complexity of multimodal analysis, with a view to developing new analytical and visualization techniques through interdisciplinary collaboration with scientists. More recently, Kay O'Halloran, John Bateman and colleagues are attempting to combine SF-MDA analysis with data mining and visualization in order to tackle the problem of big data. As people, processes, data and things become increasingly interconnected in the so-called Internet of Everything, the application of SF-MDA theory to solve real problems in the world is becoming an exciting reality.

# CHAPTER 4

# Social semiotics

## Introduction to the approach

### Early developments

The aim of social semiotics is to understand the social dimensions of meaning, its production, interpretation and circulation, and its implications. It sets out to reveal how processes of meaning making (i.e. signification and interpretation or what is called semiosis) shape individuals and societies. Its basic assumption is that meanings derive from social action and interaction using semiotic resources as tools. It stresses the agency of sign makers, focusing on modes and their affordances, as well as the social uses and needs they serve. Gunther Kress, Robert Hodge and later Theo van Leeuwen developed social semiotics from three main strands of influence: Linguistics including Hallidayan linguistics (see Chapter 3), semiotics and critical linguistics that is now more commonly referred to as critical discourse analysis (CDA).

In the late 1970s Michael Halliday, whose work is fully discussed in Chapter 3, first used the term 'language as social semiotic' (1978) to stress the relationship between a language sign system and the social needs it is used to serve. He understood language in terms of sets of options that shape what people can and cannot do with a language in a given social context. From this perspective, every linguistic act is seen as involving choices. Language is understood as an *evolving* system of *meaning potentials*. In the 1980s, Gunther Kress, Robert Hodge and others examined language as a system (Kress and Hodge, 1979) and began to build on Halliday's approach to describing language as a system of meaning/semiotic choices in order to analyse the meaning potential of other sign systems, such as image.

In the mid-1980s the influential *Newtown Semiotic Circle* was founded in Sydney. Members included Gunther Kress, Robert Hodge, Theo van Leeuwen,

Jim Martin and later Paul Thibault and Terry Threadgold, among others. They started the work of looking at different modes of communication and the ways in which they were 'integrated' in texts. As these scholars moved beyond language to consider the 'whole domain of meaning', they also drew on ideas from European and American semiotics and broadened it to *social* semiotics. Kress commented that by the 1980s he was:

> doing semiotics more than linguistics. Because linguistics could not provide the tools that we needed in order to account for the whole domain of meaning.
>
> (Andersen et al., 2015: 72)

Theo van Leeuwen, a key scholar in the development of social semiotics, who first studied film semiotics and French structuralist semiotics (e.g. the work of Roland Barthes) and later Hallidayan linguistics, has also commented on the importance of semiotics as a feature of his work (Andersen et al., 2015). (Note that the semiotician Saussure (1983) suggested that the 20th century would be the century of semiotics for which the existing and developed discipline of linguistics could provide the theoretical model.)

The Newtown circle's engagement with semiotics led to the concept of sign becoming ever more central to social semiotics. However, the social semiotic focus on agency and social context needed a more *social* account of sign than was afforded by 'traditional' structuralist semiotics. This was required because traditional semiotics is based on the concept of given social structures and a view of society as prior to individuals: epitomized by its separation of language as an abstract system of signs (langue) and how language is used by people (parole). That is, traditional semiotics assumes that the meanings of language are 'frozen and fixed' and need to be 'decoded' with 'reference to a coding system that is impersonal and neutral, and universal' (Kress and Hodge, 1988: 12).

In contrast, *social* semiotics emphasizes the agency of the sign maker. From this perspective, sign systems are shaped through social usage; they are not prior or given or abstract; it is not possible to separate a sign system from society and its contexts of use by people. Social semiotics problematized and rejected the traditional semiotic separation of langue and parole as essentialist. It developed a concept of the *motivated sign* (discussed more fully later in this chapter) to account for the role of human agency and social context in the construction of meaning and the *variability* of meanings. Motivated signs are understood as arising out of and motivated by the cultural, social and historical experiences and context of the sign maker: a product of the social process of meaning making. That is, social semiotics presents a social theory of meaning making and communication in which modes or sign systems (e.g. language or image) are intertwined with their user and social context of use.

Around the time that the Sydney semiotics circle was in full swing, critical discourse analysis (CDA) was developed in the UK. Like social semiotics, CDA built on critical linguistics and SFL. Critical linguistics gets it name from critical theory, an umbrella term for neo-Marxist–based analysis that originated from the Frankfurt School, which set out to critically analyse capitalist society (see e.g. Fowler et al., 1979). Some have argued that CDA could be seen as a branch of social semiotics and vice versa; others, including van Leeuwen, see them as distinct. We share Wodak's definition of CDA as a school, or 'shared perspective', on doing linguistic, semiotic or discourse analysis (rather than its being a theory or method):

> CDA is . . . fundamentally interested in analyzing opaque as well as transparent structural relationships of dominance, power and control when these are manifested in language . . . to investigate critically social inequality as it is expressed, constituted, legitimized, and so on, by language use (or in discourse) . . . [to] endorse Habermas's claim that 'language is also a medium of domination and social force . . . to legitimize relations of organized power'.
> (Wodak, 2006: 5)

Both CDA and social semiotics aim to account for how power and ideology operate through communicative acts. CDA aims to make visible the interconnectedness of language, social and political ideologies with the aim of creating awareness and change. Ideology and power are central concepts in a social semiotic analysis. For example, Kress and Hodge's *Language as Ideology* (1979) and *Social Semiotics* (1988) examined the social implications of writing and image in 'print' media (e.g. advertisements, magazines) and started to extend the focus on power and ideology to other modes (though at that time they did not have the term 'mode'). CDA tends to focus on specific social problems (e.g. racism) that frame institutional discourse, i.e. speech and writing, as a form of social practice to constitute and transmit knowledge and power. Social semiotics tends to focus on everyday, almost 'banal' or 'mundane' artefacts produced outside institutions (say, a child's drawing) as sites of ideology. The connection and influence of CDA is most clearly seen in van Leeuwen's approach to social semiotics. For example, van Leeuwen with Machin (2007) has written on global cultural industries through a study of semiotic artefacts (e.g. video games, women's magazines), and in *Introducing Social Semiotics* (2005), he described how discourses are realized through a broad range of modes (e.g. dress, spatial design, gesture, image and music) (see Example 4.1).

## Social semiotics and multimodality

In different ways the members of the Newtown Semiotic Circle started to question the linguistic assumption that speech (verbal language) is always the dominant, the most significant and an autonomous mode of communication. This marked a key point in the development of a social semiotic approach to multimodality.

During the period from the middle to late 1990s, social semiotic research focused on written and visual texts. Kress and van Leeuwen's much cited *Reading Images: The Grammar of Visual Design* was published in 1996. At the time of publication, the authors referred to the book as part of a 'fledgling movement' of social semiotics (Kress and van Leeuwen, 1996: 5). They analysed a wide range of artefacts that used image and writing, including children's drawings, textbook illustrations, journalistic photographs, advertisements, as well as a few examples of three-dimensional objects (e.g. sculptures and toys). The book proposed a social semiotic framework for the analysis of image and text bringing together insights from semiotics, CDA and SFL (e.g. using system networks, a diagrammatic method for visualizing meaning as choice; see Chapter 3) as well as insights from film studies, iconography and art history. Around this time, Lemke (1998) had started to explore different types of scientific representation, including diagrams, images and multimedia/digital texts in scientific textbooks. Lemke (in Andersen et al., 2015: 117) has described his use of social semiotics in the context of an 'eclectic approach' that valued 'bricolage'.

Kress and van Leeuwen used the term 'grammar of visual design' to refer to the social use of the visual, although they rejected the critique that social semiotics *imposes* a linguistic framework on visual or multimodal texts:

> The analogy with language does not imply, however, that visual structures are like linguistic structures. The relation is much more general. Visual structures realize meanings as linguistic structures do also, and thereby point to different interpretations of experience and different forms of social interaction. The meanings which can be realized in language and in visual communication

> overlap in part, that is, some things can be expressed both visually and ver-
> bally; and in part they diverge – some things can be 'said' only visually, oth-
> ers only verbally. But even when something can be 'said' both visually and
> verbally the *way in which* it will be said is different.
>
> (Kress and van Leeuwen, 1996: 2)

This returns us to the discussion we set out in Chapter 2 of how many 'linguistic' principles are actually general semiotic principles. '*Semiotic principle*' is a term that is used to refer to principles for and features of meaning making that apply across modes. For instance, all modes have resources for producing *intensity*. In the mode of *speech*, that is realized by the intensity of sound – 'loudness'; it is also realized lexically, e.g. as 'very'. In the mode of *gesture*, intensity might be realized by the *speed of movement* of the hand or by the *extent* of the move-ment. In the mode of *colour*, it might be done through degrees of saturation, and so on.

In the late 1990s, social semiotic attention to a fuller range of modes first started to gain momentum. For example, in *Sound, Music, Speech*, van Leeuwen (1999) examined the material and semiotic potentials of sound for communica-tion. He investigated the semiotic potentials of a wide range of modes, media and genres, including film soundtracks, advertising jingles, classical music and everyday soundscapes.

In the early 2000s. a significant development in a social semiotic approach to multimodality was the attempt to refocus its analytical lens from identifying and describing the resources of individual modes to the semiotic principles that oper-ate within and across modes. In *Multimodal Discourse: The Modes and Media of Communication* (2001), Kress and van Leeuwen developed their earlier work on the visual to investigate the semiotic potentials of space and architecture, multi-media and voice and music (Kress and van Leeuwen, 2001)

> We aim to explore the common principles behind multimodal communica-
> tion. We move away from the idea that the different modes in multimodal
> texts have strictly bounded and framed specialist tasks . . . . Instead we move
> towards a view of multimodality in which common semiotic principles operate
> in and across different modes.
>
> (Kress and van Leeuwen, 2001: 2)

Lemke has also contributed to the development of broad principles that inform a social semiotic approach to multimodality with a focus on the multimodal features of gaming. Most notably by introducing the concept of intertextuality and *time scales* to social semiotics:

> This translates into *activity scales, or time scales*, as I more recently called it, in which the fundamental question is not just what kinds of meaning can you make over longer periods of activity than over shorter periods, but how do the meanings or the actions that you take over shorter time-scales cumulate and integrate into the meanings that you make over the longer scales.
>
> (Lemke quoted in Andersen et al., 2015: 124)

---

*Example 4.1*   How social semiotics draws on influences from SFL, semiotics and CDA

Theo van Leeuwen has undertaken a number of studies on toys with colleagues including Staffan Selander, David Machin and Carmen Rosa Caldas-Coulthard. He has investigated the semiotic resources of toys, how their uses arise from the interests and needs of society and how these resources and uses change over time and context. Van Leeuwen's work shows how social semiotics draws on influences from SFL, semiotics and CDA. For instance, take the example of the pram rattle toy he presented in *Introducing Social Semiotics* (2005), which is hung across the pram or cot for babies to play with. He pointed out that pram rattles are 'designed to help babies to develop their eye to limb co-ordination' and, like all toys, are at the same time 'pragmatic, functional objects, and symbolic objects' (van Leeuwen, 2005: 79–80). Van Leeuwen's example compared two different pram rattles:

1   The rabbit pram rattle consisted of four identical white rabbits 'dressed' in pastel-coloured clothes strung on an elastic string that could be attached across a pram. The rabbits were made of shiny, rigid thick plastic. When the string was moved and stretched, the rabbits moved and bounced and made a soft rattle sound.

2   The rainbow galaxy pram rattle consisted of three different aliens and gold stars and a box of beads inside one alien. They were made of soft fabric in dark mixed colours. They were connected to one another with

Velcro fasteners so that they could be taken apart, but they did not rotate.

Van Leeuwen used Halliday's *interpersonal* and *ideational metafunctions* (outlined in Chapter 3) to ask 'what these toys have been designed to be able to mean and do'.

He discussed the field of possible *interpersonal meanings* of the pram rattles. For instance, he discussed the wide-range potential meanings of their combination of 'human and animal elements', including dominant cultural patterns (e.g. Beatrix Potter's Peter Rabbit stories, which depict rabbits as living a human-like family life). He explored the representation of the rabbits, for instance, the use of the colour: white, linked with 'purity' and 'innocence' (in the West), to 'symbolise children', and pastels, associated with 'calmness' and often worn by babies. He contrasted this with the demonic symbolism of the aliens (with 'bony-backs', 'lizard-like tails' and 'insect-like eyes') to make figures of 'dread' 'look human, friendly and comical'.

Van Leeuwen then investigated the *interactional meaning potential* of the pram rattles by asking, 'What can be done with these toys?' He explored their materiality and the way they move (i.e. their 'kinetic design'). The rabbits, he argued, 'lend themselves less easily to tactile experience', although they can be kicked by babies, whereas the aliens can be 'cuddled' and squished to form different postures and expressions, with more potential for 'emotive meaning'. The two toys present, he concludes, different conceptions of childhood: the rabbits a 'protective', almost 'Victorian' one, the aliens a more 'ambivalent' and 'dangerous' one.

Van Leeuwen, having considered the structure of the toys' design, turned to explore the contextually specific '*rules of use*' that shape their use. He investigated the 'discourses that surround the toys and regulated their use in various ways'. To do this, he turned to a CDA analysis of mother and baby magazines, rendering visible ideas from developmental psychology, the marketing of the toys, and so on.

Van Leeuwen's next analytical step was to study how the toys are used: 'to what extent do people follow the "rules"?' He used video recordings of ten mothers interacting with their child and the toy. The analysis showed that the mothers' actions differed and while 'not entirely determined' by the toys were 'not totally free either': 'There were constraints, partially 'built in', partially resulting from their awareness of the developmental discourses of childhood experts, and of today's popular childhood culture' (van Leeuwen, 2005: 87). He concluded by bringing these strands of analysis together to show how both toys functioned and what they supressed and afforded, and made suggestions for the future production and interpretation of such toys.

You may have noticed that, so far, most of the examples that we have referred to in this chapter are about textual artefacts. While social semiotics tends to be used to work with textual materials (e.g. magazines, adverts, textbooks), it can, however, be used to analyse interaction. Jewitt worked with Kress and others to extend a social semiotic approach to explore multimodal interaction in the school science classroom (Kress et al., 2014) and later the school English classroom (Kress et al., 2005). These two projects attended to the modes and semiotic resources available in the classroom spaces, as well as how teachers and students (sign makers) used them to construct subject knowledge and pedagogic relationships in different ways. Social semiotics was used to analyse textual artefacts (i.e. textbooks, objects, models etc.) and the use of gesture, gaze and body position and posture in classroom interaction. The potential to produce an encompassing social semiotic account of both artefacts *and* interaction is particularly powerful for gaining insight into meaning-making processes and literacy practices (Jewitt and Kress, 2003), such as 'reading' and 'writing' online (e.g. Jewitt, 2002, 2005a) and digital literacy and learning (Jewitt, 2008a, 2008b).

By the late 2000s, a social semiotic approach to multimodality was gaining traction in the field of linguistics and communication. Gunther Kress starts *Multimodality: A Social Semiotic Approach to Contemporary Communication* (2010) by 'unpacking' what is meant by multimodality and examining its relationship with social semiotics (a question that we discuss more generally in Chapter 1 of this book). He uses an example – a comparison of two supermarket car park signs at a busy junction that he sees on his bus journey to work most days – to illustrate the relationship between social semiotics and 'multimodality':

Multimodality can tell us what modes are used; it cannot tell us about this difference in *style*; it has no means to tell us what that difference might *mean*. What is the difference in colour about or the difference in the drawing style?

What *identity* is each of the two signs projecting? What are the supermar-kets 'saying' about themselves? What are they telling their customers about themselves? Are these differences accidental, arbitrary? Would the style of one sign serve equally well for the other supermarket? To answer ques-tions of that kind we need a theory that deals with *meaning* in all its appear-ances, in all social occasions and in all cultural sites. That theory is Social Semiotics.

(Kress, 2010: 1–2)

This example is typical of social semiotics in its focus on the design and interpre-tation of everyday texts (e.g. signs, adverts) and points to the potential of social semiotics to help us to interrogate the communicational landscape.

The work we discuss in this chapter differs in the levels of emphasis that is placed on the theoretical and the empirical. While their theoretical and empirical contributions are intimately connected, some publications place more emphasis on theory development while others place more on producing empirical 'evidence'.

Theoretically focused publications (e.g. Bezemer and Kress, 2016) pre-sent theoretical concepts, using selected examples. While they are empirically grounded, their primary purpose is to develop theoretical concepts rather than to explain and 'exhaust' a single set of research materials. The aim of these publica-tions is to draw out connections between instances of broadly similar phenom-ena in different domains and contexts and to develop hypotheses about semiotic principles.

Empirically focused publications aim to produce a social semiotic account of a systematically collected set of research materials, a 'data corpus' (such as materials collected in a case study of a school; e.g. Jewitt, 2008a). While such publications are focused on describing and explaining research materials, they also contribute to the advancement of multimodal theory; e.g. by pointing to the boundaries, gaps and problems with a concept and establishing the degree to which it 'stands up', where the concept works well (with what type of materi-als, genres or media) or what needs modifying. For example, as we discuss in Chapter 6, the interpretative claims and theoretical concepts of social semiotics have been interrogated within corpus-based multimodal analysis and multimodal reception analysis.

If you are starting out on your engagement with social semiotics, or multi-modality more generally (e.g. for your dissertation), we recommend a focus on systematically collecting, analysing and explaining a complete data set, drawing on, validating, advancing and problematizing social semiotic theory.

## Key principles and concepts

A social semiotic theory of communication sees systems of meaning as fluid, contingent and changing in relation to context, history and culture. Like any research tradition, social semiotics has been developed and adapted by scholars in different directions and contexts.

We introduce the concepts that are key to a social semiotic approach to multimodality with particular reference to the body of work founded by the theorist Gunther Kress, whose work has had and continues to have a major influence on both social semiotics and multimodality. Here's a classic example from his work:

> A three-year old, sitting on his father's lap, draws a series of circles, seven to be exact. At the end he says: 'This is a car'. How is, or could this be 'a car'? While drawing, he had said 'Here's a wheel . . . Here's another wheel . . . That's a funny wheel . . . This is a car.' For him the *criterial* feature of *car* was its 'wheel-ness'; it had (many) wheels . . . 'circles *are* wheels' and 'many wheels *are* a car' . . . To see how or why wheels could be the criterial feature for 'car', we have to adopt the point of view, literally, physiologically, psychologically, culturally, semiotically, of the three-year-old. If we imagine him looking at the family car we might conclude that this sign-maker's position in the world, literally, physically, but also psychically, affectively, might well lead him to see 'car' in that way. His *interest* arises out of his (physical, affective, cultural, social) position in the world at that moment vis-à-vis the object to be represented. His sign reflects his 'position'. Generalizing, we can say that *interest* at the moment of sign-making arises out of the sign-maker's position in the world; it shapes *attention*; that it *frames* a part of the world and acts as *a principle for the selection of apt signifiers*.
>
> (Kress, 2010: 70)

## Sign maker, interest and motivated sign

This example demonstrates the centrality of the concepts of *sign maker*, *interest* and *motivated sign* to meaning making. The concept of the *sign maker* is used to refer both to the *producer* and to the *interpreter* of a sign. In other words, a person who makes *or* interprets a sign is engaged in sign making. Interpreting a sign is viewed as a *remaking* of a sign. Both the producer and the remaker of a sign are shaped by their social, cultural, political and technological environments (which in our global digital world can, of course, be multiple). Recognizing the agency of the sign maker and their (implicit or explicit) intentionality is central to a social semiotic approach.

When making signs, people bring together and connect the available form that is most apt to express the meaning they want to express at a given moment. In this, the signifier that they use takes on a new meaning (in the sign): it is transformed by its use. In other words, signs are always newly made, always transformative – even if the transformations are in 'entirely minute and barely noticeable ways' (Kress, 1997: 94). Viewing sign making as motivated and transformative raises the question of what motivates a person's choice of one semiotic resource over another. The term 'motivated sign' is used to express the aptness of fit between criterial characteristics of what is meant ('signified') and form ('signifier'). (See Example 4.2.) It is the sign maker's *interest* at the moment of making the sign that guides the judgement of aptness of fit:

> 'Interest' is the articulation and realisation of an individual's relation to an object or event, acting out of that social complex at a particular moment, in the context of an interaction with other constitutive factors of the situation which are considered as relevant by the individual.
>
> (Kress, 1993: 174)

*Interest* is a term used in social semiotics to refer to the momentary condensation of all the (relevant) social experiences that have shaped the sign maker's subjectivity – a condensation produced by the need for a response to a prompt in and by the social environment in which a new sign is made. The response is both the representation of the sign maker's interest and their awareness of and attention to configurations of power in the social environment at the moment of sign making. As in all sign making there is the question of the availability of resources. The sign makers' interest leads to their choice of resources, seen as apt in the social context of sign production. Viewing signs as motivated and constantly being remade draws attention to the interests and intentions that motivate a person's choice of one semiotic resource over another (Kress, 1993). The concept of interest connects a person's choice of one resource over another with the social context of sign production – returning to the importance of *meaning as choice* within social semiotic theory of communication.

*Example 4.2*   Applying the concept of motivated signs and interest to contemporary communication

Elisabetta Adami used a social semiotic approach to explore contemporary patterns of communication in a study of video interaction on YouTube (2009). The study examined the option of 'video response' on the video-sharing website YouTube and showed how it triggered the new interaction practice of 'communication threads started by an initial video built up by video responses and resumed by a video-summary'.

Adami analysed a YouTube video thread that started from a video titled '@—Where Do You Tube?—@', by the popular vlogger ChangeDa-Channel. She conducted a detailed social semiotic analysis of the initial video and 772 videos uploaded in response to the initial video question 'Where Do You Tube From?' in different ways. She identified some preliminary key principles of video interaction in terms of how a given topic and form, prompted by the initial video, are taken on in different ways by the responses. The study drew attention to how semiotic resources are used in interaction according to their sign makers' interest and how this shapes sign making in video interaction, through processes of transduction and transformation, and the set of possible (interpretations and) responses that a text prompts.

Adami analysed, for example, how the prompt–response relation was complicated by the range of resources used to represent the (You)Tubers' 'location'. While most video responses (700) took up ChangeDaChannel's written form-specific prompt, 90 videos represented their location in speech. Among these, only 43 answered the topic question exclusively through speech:

> Using a finer-grained analysis, each video is unique, in terms of soundtracks (or environmental noises), colour palettes and effects, (You)Tubers' personae (e.g. human faces, animated avatars), facial expressions and gestures, calligraphies, writing colours, fonts, layouts, supports (e.g. post-it, duct tape, palm of the hand, blackboard) and materials (e.g. marker, lipstick, chalk), camera angles and positions (so

that handwriting is shown to a fixed webcam or the camera moves and films it), backgrounds behind (You)Tubers, (You)Tubers enacting the process of writing or showing just its final product, and so on.

(Adami, 2009: 390–391)

Adami pointed out how the semiotic resources used in the original video to indicate location were also transformed through video interaction:

The video-thread also attests to an impressive amount of multimodal representations of the location. Apart from or combined with writing, the location is represented through still/dynamic images of the country or of well-known national symbols (e.g. the Guinness beer logo for Ireland; a photo of Valentino Rossi for Italy); through maps, flags and satellite shots; it can be indicated (by pointing to it) on a globe or represented through clothes (e.g. a hat of the local baseball team). When verbalized, the location can be sung rather than spoken and, when written, it can appear on a road sign or be included in the town/country emblem. Also stereotyped phrases of the native language contribute to representing the location, such as 'ole!' for Spain and 'aloha' for Hawaii. In addition, 44 videos use a topic-related soundtrack, such as the national anthem, a song mentioning the town (e.g. 'Barcelona' by Freddie Mercury and Montserrat Caballé), or the song of a famous singer (e.g. Édith Piaf for France).

(Adami, 2009: 392)

Through her analysis, Adami showed that the response videos supplied more content and used a wider range of resources than the initial video and thus did more than *respond* to the prompt. Rather they are a semiotic act. She showed that while the affordances of the YouTube platform deter-mined what is 'structurally favored' by the interface, these affordances are intertwined with people's practices. That is, the technological possibilities and constraints of the video response option generate semiotic affordances that are used according to the purposes of the interactants in a commu-nicational context 'where differentiation and originality are highly valued' and 'maximally "tune in" with the initial video but at the same time display their distinctiveness' (Adami, 2009: 391). (You)Tubers adopted prac-tices according to their different interests and actualized these technical

affordances in various ways to realize different purposes and effects, notably to construct and present a 'distinctive' identity within a 'semiotic space
where creativeness is highly valued' (Adami, 2009: 395).

## Mode and semiotic resource

One aim of a social semiotic analysis is to identify and describe the *modes* and
*semiotic resources* that are available in a given situation and how people use
them, the choices they make and what motivates them, and how their in situ
choices are shaped by (and realize) power. Here we briefly define these terms
from a social semiotic perspective.

*Semiotic resource* is a term used to refer to a community's means for making
meaning. These are both material resources (i.e. modes) and immaterial conceptual resources, which are realized in and through modes (e.g. intensity, coherence,
proximity etc.). Semiotic resources are the product of the social meaning making
practices (the semiotic work) of members of a community over time, always as
meeting requirements of that community. For instance, the (material) resource of
physical distance has been shaped by photographers and film-makers over time
into the semiotic resource 'length of shot'. That resource is used to instantiate
levels of social intimacy: a close-up is often used to suggest a 'close' social relationship – 'intimacy' or 'intensity' among other things, while a long shot tends to
be used to suggest a more 'formal', 'absent' or 'distant' social relationship.

A *mode* is a *socially organized* set of semiotic resources for making meaning. For instance, image, writing, layout and speech are examples of modes. In
order for something to count as a mode, it needs to have a set of resources
and organizing principles that are recognized within a community. The more a
set of resources has been used in a particular community, the more fully and
finely articulated they become. For example, the resources of gesture have been
shaped into different communicative modes that serve a diverse range of communities, including different hearing communities, hearing impaired communities,
ballet dancers, deep-water divers and airport runway ground staff.

## Modal affordance, transduction and transformation

A social semiotic approach views the process of sign making as always subject
to the aptness of the available modes. This brings us to the concept of *modal*

*affordance,* a concept that is used to refer to the idea that different modes offer different potentials for making meaning. Modal affordances affect the kinds of semiotic work a mode can be used for, the ease with which it can be done and how. Modal affordances are connected both to a mode's material and social histories, that is, the social work that it has been used for in a specific context. It is in this way that modal affordances affect a sign maker's choice of a mode.

The different affordances of modes bring us to the social semiotic concept of transduction. *Transduction* is a term used in *social semiotics* to refer to the remaking of meaning involving a move *across* modes – a process in which 'meaning material' is moved from one mode to another. For example, something written might be remade as a diagram, or something said might be remade as an action. This compares with the remaking of meaning by changes *within* the same mode, referred to as *transformation.* A shift across modes involves the use the different semiotic entities of the mode into which meaning materials are moved. The process is complex because the specific material resources of each mode differ in nearly all cases. Transduction involves a change in the resources available for making meaning material, with profound implications for meaning.

Additional or alternative cultural meanings and practices may shape the transductive process. In her work on 'the transmodal moment', Newfield (2014) has focused attention on the multiple transformations that occur in processes of transduction – in materiality, genre, meaning, subjectivity and in what is learned and how – as well as revealing the situatedness of transmodal semiotic action. Newfield used a social semiotic approach to 're-modalize' the teaching of poetry in a school in Soweto, a Johannesburg township. This approach drew on African popular culture to shift the curriculum focus from the analysis of poetry – which students were entirely disengaged from – to the composition of poetry. It enabled the students to come to poetry in different ways – as a spoken form, as drawing and story writing in response to poems, as oral praise poems performed in the students' 'home' languages, returning to write their poems in English. Indeed, some students even made an embroidered cloth. Finally, the students produced an alternative written poetry anthology to the school anthology. It was the move from reading to writing and acting out/performing that made this particular pedagogical intervention such a success:

> Using certain modes catapulted the students' meanings into a new domain, style, discourse and aesthetic. In the shift from a page to a cloth, students were drawing on and displaying African semiotics forms and practices, specifically, minceka cloths and the practice of embroidery. In the shift from

canonical English poems in print to praise poems in the vernacular, and then to the performance of their own poems in English, the schoolchildren were expanding their concept of poetry to include traditional oral poetry and contemporary spoken word. The modal shift enabled integration of these forms into the curriculum.

(Newfield, 2014: 111)

These shifts in modes resulted in different modal resources, affordances and histories entering into the cultural context of the South African classroom. For these young South African students, processes of transduction in semiotic practices familiar to them but not usually admitted into or valued in school classrooms opened up spaces for them that had not existed before.

## Design

Another key concept in social semiotics is design. *Design* is a term used in social semiotics to refer to the situated process in which a sign maker chooses semiotic resources and possible arrangements for semiotic entities to be produced to meet particular social functions or purposes. Design is seen as based on a rhetorical (a rhetor's) assessment of the requirements of such an entity; that serves as the starting point for the meaning-making process of design. All sign making and hence all signs are subject to this process. Both the original designer and producer of a sign and those who subsequently interpret and remake the sign are seen as making meaning. Design is not understood as a matter of 'anything goes'. Design is always socially located and subject to various constraints, for example of the resources that are (made) available to designers and producers (e.g. Jewitt, 2005b). The process is subject in varying degrees to regimes that regulate and shape how resources are to be used so as to meet various norms and expectations. Social semiotics is interested in how modes change as power shifts at the interpersonal, institutional and societal levels. Norms that are socially made are also broken and changed through social interaction. It is through this process of breaking and making that semiotic resources are changed and new possibilities for semiotic resources are generated and come into the 'modal pool' of meaning-making potentials.

In the next section, we give an account of how these concepts guide a social semiotic analysis of multimodal artefacts.

## Methods and analysis

Social semiotic analysis involves intensive engagement with artefacts. It views artefacts as a semiotic material residue of a sign maker's interests mediated through the environment the sign was made in. It sets out to examine the social world as it is represented in artefacts. The analysis of artefacts is based on available information of the context in which they were produced. Take, for instance, Kress's classic example of his young son's drawing of a car discussed in the previous section. The child's drawing is the focus of analysis and interpreted against the background of what his son said to him when he showed him the drawing. Yet access to information about the process of producing the artefact is not a prerequisite for a social semiotic analysis. Indeed frequently texts are analysed without having interviewed or observed the text maker (see e.g. Bezemer and Kress, 2008 on textbooks). In some ways, this is similar to how an archaeologist reconstructs social practices through the detailed analysis of tools produced in a bygone era.

The following features characterize a social semiotic methodology:

- Small or large collections of artefacts including the everyday, some would even say 'banal' artefacts (e.g. children's drawings, supermarket car park signs, salt and pepper sachets), as well as more prominent, regulated artefacts (e.g. textbooks, magazines)
- Micro observation of modal features
- Often the comparison of works (e.g. comparing artefacts from different points in time or perhaps made by different people in the same context)
- Exploring all the semiotic aspects of an artefact
- Assuming that the person who made it wanted to express a meaning and using the best available semiotic resources to do so
- Placing emphasis on the social contexts and resources of meaning making within which an individual's meaning making is suffused
- Paying detailed attention to all elements of an artefact as a key to gaining insight in the sign maker's interests (e.g. from the 'wheel-ness' of a child's drawing of a car to the design of banal everyday objects)

The analytical starting point is often a general description of the artefact (e.g. context, genre, materiality and general structure) to locate it in the wider world of representation and communication. The analysis will often identify and describe the use of *modes* in the artefacts being studied. The *semiotic resources* of each mode are examined in detail, as well as the principles and conventions underpinning their use, and the modal *affordances* that have been drawn on by the maker of the artefact (as well as those that have not been). The analytical process will also attend to questions concerning the *design* of the artefacts. This will focus in some detail on the relationships between the modes in use, their arrangements, questions of modal dominance and order and coherence. Reading entry points and paths (e.g. open or fixed) will usually be explored. (See Example 4.3.)

*Example 4.3*   A social semiotic analysis of meaning making in a science classroom

The example we present here concerns a study by Diane Mavers (2009) set in a primary school science lesson on magnetism. Mavers set out to understand the semiotic work of student text making that arose in response to their teacher's framing and classroom practices of production. Mavers wanted to explore the relationship between the use of a visualizer (a whole-class digital display technology) and the drawings that children made subsequently in the lesson. More generally, she was concerned with learning and the resources of learners:

- What semiotics modes and resources do learners have access to in the classroom?
- How do the students take up these resources to re-present the world?
- What did the students attend to and highlight?
- What is their place in the frameworks of pedagogy and assessment?
- What was gained and lost in the process of 'translating' from one mode to another?

Mavers used video recording to collect her research materials. She recorded the teacher's demonstration at the front of the class, the children's processes of drawing and the drawings they produced. Mavers used the video recordings of the lesson to make a transcript of the teachers' demonstration of magnetism on a visualizer (see Figure 4.1). She explored the variety of ways in which children interpret and produce meaning in pedagogic interactions in the primary and early years education.

| Visualizer | | Speech |
|---|---|---|
| (a) 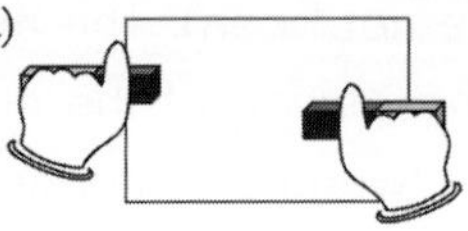 | places the bar magnets on a small board | okay (.) |
| (b) 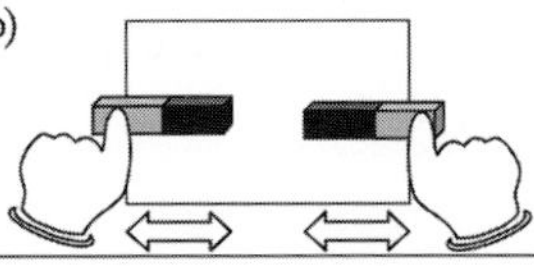 | touches each bar magnet and adjusts them slightly | two bar magnets (..) |
| (c) 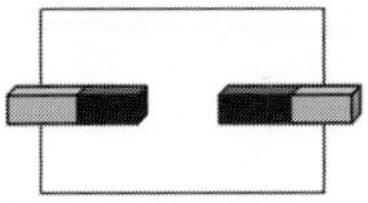 | | now looking back to what our aim for today was (.) Tom (..) okay (..) we will learn that forces act between two magnets (..) |
| (d) 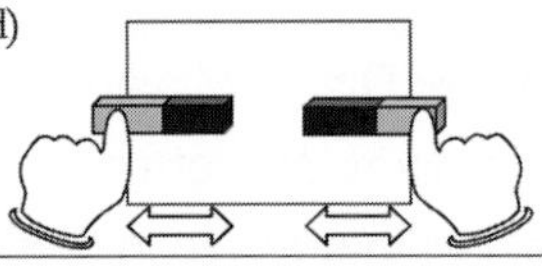 | touches each bar magnet and adjusts them slightly | so there are our two magnets okay (..) |
| (e) 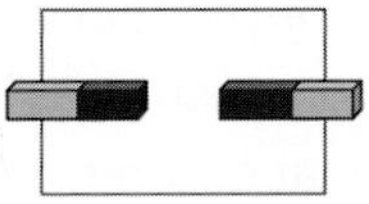 | | what do you think (.) think about this (.) don't put your hands up for now (.) |
| (f) 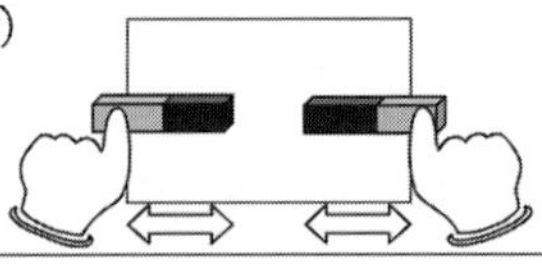 | touches each bar magnet and adjusts them slightly | if I (..) move them |
| (g) 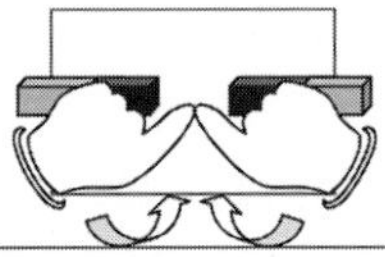 | brings fingers together above the magnets | closer together (..) |
| (h) 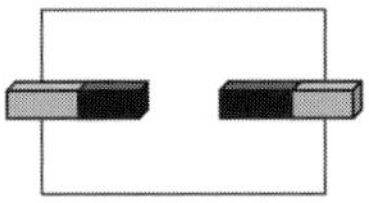 | | then let go (..) what do you think would happen to the magnets? |

Figure 4.1   Multimodal transcript of the teacher's framing of the task (Mavers, 2009: 146). Reprinted with permission from SAGE Publications and the author.

Mavers used the social semiotic concepts of *motivated sign* and *interest* to analyse the artefacts that the students made in the classroom as *responses* to the teacher's instructions. The analysis examined all of the student texts with attention to the following features:

- Choice and combination of resources of image (e.g. shape, line, shading and positioning)
- Writing (e.g. nouns, pronouns, tense, punctuation)
- Composition (e.g. relationships between drawing and image)

The study findings showed how:

[T]he semiotic work of learning in the classroom is framed by, and demands recognition of, the representational practices of the school subject.

(Mavers, 2009: 152)

It also pointed to the semiotic work of learning – the work of interpreting the teacher's signs and making semiotic choices about what is significant to attend to and how to represent meaning across different modes. Mavers argued that:

Taking their efforts seriously provides the ground for supporting them as they learn to make texts apt to different discourses and genres.

(Mavers, 2009: 142)

While the descriptive processes of a social semiotic analysis can be formalized, in general an oversystemized formulaic approach should be avoided because it is important not to lose sight of the particularities of your research materials. Analysis needs to make conceptual connections between motivated signs, sign makers, interest and the choice of modal and semiotic resources used in a text. A social semiotic account goes beyond a 'pure' description and the mapping of features. It combines a conceptual and an empirical focus and requires the analyst to be highly responsive to the research materials that they are working with. For example, when Kress analysed the two very different supermarket car park signs on a busy road, discussed earlier in this chapter, he drew on his own experience (e.g. recalling being in a car and visiting the supermarket) to explore context and environment, as well as issues of power and authority. Clearly this approach requires a reflexive stance and awareness of the limits and gaps of ones own life experiences. Nonetheless, you can use one's own experience as a springboard to generate questions about the place and function of an artefact, asking, for example:

- Who made it and why?
- What is its relationship to other discourses?
- Who is the imagined reader/audience?
- What does the artefact suggest about the imagined reader's 'life worlds'?
- What is the artefact expected to be used to do?

Asking such questions can guide you towards an artefact's meaning potential, as can the use of comparison and commutation as analytical procedures. The former involves iteratively moving between different artefacts in a collection; the latter involves reimagining or remaking (parts of) the artefact itself. Imagination is often used as a research tool to reimagine artefacts and alternative textual design scenarios.

In *Multimodality* (2010: 90), for example, Kress explores the consequences of three alternative layouts of a textbook double spread by extending the practice of commutation from structural linguistics to other modal representations. (See Figure 4.2.)

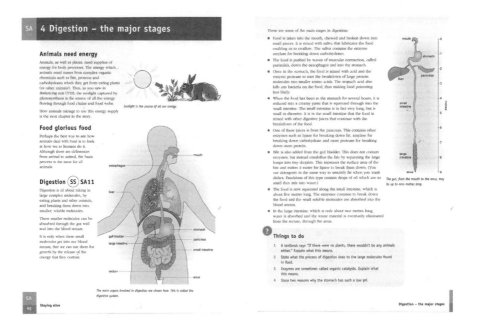

(a) Layout 1: Original layout (Reprinted from *Salters GCSE Science: Y11* student book. Used with permission.)

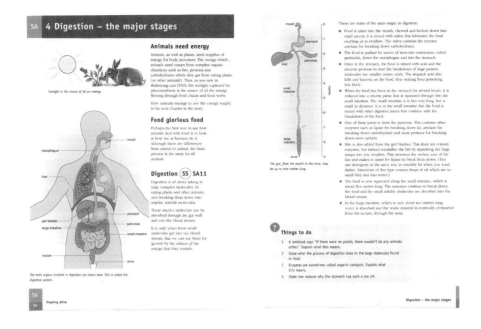

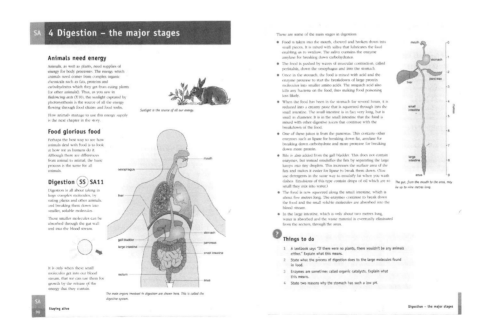

Figure 4.2   Commutation: Three alternative textbook layouts of the digestive system

Changing ('upsetting') the order of elements in a textbook can help to uncover the often otherwise 'invisible' order that existed within it. In this case, Kress showed how the changes in layout affected the relationship between image and writing, as well as the narrative and coherence of the textbook page.

In another example, Kress (2010) used commutation to analyse a child's drawing of herself standing between her parents. He did this by creating a version of the image where the child is to the right of her mother, asking what sense of her and her family, her relation to mother and father, is shown in this version of the image? He draws meanings about the family from the placement of elements in relation to one another (e.g. how a child's drawing depicts her in between her two parents), the use of scale (e.g. the child making herself markedly smaller than her parents), the use of colour (e.g. heightened use of colour to depict her mother), and the selection of criterial features and what is given salience by the child.

## Fields of application

A social semiotic approach has been applied to explore meaning making in a number of fields, including education, language studies, media studies, advertising and health. A wide range of materials have been analysed using this approach including advertisements, newspaper articles, brochures and leaflets, books, websites and social media, logos and children's drawings. To a lesser extent, social semiotics has also been used to investigate multimodal interaction across these contexts. Social semiotics has been used to account for a number of modes including image, colour, writing and typography, texture and layout, as well as speech, gesture, gaze, sound and music, among many. It has also been used to explore how the use of modes has changed over time (e.g. Bezemer and Kress, 2008) and digital platforms (e.g. Jewitt, 2002, 2013; Jewitt, Moss and Cardini, 2007; Jewitt et al., 2009). In this section we briefly discuss how social semiotics has been applied to the field of education, a field where it has had a significant take-up, notably in relation to literacy, learning and pedagogy.

Social semiotics has extended educational ideas of literacy to encompass multimodal literacy practices. Studies in this area have attended to children's pathways to literacy and the recognition of their 'semiotic work' in relation to a wide range of meaning making. A social semiotic approach has been applied in several studies to highlight the multimodal character of writing. Kenner and Kress (2003), for example, used social semiotics to investigate the resources of different written script systems (i.e. Mandarin Chinese, Arabic and Roman), such as the directionality, shape, size and angle of a script, spatiality and graphic marks and the literacy practices of young bilingual learners. They showed how they used these resources to realize meaning and express identities in complex ways related to their interests and context. Social semiotics has been used to explore how children become literate through engaging with and creating multimodal artefacts (Flewitt, 2011; Jewitt and Kress, 2003). Social semiotics has also been taken up within new literacy studies, for example, to focus on the materiality and situated character of young children's processes of meaning making (e.g. Pahl, 1999).

Social semiotics has also been used to investigate questions for teaching, learning and assessment. For instance, scholars in South Africa (e.g. Pippa Stein, Denise Newfield and Arlene Archer) have used a social semiotic approach to study the meaning-making resources and practices of marginalized South African learners and to explore the links between multimodal pedagogies and social justice. Stein (2012), for example, used a social semiotic approach to examine how school students living in informal settlements in South Africa created narratives of identity and culture in the school classroom through the artefacts they made (e.g. drawings, 3D figures, spoken dialogues and performance). Her study explored the character of the relationships among identity, literacy and multimodal meaning making in this context. This body of work has used a social semiotic approach to 'open up spaces for re-conceptualizing which texts and which textual practices count and for whom, thus highlighting relations of power, social boundaries and inequality, political or commercial agendas' (Archer, 2014: 189).

## Critique of social semiotics

In this section we discuss four key criticisms of social semiotics building on the ideas we have already discussed. These include concerns about the overdeterminative character of social semiotics, the place of context in social semiotic empirical work, its presentation of an overly linear historical narrative of semiotic communication and the recognition of the analytical reach of social semiotics.

*Overdeterminative*: Social semiotics has been criticized as being 'highly determinative, mutually exclusive, and binary' in the proposition of 'affordances' and 'hard binary distinctions between words and images' (Prior, 2005: 27). This criticism can be understood as pointing to the need for social semiotic analysis to focus on the use of modes in context (so the affordances of image or speech refer to its affordance in a particular text) and to avoid making overly generalized claims about modes that could be misconstrued as universal and fixed. However, this criticism oversimplifies social semiotics in two important ways. First, it wrongly reduces the social semiotic use of Halliday's meaning as choice (i.e. choosing one resource over another) to a binary rather than a selection from a variety of choices. Second, it oversimplifies the distinctions made between modes and affordances. The social semiotic idea is that there are inherent social affordances in resources that are the outcome of long periods of social action with physical-material resources: periods through which resources are shaped by how they have been taken up by different societies as a means for shaping meaning. It is the traces of this social 'work' that adhere to modes and become a part of its affordances. This is not to say that you cannot attempt to use modes in ways they have not been used but rather to acknowledge that the ease with which modes can be used for a task differs, as do the modal means, and therefore meaning will be shaped differently. In other words, affordances are complementary, they change and they are not mutually exclusive. Nonetheless, this criticism usefully reminds us of the need to ensure that our analysis maintains the situated complexity of modes, engages with a full range of texts, and uses a fine-grained analysis to provide a complex interpretation of what different functions modes realize in an artefact.

*Context*: The context of meaning making is usually an important feature of a social semiotic analysis. However, social semiotic accounts take different approaches to context, and this has led to some criticism. Many of the artefacts Kress and van Leeuwen analysed in *Reading Images* were decontextualized: adverts and diagrams were shown out of context from their pages, and so on. In a historical study of the changing semiotic landscape of school textbooks, whole textbook pages were analysed (Bezemer and Kress, 2008) but not the way in which they were used in classrooms. An analytical focus on textual artefacts alone, without attention to semiotic practices, has been critiqued as limited, for instance by Prior (2005: 9):

> I do not believe that we can account for multimodality and affordances without a focus on the whole of practice – on artifacts, activity, and people alike.

However, as we have discussed in this chapter, social semiotics sees signs as motivated and artefacts as semiotic traces from which meanings can be read. In addition, in a historical study, researchers do not have access to the producers of artefacts that are being analysed. That said, some of the examples that we have used in this chapter have shown how the processes of making (design, use and interpretation) can be central to the analysis of textual artefacts; see, for instance, Mavers' study of children's text making in the science classroom (Example 4.3). We have also discussed how social semiotic studies might attend to the broader discourse environment as part of an analysis – for instance, van Leeuwen's interest in the discourses of parenting magazines and child development experts in his analysis of pram rattles (Example 4.1). The amount of contextual information a social semiotic analysis needs is shaped by its questions and focus. Some scholars working within a social semiotic approach have come to see the broad context of a setting as central to understanding meaning making and have brought a social semiotic approach to ethnography in response (see Chapter 6). How much and what kind of contextual information is needed to analyse materials is shaped by the requirements of research questions. For example, a social semiotic analysis of gender in advertisements in magazines might require contextual information on their design and production (e.g. the aim and focus of the magazine) or information on the typical reader of the magazine or maybe on how, where and when the magazine is read. (We revisit the question of context in relation to designing a study in Chapter 7.)

*Periodization*: One concern of social semiotics is to map the ways in which modes change and their uses change. Even though it is generally accepted that we are in a period of rapid change, it is important to explore and describe this semiotic landscape carefully. Social semiotic descriptions of this landscape in terms of rigid periods dominated by 'one stable constellation' of communicational technology (e.g. an era of print literacy or the image and the screen) have been critiqued (Prior, 2005: 22). Prior argues for the need to engage with the semiotic change as blurred, complex and mutual – 'as computer screens borrow from texts and pages and texts and pages borrow from computer screens, and as television screens remediate tickertape news of the early twentieth century, and so on' – in order to avoid an overdetermined narrative of modes of communication and their consequences. In doing so, he calls on social semiotics to ensure that it does not obscure the complexity and overlapping of modes and technologies as we describe the changing landscape. For instance, in *Literacy in the New Media Age* (2003), Kress does this by pointing to how changes in the semiotic landscape are 'in flux' and to the need to investigate semiotic change as one element of a broader set of interrelated social, cultural and technological changes that need to be understood from a historical perspective.

*The analytical reach of social semiotics*: This is important to consider – what can and cannot social semiotics be used to do. Some social semiotic analyses have been criticized for reading too much from a text. For example, sociologist Dowling (2004), whilst acknowledging the 'careful and sociologically relevant analysis' of Hodge and Kress's (1988) analysis, has critiqued their use of a linguistic language of description to reach fundamentally sociological conclusions as problematic, arguing that a social semiotic language of description cannot construct a text as a sociological instance. One response to such criticism is to ensure that the claims made through an analysis are closer to the texts and contexts of use, and another is to combine social semiotics with sociological theory (e.g. Jewitt, 1997).

## New directions

Social semiotics is concerned with change and the new semiotic regimes in contemporary society. Its attention to how existing semiotic resources are used in new ways and the discovery of new semiotic resources can provide exciting new directions. We noted in Chapter 1 that a fundamental premise of multimodal approaches is a concern with the *cultural* and *social* resources for making meaning rather than with the *senses.* However, while it is important not to conflate the senses and the means for making meaning, there are important relations to be explored between the two, and a social semiotic approach can aid this exploration. Social semiotics provides a framework through which we can explore the cultural and social shaping of sensory resources into semiotic resources for making meaning. For instance, while touch is not 'new', the sensory resources of touch are being semiotically shaped and brought into the frame of digital communication in some new ways. Social semiotics can help us to investigate these semiotic potentials at the same time as we question why touch is newly important now. What is it that has brought it to the fore in contemporary society? Why now? How does it relate to other significant social conditions that are shaping the communicational landscape? Of course, one response to this could be the ubiquitous use of touch interfaces, as well as new digital devices that are reconfiguring who, what and how people touch, while another response could point to globalization and the consequent distances over which many social relations are conducted. One future question is whether touch will develop into a 'mode' that can serve a 'full' range of semiotic functions within a community. A social semiotic approach has been used to start to explore the ways in which touch is used as a resource for making meaning and to unpack the multiplicity of meanings attached to the term itself and the overlapping yet distinct roles of touch and gesture (Bezemer and Kress, 2014; Crescenzi, Jewitt and Price, 2014; Flewitt, Kucirkova and Messer, 2014).

Van Leeuwen has argued that social semiotics has a distinct contribution to make to software studies focused 'on the semiotic choices made by software designers, on how they configure layout choices, typographic choices, colour choices, texture choices and so on' (Andersen et al., 2015: 111). He has also pointed to the need to move on from the need for 'a grammar' of individual modes to consider the semiotic principles that work across modes. A social semiotic approach to multimodality is relatively new, and it continues to be developed methodologically and theoretically. One aspect of this development is the way in which it is being taken forward in new directions by combining it with other methods into new frameworks. In Chapter 6, we outline how a social semiotic approach to multimodality has informed the development of geosemiotics, multimodal (inter)action analysis and multimodal ethnography. We also discuss how multimodal corpus analysis and multimodal reception analysis have empirically tested, evidenced and refined social semiotic theories and concepts.

# CHAPTER 5

# Conversation analysis

## Introduction to the approach

### Origins

The origins of conversation analysis (CA) go back to interactionism, an approach in sociology that developed in the US in the early and mid-twentieth century. Central among those who developed the approach were Herbert Blumer (1900–1987), Erving Goffman (1922–1982) and Harold Garfinkel (1917–2011). They proposed to investigate social interaction through detailed observation, examination and description of concrete instances of social interaction. They were concerned with people's 'lived experiences' and the means by which we make sense of the world; more specifically, how we display our understanding of the situation we are in and the social actions produced within it. They insisted on grounding sociological theory in empirical observations of particular situations.

CA emerged in the early 1960s as a distinct theoretical and methodological approach to the study of social interaction, namely one that is focused on *talk*. It was developed in the period that Harvey Sacks (1935–1975), Emanuel Schegloff (b. 1937) and David Sudnow (?–2007) were graduate students at the University of California, Berkeley, where Blumer was based and where Goffman taught, while Garfinkel was at the University of California at Los Angeles. In 1963–1964, Sacks and Garfinkel were fellows at the Centre for the Scientific Study of Suicide in Los Angeles, and Sacks made audio recordings of calls to the Suicide Prevention Centre there using the tape recorder. Examining his and other recordings, Sacks, Schegloff (who had just moved from Berkeley to University of California at Los Angeles) and colleagues started addressing a question that was later formulated as: 'How is intelligible social action possible?' (Heritage, 1997: 104). In CA, this question is answered by specifying 'the normative structuring and logics of particular courses of social action' (Heritage, 1997: 104). The interest in structures and logics translates into questions about how people move from one part to the next part and from one event to another. It is the analyst's job to transcribe in detail short interactional episodes (say, up to 30 seconds each) and to break them down into their constituent meaningful parts.

To give one example: Sacks found that the opening of phone calls to the Suicide Centre were often organized as a two-part structure consisting of a greeting (e.g. 'This is Mr. Smith. May I help you?') and a greeting return (e.g. 'Yes, this is Mr. Brown'). This is an example of an 'adjacency pair' (Schegloff and Sacks, 1973), in which the first part is invitation to the other to respond, implying an inversion of speaker–listener roles. The example also illustrates how the first part sets up expectations about the next. In this example, the answerer identifies himself and, in so doing, sets up the expectation that the caller will do the same. By using the format of a title and surname, he also creates expectations about how the answerer will identify himself. It illustrates the basic principle that everything a participant in an interaction says is 'context-shaped' in that it acts as a response to what's just been said, and at the same time it is 'context-renewing', in that it raises expectations about what is to happen next (Heritage, 1997). These expectations do not determine but shape what the next speaker will say and how. In this fashion, Sacks and his colleagues began to describe and make explicit how people manage openings and closings of conversations, how they take turns, and so forth.

Since the early days at the University of Berkeley, an international community of CA researchers has developed, and numerous instances of talk have been analysed, produced in different social settings, including sites of 'ordinary conversation' and institutions such as schools and hospitals. CA is often described as a form of 'naturalistic inquiry': the aim is to record talk that has been produced in the setting where such talk is ordinarily produced. Hence fieldwork is preferred as a method of collecting data over prompting research participants to talk in laboratories. Researchers try to minimize their participation in the interactions they record.

CA is closely connected with a number of disciplines. Some contributors are based in departments of sociology, others in anthropology, linguistics or education. Some call themselves conversation analysts, others call themselves differently while still very much adopting a CA perspective and analytical mindset. CA shares its concern with the fine-grained analysis of talk and interaction with linguistic traditions, including interactional (socio)linguistics and linguistic anthropology. For instance, Gumperz and Hymes (1964) worked towards an 'ethnography of communication' at the same time that CA emerged. Interactions between those representing these traditions have been frequent from the start, and scholars often work across disciplinary boundaries. There are also productive synergies with work in distributed cognition (Hutchins, 1995) and computer-supported cooperative work (Suchman, 1987).

## CA and multimodality

In the early 1970s, about a decade after Sacks, Schegloff and others had begun to transcribe and analyse conversations, Charles Goodwin and other scholars started analysing *video* recordings of everyday interactions. Using video instead of audio had profound effects on what could be analysed. For instance, Goodwin, like other early adopters of video, was able to study *gaze* in just as much detail as talk, and his analyses shed new light on some of the issues that had been central to the CA endeavor from the start, for instance how people manage transitions from one turn to another (Sacks, Schegloff and Jefferson, 1974). In one of his first papers, Goodwin (1979) famously analysed *one* utterance produced during a dinner conversation: 'I gave up smoking cigarettes one week ago today actually'. He shows that, as the speaker produces this utterance, he directs his gaze to/addresses three different people at the dinner table. He shows that these shifts are organized in such a way that the part of the sentence that is produced is always relevant to and appropriate for the person addressed at that moment. For instance, the first part, 'I gave up smoking cigarettes', is particularly relevant to his two guests and not so relevant to his wife, who is familiar with her husband's quitting – and it is indeed the guest – more specifically the guest sitting closest to him – whom he is glancing at during the production of this part of the sentence.

Another two decades or so later, from the early 1990s, Goodwin began to move beyond 'family settings' to explore interaction in scientific and workplace settings. For instance, he looked at work in an archeological site, a chemistry lab, an oceanographic ship in the Amazon and the ramp and operations room of an airport. These explorations highlighted that social interactions are situated in a historically shaped 'material world'. That material world offers a range of resources for interaction, including the bodies of the interlocutors and the 'tools' that, in Goodwin's terms, 'mutually elaborate' one another (we will get back to this term in the next section). In one seminal paper, Goodwin (1994) shows how during a field trip, archaeologists and their trainees jointly draw a map of the different layers of dirt in the excavation site, involving gesture, inscription in dirt, a tape measure and other tools, and talking all at the same time, and all of these play an essential and distinctive role in the accomplishment of their joint practical work and in the process of becoming an archaeologist: all these resources are part and parcel of the professional world of archaeology.

In the UK, similar moves towards using video in CA can be identified. In the early 1980s, Christian Heath analysed video recordings of patients and their GPs in the consultation room. Like Goodwin's early work, his work highlighted the role of the body in conversations. In one much cited example, he shows that a patient does not answer the doctor's opening question, 'what's up', until the doctor has looked up from his papers, while the patient uses a pointing gesture to identify the eye that is sore as he's saying, 'I've had a bad eye in there' (1986) (see Figure 5.3). Heath then went on do a series of studies with Paul Luff, Jon Hindmarsh and others on workplaces (Luff, Hindmarsh and Heath, 2000). Among the wide range of sites they have investigated are London underground control rooms, auction rooms and operating theatres. Doing research in these sites allowed them to explore how people structure and coordinate their actions to accomplish practical tasks such as the passing of objects. Like Goodwin, in pursuing this line of inquiry, they take part of their inspiration from ethnomethodology (Garfinkel, 1967), which is concerned with the 'methods' that people use to organize their social life.

Goodwin and Heath were pioneers in extending the original empirical scope of CA by using video and looking at the role of gaze, gesture and other resources in conversations. The same applies to their attention to forms of interaction other than the conversation. Since they have taken CA's theoretical and methodological apparatus to explore these other forms of interaction, where talk isn't always central to what is going on, many others have followed suit. A significant body of work has grown out of this, which we will be reviewing in this chapter.

Before we introduce this work, a note on naming. We should note that while this work is now increasingly described as 'multimodal', there is some variation in the uptake of the term. For instance, it appears in Goodwin's seminal article on action and embodiment in human interaction (2000), and it is featured in the theme of the 10th International Conference on Conversation Analysis (2010); it is also used in the first major collection of papers in this area (Streeck, Goodwin and LeBaron, 2011), but only scarcely. Where it does appear, it tends to refer to actions (see C. Goodwin, 2000: 1518; M. Goodwin et al., 2002). The notion of 'mode', which is central to SFL and social semiotics, is rarely used. Indeed, you will find that some scholars whose work we describe in this chapter have reservations about the theoretical notion of 'mode' or 'multimodality' and point to the analytical difficulty of separating out that which operates as a meaningful whole. To highlight this position, we write 'mode' in inverted commas in this chapter.

## Key principles

CA is highly 'data'-driven. The starting point for any discussion or paper is always a video clip that features some form of social interaction. Indeed it is common in this approach to organize so-called data sessions, where researchers invite colleagues to jointly view selected video clips. When commenting on a video clip, two principles apply.

The first principle is to *stay close to the selected clip*. That means that when you adopt this approach, the claims you make about what happens in the recorded interaction should always be grounded in observations in the clip. While it is important to know a good deal about the context in which the interaction occurred, the focus is always on what happens *in this* clip. More specifically, the focus is on what the participants in the interaction orient to. So although you'd want to know, for instance, what the 'official' roles and relationships are of participants (husband–wife, teacher–student, doctor–nurse), these 'text-external' sources of information cannot be used to explain how the interaction in this concrete situation unfolds. Indeed, your analysis might show that, under the given circumstances, the participants defy social conventions or social theories about gender, power relations or pedagogic relations. In other words, the video clip has a special ('epistemological') status: it is the primary data source. Other sources of information, such as interviews with the participants, might provide useful background information (e.g. about the working of the tools used in the interaction), but the main claims should ultimately be grounded in the video data.

The second principle is to *slow down* (Silverman, 1999). Instead of drawing conclusions based on first impressions, having watched a video clip only once or twice, you suspend judgements until you have watched a clip many times. Perhaps you also play the clip in slow motion, to check that, say, Participant X did indeed 'interrupt' Participant Y, as you thought, and that Y did not actually offer the turn to X through a shift of gaze in the direction of X, a hesitation, and so on. Slowing down enables you *to attend to detail* ('smallness') and be specific about what it is in the clip that supports your claim about what is happening: was it the raised eyebrow, the rising intonation at the end of the utterance, the shift in gaze direction or all of those? Transcription has always been an important means of building up such detailed pictures of what is going on, and it still is as CA researchers increasingly attend to the details of speech as well as gesture, gaze and other means of communication. We will demonstrate how they make such transcripts later on in the chapter.

## Key concepts

We will now discuss four concepts that are central in a CA approach to multimodality: mutually elaborating semiotic resources, sequential organization of action, coordination of action and multi-activity.

### Mutually elaborating semiotic resources

A 'CA version' of 'multimodality' is based on the notion that people 'build action' using different 'semiotic resources': one 'action' may be realized by a spoken utterance, another may be a hand gesture, and yet another may be a momentary shift in gaze. These different resources have different properties. Goodwin writes:

> By itself each set of semiotic resources is partial and incomplete. However when joined together in local contextures of action, diverse semiotic resources mutually elaborate each other to create a whole that is both greater than and different from any of its constituent parts.
>
> (Goodwin, 2000: 2)

Goodwin's notion of 'mutual elaboration' of semiotic resources is similar to the social semiotic notion of 'affordance' (Chapter 4): each recognizes that the potential of, say, 'gesture', which is performed in a three-dimensional space and in time, is different from what can be done in speech.

'Multimodality' in CA has also been described in terms of 'simultaneity'. This notion is a way of marking a re-framing of the original CA 'remit' from a concern with the sequential unfolding of action (see below) to the sequential and *simultaneous* unfolding of action (Deppermann and Schmidt, 2007).

This reframing has significant implications for the theoretical and empirical scope of CA. When Goodwin looked at archeologists excavating soil, he attended not only to the ways in which they use their bodies and talk in interaction but also to the *tools* they use. For him, the tool and the body constitute different 'semiotic fields' in a 'contextual configuration'. 'Tool' should be broadly conceived here. It includes any kind of artefact and technology, ranging from makeshift implements to professionally designed and produced instruments, and from inscriptions on the ground, such as the hopscotch grid drawn on a pavement by children to digital cameras and screens. The interest is in the relations between tools and actions: Hindmarsh and Heath (2007: 169) speak of the 'mutually constitutive relationship between action and the local material environment of texts, tools and technologies'.

## Sequential organization of action

At the beginning of this chapter, we gave an example of an 'adjacency pair'. In the example, we could see how speech was used to realize both the first and the second parts (no other 'modes' were available: it was a phone conversation). If we now adopt a multimodal perspective on the adjacency pair, we need to differentiate between different kinds of pairs on the basis of the 'modes' involved in the first and second parts. So we can see, for instance, that in some adjacency pairs only the first part is realized in speech. For instance, Schegloff (2007) presents the example of someone saying 'Butter please' at a dinner table. In response, someone passes the butter, completing the two-part structure. In other pairs, neither part involves talk. Take the following example, taken from a clinical workplace: the operating theatre. A surgeon has just tied a knot and is now holding the stitch between the thumb and index finger of his left hand, bringing the stitch under tension. (At the same time, he is talking to his first assistant – who is holding a big retractor in his left hand – about some organizational issue in the hospital.) The second assistant, who holds scissors in her right hand, is about to cut the stitch held by the surgeon (see Figure 5.1). Here the act of holding the stitch tight is interpreted by the second assistant as a request to cut it, and judging

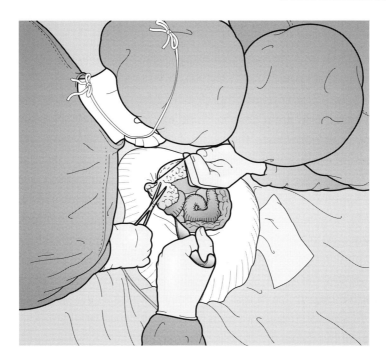

Figure 5.1    Surgeons cutting a suture

from the subsequent actions of the surgeon, that is what the surgeon aimed to communicate with this gesture.

Thus gestures can operate in pairs in the same way that verbal utterances can, allowing people to achieve complex tasks in the absence of speech. What the example also shows is that meaning is attached not only to the *form* of the gesture (or choice of lexis, syntax etc.) but also to the *positioning* of that gesture in a sequential structure: the 'same' gesture would have been interpreted differently if it had been preceded by a different series of actions. Mondada (2011), also looking at surgical work, gives the example of a surgeon holding an instrument that he uses to coagulate and an assistant who operates the foot pedal that activates the coagulation. Her analysis shows that the assistant takes the surgeon approaching tissue as a sign to activate the diathermy. Thus, the approach and the activation of the coagulation are organized as what Mondada calls 'paired actions'. The surgeon used speech only when he deviated from this pattern, that is, when he touched tissue with the instrument that he did not want to cauterize ('no co-ag,' meaning, do not activate the diathermy).

Coordination of action

Taken together, the notions of sequentiality and simultaneity raise the question of coordination: how do people who are engaged in 'concerted action' coordinate their actions with the actions of others?

Musical ensembles are a case in point: in order for an ensemble to work, the musicians need to coordinate their contributions. John Haviland (2011) looked at how musicians in a string quartet and a jazz quartet do that. Each of these ensembles face issues of coordination. For instance, the string quartet needs to establish a moment of starting and a tempo; a jazz quartet needs to manage the transitions between individual solos. Haviland's analysis renders visible the methods they use to achieve that: the first violinist performs a stylized gesture to mark the beginning, while the saxophonist walks in or out of the performance space to mark the end of his solo. They also use musical cues. For instance, the piano player (who can't leave the performance stage in the way the saxophone player can) repeats a single phrase in modulated series of descending scales to mark the end of his solo.

The 'ensemble' and the notion of concerted action point to a key feature of much social activity across different sites. It applies equally to, say, the work of clinical teams in hospitals. For instance, Hindmarsh and Pilnick (2007) have explored how an anesthetist and an operation department assistant collaborate in putting a patient to sleep. They noticed that '[t]he sights, sounds and feel of colleagues are used to sense, anticipate, appreciate and respond to emerging tasks and activities.' The participants are 'intimately sensitive to delicate and subtle shifts in the embodied conduct of colleagues. This sensitivity, what we term intercorporeal knowing, underpins the team's abilities to seamlessly coordinate emerging activities' (Hindmarsh and Pilnick, 2007: 1413). Looking at specific instances, they found that:

> the onset of certain actions or object manipulations can be oriented to as projecting a course of action. This provides a critical resource for the team to coordinate and organize their work seamlessly and often without words (cf. Heath and Luff, 1996). Witnessing someone beginning to engage in a particular activity can project a trajectory of actions that routinely follow. For example, within certain contexts, picking up monitoring pads is highly likely to be followed by the placement of those on the body.
>
> (Hindmarsh and Pilnick, 2002: 151)

Recognizing the onset of a 'course of action' not only means that members of a team know what others are likely to do next, it also means that they can anticipate and participate in that course of action in appropriate ways. As Goodwin observes:

> The accomplishment of social action requires that not only the party producing an action, but also that others present, such as its addressee, be able to systematically recognize the shape and character of what is occurring. Without this it would be impossible for separate parties to recognize in common not only what is happening at the moment, but more crucially, what range of events are being projected as relevant nexts, such that an addressee can build not just another independent action, but instead a relevant coordinated next move to what someone else has just done.
>
> (Goodwin, 2000: 1491)

The examples of the musical ensemble and the anesthetic team both illustrate coordination of action by people who frequently move about. This is a significant departure from prior work in CA, when the focus was on more stable bodily configurations, such as in the case of dinner conversations. Current research highlights that it is not only the movement of certain body parts that are used in interaction – for example to make a gesture – but also movement of the entire body, that is the *placement of people* within a space.

Coordination of action is contingent not only on bodies and tools but also on the *built environment*, the place where the interaction happens. Take LeBaron and Streeck's (1997) analysis of a murder interrogation. They show how the interrogation room is used by the interrogator – a detective – as a resource for interaction. Inside the small room (7 × 8 feet), a round table is placed in one corner opposite the door, with three seats. Upon entry the suspect is allocated the seat in the corner. The detective sits next to him and the ranger opposite. In the first 20 minutes or so of the interrogation, both speech and seating arrangement suggest relative parity. The suspect is read his rights and is then free to talk without interruption. Then a radical shift in framing takes place, marked by lexical choice (and no doubt vocal choices) ('Your story is so full of shit [.] it's ridiculous'), while the interrogator literally corners the suspect by moving his chair and body inches away from the suspect, with his right arm leaning on the table. The suspect is prevented from speaking. The spatial and discursive disparity thus created is used by the interrogator to move the suspect towards confession.

Multi-activity

In recent years, CA studies have begun to explore how different activities, possibly involving different, sometimes partially overlapping teams, operate in conjunction, pursuing 'concurrent courses of action' (Mondada, 2011). For instance, Bezemer et al. (2011) looked at concurrent activities unfolding around the operating table. We discussed one of these activities already: a stitch is cut after knots have been tied (see Figure 5.1). The other activity involved the surgical assistant who eventually cut the stitch and the scrub nurse who passed the scissors to her just before she cuts the stitch. The scrub nurse passed the scissors in response to a request from the surgical assistant, which was timed such that it was in the assistant's hand ready to cut seconds before the surgeon had completed the knot tying and offered the stitch for cutting. Thus the assistant helped sustain and complete one activity (knot tying) through the timely initiation and completion of another (instrument exchange). She managed to simultaneously engage in those two activities by using her body in particular ways: She 'juggled' two activities, each of which required her attention: she needed to keep her eyes on the surgeon, so as to know when and where to cut. She also needed to keep an eye on the scrub nurse, first to make a request for scissors and then to receive the scissors.

The authors highlight the role of the body in managing such dual engagement. They describe the bodily arrangements in terms of what Kendon (1990) calls the 'f-formation.' Looking at 'informal' gatherings, he showed how participants standing in a social circle with two others can temporarily turn their head away from the centre point of this f-formation while sustaining their involvement in the talk. They keep their lower body in line with the centre of the f-formation to express engagement with the talk and use the upper body to engage, temporarily, with someone situated outside the formation. Similarly, in the case of the surgical operation, the assistant positioned herself to display her involvement to two activities, with her lower body still aligned with the operative field and the surgeon and her head turned away momentarily at various points to engage with the scrub nurse.

Methods of transcription and analysis

Transcription is an important part of doing CA. It has analytical as well as rhetorical purposes: detailing how actions unfold moment by moment helps you develop new insights, and it enables you to render those insights visible and present them to audiences who do not have access to the video clip on which it is based. The role of the transcript in CA is reflected in the 'look' of its academic publications: by definition, these contain one or more detailed transcripts, while the best part of the remainder of the publication is a commentary on those transcripts, with references to specific places in the transcript. CA transcripts tend to follow transcription conventions originally defined by Gail Jefferson (1938–2008), one of the 'founders' of CA.

## Types of transcripts

Jefferson led the development of a set of conventionalized notations for rendering visible a range of features of talk. Some symbols are used for describing how utterances are connected, for instance, through overlaps, latches, intervals; others are used for describing intonation, pitch movement, loudness, sound prolongation, and their effects, such as stress; yet others are used for detailing vocal qualities, such as 'creaky' voice, and aspiration (in-breaths, out-breaths). In a now seminal paper, Jefferson (2004) provides a detailed glossary of the symbols and shows how attention to these minute details can make a real difference for analysis and interpretation. Figure 5.2 provides an example of her approach to transcription. The example is a transcript of a small fragment from the 'Nixon tapes'. As the figure shows, Jefferson's transcript provides a lot of detail about how things are said and how the talk unfolds in time. She had developed conventions for the transcription of *speech*. Would it be possible to achieve a comparable degree of detail in the representation of gesture, gaze and other 'modes'?

```
(4)  [Jeff:Canc:40:10-20]
Dean:       I ↑don't kno:w thė (·) full extent ↓'v it.↓
                 (0.7)
Dean:       °↓Uh:::eh°
                 (0.9)
Nixon:      °I don'noo° 'bout anything else exchhe[pt
Dean: →                                           [I do‿n't either in I: °w'd (h)als(h)o
          → hhate tuh learn [some a'] these thi]ngs. ·hh·hh·hh·hh
Nixon:                      [W e l l  ] y a: h   ]
                 (0.2)
Dean:       So ↑That's,hhhh that's that situation.
```

Figure 5.2   Sample transcript from Gail Jefferson's 'Nixon' tapes study (Jefferson, 2004)

Different models have been used to accommodate the need to represent more than just speech, while preserving the sequentiality (which is an important criterion from a CA perspective). None of these have as yet become conventional: significant differences remain even among transcripts produced by the same author. We briefly mention two models here.

In the first model, descriptions of gesture, gaze and other 'modes' are added to a transcript of speech at points where it is deemed relevant. Thus only speech is systematically transcribed, and the descriptions of other modes appear as relatively generic glosses (e.g. 'moves head up', 'picks up scissors'). For instance, we could transcribe the exchange discussed earlier between surgical assistant and scrub nurse as follows:

## Transcript 5.1

Assistant:      Scissors please
Scrub nurse:   *Passes scissors*

This transcript, while seemingly relatively 'complete', details relatively little about the request for and passing of the scissors. Looking at this transcript, you would have no way of knowing what the making of the request and the passing entailed, including shifts in bodily orientation, synchronization of actions and so forth.

In the second model, modes other than speech are systematically transcribed, alongside speech, using a set of transcription conventions. One example of this model is described in Heath, Hindmarsh and Luff (2010). In order to accommodate speech, gaze and gesture in one transcript, they use a horizontal timeline. Participants and the 'modes' they use appear on separate rows. Figure 5.3 provides an example. According to the authors, 'a continuous line indicates that the participant is looking at the co-participant, a series of dots ('. . . . .') that one party is turning towards another, and a series of commas (',,,,,') indicates that one party is turning away from the other' (Heath, Hindmarsh and Luff (2010: 71).

The advantage of this model is that it represents both the sequential unfolding of the interaction and the 'simultaneity' of 'modes': readers of the transcript can work out exactly which gesture coincided with which part of the spoken utterance, and they can see exactly who looks where at any point.

When adopting this model, ELAN, a free software package developed by the Max Plank Institute of Psycholinguistics, is a very useful tool. In ELAN (Wittenburg et al., 2006), you can create the type of template Heath made on grid paper, with a horizontal time line as a base and rows of 'tiers' below it. It works like this. First you allocate 'tiers' to participants and the 'modes' they use – say, 'speech

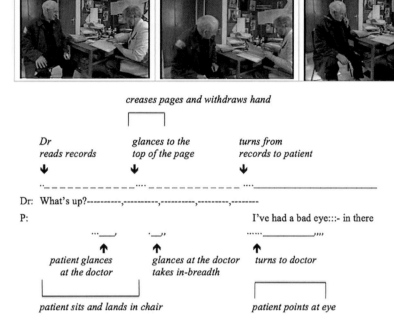

*creases pages and withdraws hand*

Dr                   *glances to the*          *turns from*
*reads records*      *top of the page*         *records to patient*
↓                    ↓                          ↓

Dr:  What's up?----------,----------,----------,---------,--------
P:                                              I've had a bad eye:::- in there

                ↑                   ↑                      ↑
          *patient glances*   *glances at the doctor*   *turns to doctor*
          *at the doctor*     *takes in-breadth*

*patient sits and lands in chair*            *patient points at eye*

Figure 5.3    Transcript of an exchange between a doctor and a patient (From Heath, Hindmarsh and Luff 2010)

John', 'gesture Pete'. Second, you look for and mark transition points in each tier. For instance, in speech, you distinguish between different breath groups or intonation units; in gesture, you distinguish between different gesture units (Kendon, 2004a). Third, you annotate the segmented entities: you 'fill' the entities identified in a speech tier with transcriptions, and you fill the entities identified in other tiers with annotations. For instance, on the gaze-John tier, you might fill the segments with annotations such as 'at Pete', 'at table', 'up in the air'.

In both approaches to transcription, video stills and line drawings made from video stills are often included to represent the bodily arrangements of participants in an interaction and their placement in the environment. The advantage of these images is that they can represent spatial configurations rather precisely; the downside is that they represent single moments in time. To show how arrangements change over time, you can include a series of these images, as in the example from Heath, Hindmarsh and Luff (2010).

Regardless of the approach to transcription, the commentary on the transcript will often include important additional detail about the multimodal organization of the interaction, which is not made visible in the transcript. The commentary will also provide guidance on what to see in the transcript: it will draw out some features and background others. The original video clips are normally shown as part of oral presentations (including, of course, during data sessions), but they are rarely made available to third parties for secondary analysis.

## Selecting strips for detailed analysis

Given the appreciation of 'smallness' in CA, the video clips selected for detailed transcription will be relatively short, especially when more than two participants are involved and when more than one mode is to be represented. The question of what to select for transcription is approached in different ways.

One approach is to do less fine-grained analysis of the entire corpus first, to identify what the main 'themes' and 'categories' are (and what their frequency of occurrence is). You can then select instances of each of these themes and categories for more detailed, interactional analysis and verify and refine your definitions of the themes and categories accordingly.

Another approach is to transcribe and analyse an episode that appears to illustrate a phenomenon that you're interested in. You can still come up with generalizable and falsifiable explanations, yet the way in which generalizations are achieved is different. In the words of Burawoy, you attempt to 'extract the general from the unique' (Burawoy, 2009: 21), or, in the words of William Blake, you look to see 'a world in a grain of sand'. For instance, Goodwin formulated the following more general interactional principle on the basis of a detailed analysis of that single utterance at the dinner table ('I gave up smoking . . .'): 'The gaze of a speaker should locate the party being gazed at as an addressee of his utterance' (Goodwin, 1979: 99).

A common variation on the second approach is to build up a *collection* of instantiations of the phenomenon, drawing from one or more different data sets.

## Fields of application

The examples discussed so far in this chapter show that CA research relevant to multimodality includes work in two different areas. The first body of work examines activities characterized by a continuous stream of talk, in ordinary conversation and in specialized, institutional settings. The second body of work looks at activities that are organized around a practical task, such as operating or doing the dishes together with someone.

Looking at the former, CA has drawn attention to the role of *gaze* in turn taking. For instance, in Goodwin's early work he found that when the speaker's gaze reaches his or her listener, the listener is expected to be oriented towards the speaker again, ready to take the turn (Goodwin, 1981). If not, a pause or a restart follows. The speaker can, however, look away from the listener without impacting on the structure of the conversation. Heath (1986) also showed that participation rights and obligations, as well as engagement and disengagement, are achieved through talk working in concert with gaze and gesture.

*Gesture* in conversations has also been looked at. For instance, in their analysis of a murder interrogation, LeBaron and Streeck (1997) draw attention to the gestures accompanying what the detective said during the murder interrogation referred to earlier:

> When he says 'you're locked in a room' . . ., he gestures in the air, tracing the shape of an enclosed space . . . When he says 'you're looking for a window' . . ., he gestures toward the windowless wall . . . . When the detective says 'some way out' . . ., he throws his arms in the air as though demonstrating desperation . . . . And when he says 'there's not one' . . ., his right hand drops on the table in a chopping motion . . . .'
>
> (LeBaron and Streeck, 1997: 20)

These studies have drawn attention to gestures that *accompany* speech. Looking at the second body of work, i.e. the studies that focus on what Goffman (1981) called 'coordinated task activities', a different insight in gesture, gaze and their relation to speech emerges. Goffman defined coordinated task activity as interactive engagements 'in which talk, when it figures at all, does so either as a desultory, muted side-involvement or as an irregular, intermittent adjunct to the coordination of the doings in progress' (1983: 7). We have seen that such activity is characteristic of many of the workplaces that have been studied. Examples drawn from, for instance, the operating theatre illustrate how practical tasks, such as the passing of objects, are jointly achieved, frequently in the absence of speech. Thus gaze and gesture can be seen to have the potential to operate *independently of* speech, such as in the case of the example discussed earlier of surgeons cutting a stitch.

The CA approach has produced important insights in a range of issues beyond and/or in relation to multimodality, including questions related to instruction, professional vision, ways of seeing, knowing, cognition, embodiment, tools and technologies and teamwork. They have rendered visible phenomena that we are often entirely unaware of as participants in an interaction, unless and until that 'tacit order' is disrupted, for instance by a participant who is new to the activity engaged in (Hindmarsh and Pilnick, 2002). Hence it would have been difficult, if not impossible, to 'get at' these phenomena by interviewing participants.

The work has also made a significant impact beyond academia. For instance, Charles Goodwin's work on aphasia has been hugely influential in that it problematized established understandings of the capacity of 'speech impaired' people to communicate. One example is from conversations involving a person with aphasia, who can understand spoken language but who can say only three words. On top of these, he produces 'non-conventional' syllables, which are subsequently 'translated' by others in speech. Moment-by-moment analysis of these conversations revealed how interlocutors learn how to interpret and then 'gloss' the signs produced by the person with aphasia, who then confirms or rejects the gloss (Goodwin, Goodwin and Olsher, 2009). A similar point is made by Avital and Streeck (2011), who challenge the deficit view on blind people, rendering visible how they align their orientation and coordinate their action in the absence of vision.

Many of the principles and concepts discussed in this chapter have been used to generate significant new insights in key issues in anthropology and education. Work in this area includes some pioneering video analysis in which attention was given to the role of gaze and body posture in interaction. For instance, Mehan (1980) looked at classroom interactions and found that teachers and students 'mark the boundaries of interactional sequences, event phases and school events through shifts in kinesic, paralinguistic, and verbal behavior' (Mehan, 1980: 136). He emphasizes that the variation in constraints on students' actions 'implies that effective participation in the classroom entails recognizing different contexts for interaction and producing behavior that is appropriate for each context' (137). Where for 'insiders' shifts in the teacher's position and posture may signify the transition to a quite specific activity, students new to the classroom have been observed to be unable to adjust to shifts in framing, which is not only potentially face threatening but may also have implications for learning and learner identities (Herrlitz, 1994). Erickson also found that not all students learn to recognize the 'turning points in the ongoing conduct of interaction' (Erickson, 2004: 9). Referring to Mehan's (1996) case study on referrals to special education, he notes that informal assessments of students' responses to these turning points can 'take on a life beyond the immediacy of the interactional situation within which the judgement originated' (Erickson, 2004: 70) as soon as such assessments are entered into permanent institutional records.

An illustration of applying multimodal insights from CA in the domain of medical education is given in Example 5.1 on page 105.

## Critique

As noted earlier, conversation analysts insist on grounding all claims made in the video recording. That does not mean that all other sources of information are ruled out of course. Background information obtained from the people you have observed can be useful and often necessary to make sense of video-recorded interactions. For instance, had Goodwin not known anything about the history of the speaker quitting smoking and his relation to the other people at the dinner table, he would not have reached the analysis he provided. And without knowing how the tools being drawn into interactions work, it will be difficult to produce an appropriate account of the interaction. Yet CA warns against making 'high inferences' or assumptions on the basis of, for instance, 'official institutional roles' of participants in an interaction. For instance, when presenting and discussing interactions between surgeons and their assistants, the presumed hierarchical relationship between the two, or their gender, might be put forward as an explanation. However, on closer inspection, it becomes clear that while institutional roles and models do shape the organization of interaction and the expectations that participants have, they do not determine what happens in a concrete situation, which is always full of contingencies.

The other, related, issue here is exactly what the analyst should treat as its 'core' text for analysis and what counts as context. For Goodwin, 'The constitution of relevant context is in the first instance an issue for the participants' (Goodwin, 2000: 1519). So, for instance, if participants are oriented to a pro forma, then that form becomes relevant context. It is important to note that artefacts such as forms are always analysed only inasmuch as they appear in the interaction:

> [I]mages and documents . . . cannot be analyzed as self-contained fields of visually organized meaning, but instead stand in a reflexive relationship to the settings and processes of embodied human interaction through which they are constituted as meaningful entities.
>
> (Goodwin, 2001: 166)

Both of these issues go back to the insistence that the analyst may consider only social categories and artefacts that can be shown to be relevant to the participants in the interaction being examined. This position has been critiqued by, for example, Blommaert (2005). He points out that while, say, gender may not appear to be relevant to the participants in an interaction, it can often be shown to be *made relevant* by later re-entextualizations of that talk by others, in consequential ways for the original participants. For instance, during a job interview, gender may not be demonstrably relevant; yet the notes of the interviewers and their conversation subsequent to the interview may well show that they do orient to gender. Analysis of guidelines for interviewers – not uncommon in institutional contexts – might also draw attention to the possibility that participants in the interaction have been encouraged to avoid displaying an orientation to gender.

## New directions

All of the examples used in this chapter focus on interaction that unfolded in a single spatio-temporal frame, with all participants being in the same time frame and place. More recent work has started to look at interactions involving participants who are located in different places and whose (synchronous) interactions are mediated by new technologies such as cameras and screens (Broth, Laurier and Mondada, 2014). Some attempts have also been made at applying CA procedures to the analysis of asynchronous, writing-based interaction (Gibson, 2009).

Recently attention is also drawn to 'mobile' interactions, that involves participants who move about. Classic CA studies often looked at interactions in relatively stable, static conditions: as in two people having a 'chat' while seated on a sofa. More recent work is focused on 'mobile' face-to-face interaction (cf. Broth and Mondada, 2013). Such work shows how movement of the entire body and its placement in a material environment is intimately entwined with the use of other 'modes', such as speech and gesture. The movement, of course, adds another layer of complexity, posing new challenges for transcription and analysis.

As with all approaches described in this book, interest in 'multimodality' in CA has a relatively short history and is not on the research agenda of all members of the community. There is still much work to be done, especially in the following three areas.

- *In terms of 'modes':* Attention in CA to 'modes' beyond speech is often still limited to gesture and speech. Facial expression, for instance, has received little to no attention.
- *In terms of 'communities' studied:* The focus has been on Western hearing, 'native speaker' communities. Far less has been done on interactions in other social and cultural settings and on interactions involving 'non-native' speakers, or members of, for example, blind and deaf communities.
- *In terms of questions asked:* many of the questions addressed have come from 'within' CA, and refer back to or revisit theoretical concepts from the 'classics'. They provide elaborate, highly detailed accounts of interaction, leaving some to ask whether and how the approach can be useful to address questions from outside CA. One response to this would be to say that CA was never 'designed' to answer questions other than ones relating to the 'machinery' of interaction. Yet another response is to refer to a body of work called 'applied CA' (Antaki, 2011), which aims to not only understand interaction but also show how it might be changed. Either approach has a significant contribution to make to the field of multimodality.

## *Example 5.1*    Learning to operate on real patients

A key component of the training of any surgeon is to actually operate. Although operating provides important opportunities for the trainee to learn, for the patient, it raises important questions about the quality and safety of the care she or he receives. This potential tension was explored in a study by Bezemer and colleagues (2014). They went about addressing this question through detailed analysis of the interaction between trainees and their supervisors. In this box, they summarize what they found.

Figure 5.4 is an excerpt from an interaction featuring a trainee (who had been in specialist training for about ten years) working under the supervision of a consultant surgeon. They had worked together for six months. Looking back on the episode, the consultant told us that he knew this

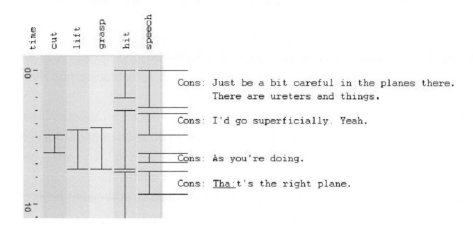

**Figure 5.4**    Transcript of interaction between a surgical trainee and his supervisor

trainee well and that he therefore felt comfortable handing the scalpel to him. In the episode they perform a keyhole operation, which means that they access the patient's abdomen through a number of keyhole incisions. They then insert a camera (a 'laparoscope') into the cavity, gaining a view which is magnified and projected on screens around them. Other instruments are then inserted to operate inside the patient's abdomen.

In the episode as represented in Figure 5.4, the trainee is dissecting the attachment to the abdominal wall. To achieve that, they need to identify 'planes' where they can separate tissue without damaging surrounding – and often vital – structures. For instance, the gonadal vessels and the ureters are delicate structures that run close to the colon and remain difficult to spot when dissecting the colon out. Surgeons therefore treat these structures as 'danger points' (Goffman, 1961) that, if exposed to 'unskilled action', result in significant 'costs'. We selected the episode for close analysis as it is here that the trainer *orients to* a danger point (the trainer *warns* the trainee in the first line of [the transcript]), providing an opportunity to investigate how consultants themselves see and deal with risks when they let their trainees operate.

As well as giving instructions, the consultant holds the *camera*. He sets the frame, zooming in and out and changing the camera angle as and when he feels appropriate. The trainee is in control of the Harmonic, a laparoscopic scalpel that surgeons use to cut and coagulate tissue by burning it. Both direct their gaze at one of the screens that display what the camera captures. To make a cut the trainee grasps tissue, closes the instrument, and then presses a pedal to activate the electric circuit that runs through the grasper, so-called 'diathermy'. In the transcript these actions are marked on (vertical) time lines alongside the spoken utterances produced by the trainer. Every second is marked with a short hairline and every 10 seconds with a long hairline. The first vertical line marks the moments that the trainee keeps the scalpel in contact with tissue; the second line the moments that he lifts tissue up; the third line the moments that he grasps tissue; and the fourth line the moments that he actually cuts tissue.

The transcript helps us deconstruct – 'dissect' – what happens in this strip of interaction. As the trainee makes the first contact in this episode, the trainer tells the trainee to 'just be a bit careful with the planes there'. The trainee then withdraws the instrument from the tissue he was touching and the trainer explains why he wants the trainee to be 'careful' in the area he was in: 'there are the ureter and things.' The prompt change in the trainee's course of action suggests that the trainee is responding to what the trainer says, perhaps taking his comment as an indication that he had better find a different, 'safer' plane. Note that the trainer's 'there' in the first two utterances refers to a broad area, including but not specifically pointing to where the trainee had placed the scalpel.

In the next four seconds or so the trainee makes the first cut. As the trainee is approaching a different plane the trainer tells him to 'go superficially.' Staying superficial is a way to avoid getting in contact with structures such as the ureter, which are hidden further into the body. The latter part of the utterance overlaps with a grasping and a lifting action by the trainee. Then, just after the trainer has said (a very short) 'yeah,' the trainee starts cauterizing. As the trainer's 'yeah' is preceded by a lifting and grasping action and followed by a cauterizing action we suggest that the trainer has interpreted the lift and the grasp as an indication of the trainee's commitment to cut at the point where he is grasping; and that the trainee has interpreted the trainer's 'yeah' as a ratification to cauterize. After the cauterizing the trainer says, 'as you're doing,' acknowledging that the trainee has indeed gone 'superficially,' as he had suggested. As the tissue that is cauterized separates, the trainee withdraws the instrument.

We used this form of analysis of teaching episodes to make two points. First, we proposed that the analysis shows how patient safety is actually achieved. We noted that the trainee's actions signify to the trainer a trajectory of actions. This is an important resource for achieving surgical care in a learning environment where the trainee holds the scalpel: trainers can read and anticipate, and trainees can signal what they are up to. We also explored the potentials and limitations of using speech to give instructions. We saw what the effects were of the trainer's spoken utterances: they prompted the trainee to withdraw his instrument, start a new contact, or proceed to cut. In other words, speech is an important resource for achieving surgical care in learning environments, allowing the trainer to prompt the trainee to *act* or to *cease to act*. We also rendered visible some of the challenges in using speech. Surgeons do not have names for everything they see inside a body, so you'll often hear them saying something like, 'that stuff there', for instance, when directing a trainee *where* to act. At these moments *pointing* is an essential semiotic resource, yet supervising surgeons often do not have a spare hand to point with at these moments as they hold the camera in one hand and provide traction with the other. This challenge could be addressed, for instance, by introducing head mounted laser pointers.

Another point we were able to make with this analysis was to do with the limitations of more common qualitative and quantitative medical research. For instance, we pointed out that the kinds of teaching strategies made *visible* by the transcript are not articulated in interviews and they would be difficult to note on-the-spot in structured observation sheets, yet they play a key role in safely training up the next generation of surgeons – and in training them how to support the training of others. We also drew attention to the way in which operations are reported. In research and assessment, surgeons often distinguish between 'doing' an operation, either independently or under supervision, and 'assisting in' an operation. Classifying participation in that way enables surgeons to calculate 'how many' cases of a procedure they 'have done' ('I've assisted in 100 and did 50'). Using examples such as the one above we highlighted that operating is always a *joint achievement*. Trainees do not simply 'do' the operation, nor are they merely passive 'recipients' of instruction: control over operations is distributed, and this distribution (the degree of guidance) varies significantly from moment to moment: some actions are performed by trainees without any visible or audible guidance, whereas others are strongly mediated by instructions. In a paper for the *World Journal of Surgery* (Bezemer et al., 2012), we therefore concluded that the common classification of participation in operations is 'an oversimplification of a complex picture'.

Adapted from Bezemer et al. 2014.

# CHAPTER 6

# Five more approaches to multimodality

In this chapter, we present five more multimodal research approaches. These build on concepts and methods of the multimodal approaches introduced in Chapters 3 to 5 and connect these with concepts and methods from other research traditions. In doing so, they take multimodality in different directions. In the chapter, we will show how such frameworks can draw attention to and render visible different features of multimodal meaning making.

When combining selected concepts and methods of SFL, social semiotics or CA with other traditions to form a new framework, it is important for you to reflect on their 'compatibility' both in relation to how meaning is theorized, their aim and research questions, the key concepts used and their empirical focus. In Chapter 1, we discussed the importance of having a clear rationale for adopting multimodal concepts, and the same goes for mixing approaches: you need to make a case for doing so and be explicit about the place of multimodality in your study.

The approaches discussed in this chapter are not intended as an exhaustive list of all approaches to multimodality. The approaches that we present:

■ Draw on selected concepts and methods from SFL, social semiotics or CA
■ Are coherent research frameworks that have produced a distinct research community and body of published work
■ Make a significant contribution to extending the scope of multimodal research, empirically, methodologically and/or theoretically

The five approaches that we set out in the chapter are:

■ *Geo-semiotics* (or discourses in place), which combines linguistic anthropology and place semiotics with a social semiotic approach to foreground the spatial material character of semiotic artefacts and interaction
■ *Multimodal (inter)action analysis*, which combines interactional sociolinguistics and a social semiotic approach to foreground identity through interaction

- *Multimodal ethnography,* which draws on a social semiotic approach and ethnography to examine artefacts and interactional practices in context
- *Multimodal corpus analysis,* which combines corpus analysis methods with SFL and social semiotic approaches to empirically evaluate, critique and validate the hypotheses and theories of multimodal meaning making through the analysis of artefacts
- *Multimodal reception analysis*, which combines eye-tracking methods from a cognitive approach to the perception of textual artefacts with SFL and social semiotics to focus on the cognitive processes that underlie their reception.

In the following sections, we introduce each of these combined frameworks. Our aim is to give you a sense of their scope, the different aims and research questions that concern them, the theory of meaning that informs them, their key concepts and their empirical focus. We also identify their key representatives and outline the methodologies of the approaches to highlight their specific contribution to multimodality. In doing so, we illustrate the potential (and challenges) of combining elements from different research traditions to advance multimodality.


## Geo-semiotics: discourses in place

Geo-semiotics examines how language and signs made in other modes are placed in the material world. It attends to the spatial and material character of communication to highlight how:

> [D]iscourses in place everywhere in our world bring with them both potentials for action and constraints upon possible meanings and interpretations.
> (Scollon and Wong Scollon, 2003: 207)

The American linguists Ron and Suzie Wong Scollon developed this way of working, which is outlined in their book *Discourses in Place* (2003). They highlighted the need to investigate emplacement in order to understand the meaning of signs and discourses and actions in and among those signs. Their aim was to provide a descriptive language to account for semiotic landscapes and to contribute to a social change agenda by revealing the power of discourses in place.

The Scollons developed geo-semiotics at the intersection of three traditions:

- *Linguistic anthropology*, drawing on particularly Erving Goffman's (1983) concept of the interaction order and Edward Hall's (1990) work on interpersonal distance to examine the social arrangements among people in situated interaction;
- *Social semiotics*, drawing on Kress and van Leeuwen's (1996, 2001) work on multimodal design to analyse the materiality and semiotic resources involved in making signs;
- *Place semiotics,* drawing on the work of cultural geographers, notably Tuan (1991), to examine the situatedness of signs in time and space.

Geo-semiotics is used to foreground how the sociocultural and meaning-making resources of space and place shape communication.

> [We] use a Geo-semiotic perspective to try to bring together the study of texts, the study of social interaction, and the study of the material world in which human actions take place. We speak of this intersection of multiple discourses as the semiotic aggregate . . . of the place of humans in time and space.
>
> (Scollon and Wong Scollon, 2003: 13)

It attends to the rules, meaning potentials and constraints of a place, as well as its historically organized and patterned features. From this perspective, it is possible to understand the meaning of public artefacts (e.g. signs, notices, logos) *only* by physically and socially contextualising them. This contextualizing is realized through attention to the:

- *Indexicality of signs*, which focuses on meanings derived from the placement of signs in their context;
- *Dialogicality of signs*, which proposes that there is always a dynamic among signs, an inter-semiotic, and inter-discursive relationship between signs, once they are placed in an environment;
- *Selection of a subset of signs* by the actor, a selection that foregrounds some potential meanings and backgrounds others.

Questions addressed by geo-semiotics include, How is power structured through situated everyday 'public discourse signs'? How do people produce discourses in place through their interpretation of signs in place? What 'work' do signs allow us or require us to do in a social situation? How do people negotiate the meanings of an artefact through interaction?

The empirical focus of geo-semiotics is on people's situated understanding of public signs. For example, signs, notices, logos, advertisements, graffiti, as well as monuments and the built environment. Materials are collected in the form of ethnographic observation, photographs and video recordings. A descriptive analysis is undertaken of these three aspects of social action.

The *interaction order* (borrowed from Goffman as well as from Hall's work on interpersonal distance) is the starting point for a geo-semiotic analysis. This involves a fine-grained analysis of the participants' embodied interaction in the space being investigated and the ways in which social arrangements within the social context are produced, contested and resisted through the organization of the resources of time, space, interpersonal distance and the personal front. The analysis is focused on exploring the social structures of this situated interaction, the rules and norms of an encounter and how these are taken up through attention to how social actors bodily orient to signs or use them to realize social action. This involves the analysis of the meaning-making resources of time and space and how these are configured. For example, interpersonal distances and perceptual spaces are mapped with attention to social actors' positions, their presentation of self in relation to dress, roles and the units of the interaction order. How the placement of these signs affects their interpretation is central to a geo-semiotic analysis, leading to the second stage of its analytical process that is focused on signs, and its third stage, focused on place.

Geo-semiotics views *(semiotic) signs* as integral to interaction because they both represent and mediate interaction. A social semiotic approach, outlined in Chapter 4, is used to analyse the grammar of signs in the environment being studied. This analysis attends to what or who is represented in the sign, the type of representation; the modality or the truth value of a representation, realized, for example, through the use of colour or contextualization; its compositional layout; and the interpersonal or interactive relationship established by a sign with its viewer.

*Place Semiotics* is the third strand of a geo-semiotic analysis. This refers to:

the ways in which the placement of discourse in the material world produces meanings that derive directly from that placement.

(Scollon and Wong Scollon, 2003: 22)

The analysis of place semiotics focuses on the interactional environment with attention to three dimensions:

1    The *code preference* of a sign refers to its placement in the environment (e.g. a street name sign). This is analysed to explore how the positioning of a sign can signal legal, historical or social relationships among a community in a place.
2    The *inscription* of an artefact refers to its physical material aspects in the environment, for example its material (e.g. durability) or temporal qualities (e.g. newness).
3    The *emplacement* of an artefact refers to its physical placement of a sign in the environment to explore the affordances and limitations that such placement affords, including the social and historical meanings associated with place, which may be either decontextualized (e.g. brands and logos that signal independence from its placement), situated (e.g. an exit sign) or transgressive (e.g. graffiti).

The intersections of multiple discourses (e.g. public, private, regulatory discourse and commercial discourse) and the interaction order in particular places (e.g. shopping malls, street corners in neighbourhoods) are seen as 'semiotic aggregates' (Scollon and Wong Scollon, 2003: 167). Semiotic aggregates are layered discourses in a place created over time. The layered account provided by this 'semiotic aggregate' offers a composite meaning of social action in place that accounts for what sorts of social action might be done in a place, its affordances and its constraints. An account that points to how interaction orders are 'written' into public spaces as discourses, artefacts and place orientate to and connect to one another over time and space.

Geo-semiotics contributes to theorizing multimodal research by connecting it with the concepts of interaction order and place semiotics and emplacement. It also contributes to multimodality by situating artefacts in time and space and bringing place into the centre of the analysis and showing how locating artefacts in situ can contribute to their interpretation.

## Multimodal (inter)actional analysis

Multimodal (inter)actional analysis is used to explore social action, interaction and identity from a multimodal perspective. It questions the notion that communication is always dependent on language. Multimodal (inter)action analysis sets out to examine how a variety of modes are brought into and are constitutive of social interaction, identities and social relations. This way of working was developed by Sigrid Norris, who studied with the Scollons in the US before moving to New Zealand, and is outlined in her book *Analyzing Multimodal Interaction: A Methodological Framework* (2004).

Multimodal (inter)action analysis brings together concepts from different theoretical approaches:

- *Mediated discourse*, notably the work of the Scollons; this is used to focus on the ways in which interaction is always mediated by semiotic resources
- *Social interaction studies*, drawing on the work of Goffman, Gumperz and Tannen
- *Social semiotics*, drawing on Kress and van Leeuwen's approach to visual and multimodal analysis to analyse texts (what Norris refers to as 'frozen actions')

The work of the actor is seen as central in this approach because it is through interaction that social occasions are instantiated. Multimodal concepts are used to expand the focus of interaction, moving away from a focus on language to encompass how people deploy gesture, gaze, posture, movement, as well as how space and artefacts mediate interaction. The analytical framework is organized around the following key concepts: 'mode'; levels of action (higher-level, lower-level and frozen actions); and modal density.

The multimodal concept of *mode* is (re-)conceptualized in this approach on the basis that mode, sign maker and context are seen as too intimately connected to separate:

> Social actors always co-construct their actions from the environment and/or from the other social actors so that we can never extricate a social actor's actions from the environment and/or from the other social actors involved.
>
> (Norris, 2014: 86)

Norris uses the notion of mode heuristically and focuses on the rules and regularities that come about while social actors use modes:

> Communicative modes are heuristic or explanatory units that allow analysts to dissect complex interactions and enable the analysis of small parts, before

analysing how these parts work together to construct the complexity of face to face interactions.

(Norris, 2004: 12–13)

From this stance, it is not possible to consider the affordances and constraints of different media in a general way outside of a specific context. To do so is of limited use because the affordances and constraints of modes are understood as contingent on and realized through interaction:

> [A] communicative mode is never a bounded or static unit, but always and only a heuristic unit. The term 'heuristic' highlights the plainly explanatory function, and also accentuates the constant tension and contradiction between the system of representation and the real-time interaction among social actors. . . . Individuals in interaction draw on systems of representation [modes] while at the same time constructing, adopting, and changing those systems through their actions. In turn, all actions that individuals perform are mediated by the system of representation that they draw on.
>
> (Norris, 2004: 12–13)

That is, modes do not exist without social actors utilizing them in some way. Multimodal (inter)actional analysis is concerned with the situated interplay between modes at a given moment in social interaction. The focus is on understanding modes in action and on the hierarchical and non-hierarchical structures among the modes used in a specific social interaction. This concept of mode leads to the two other key concepts of this perspective: levels of action and modal density.

The unit of analysis used by this approach is *(mediated) action* rather than mode. Multimodal (inter)actional analysis distinguishes among three levels of social (mediated) action: higher- and lower-level actions and frozen action, each of which deals with a different level of interaction.

- *Higher-level action* is used to refer to large-scale actions, such as a meeting, and is made up of 'multiplicity of chained lower-level actions' (Norris, 2004: 13).
- *Lower-level action* is used to refer to smaller-scale actions, for example, gestures or gaze shifts that become 'chains of lower-level interactions' (Norris, 2004: 13).
- *Frozen action* is used to refer to material artefacts, in order to foreground the social interaction that led to their production.

These three levels make a distinction between two 'sets' of interactional modes:

1  'Embodied' modes: e.g. gesture, gaze, posture
2  'Disembodied' modes: e.g. layout, spatial modes and media

Norris uses frozen action to point to the role of the material constraints and affordances of artefacts in mediating social interaction.

*Modal density* is a concept developed by Norris to explore the hierarchical and non-hierarchical structures among the modes used in a specific social interaction. It is used to map the modal shifts that foreground or background higher-level actions. Modal density is explored via the analysis of modal *intensity* and *complexity*. Modal intensity refers to:

> 'the intensity or weight that a mode carries in the construction of a higher-level action' (e.g. speech takes on high modal intensity when people talk on the phone).
>
> (Norris, 2014: 90)

Modal complexity refers to how modes interrelate. This is visualized using circles and continuums representing the changes in modal intensity and complexity, which in turn mark changes in the level of awareness and attention of the participants in an interaction sequence.

The research questions explored by multimodal inter(action) analysis address how people produce their identities through interaction across a range of sites and contexts. Materials are collected using observation and video recordings. Analysis involves the following steps.

First, the range of communicative modes and their affordances are mapped in relation to real-time social interaction.

The video materials are viewed, and episodes of interest focused on a higher-level action are selected for in-depth analysis. These episodes tend to be short, around one or two minutes in length.

The episode is transcribed by attending to selected lower-level actions that form and construct the higher-level or frozen action. Transcription uses time stamps and still images to show selected snapshots of moments. Attention is given to visualizing proxemics, posture, gesture, gaze and so on at a point in the interaction. The selection of the images in a transcript is related to the notion of a lower-level action as an analytical unit, some of which may be a couple of seconds, others 20 seconds.

Figure 6.1 Transcript of six simultaneous higher-level actions (Reprinted from Norris, 2004: 102)

The transcript in Figure 6.1 is used to develop an analytical description of 'embodied modes': proxemics, that is the use of space, the distance established between people and objects; posture, the ways that people's bodies are positioned in a given interaction, such as their orientation or involvement with others; categories of gesture; head movement, including directional shifts, deictic movements and beats; gaze, its organization and direction. The 'disembodied modes' in use – such as written text and printed image, layout and so on – are also transcribed. Once the lower-level and frozen actions have been described, the analytical attention shifts to explore how modes interconnect to construct the complexity of interaction. The analytical focus is on the (hierarchical) structures of the interaction. A continuum of high to low modal density is used to visualize the modal shifts, intensity and complexity of the higher-level actions throughout the interaction sequence.

Multimodal (inter)action analysis contributes to theorizing multimodal research by connecting the concept of mode and multimodality with methods and concepts derived from interactional sociolinguistics and mediated discourse. One outcome of this approach has been the concept of multimodal density.

## Multimodal ethnography

Multimodal ethnography refers to a framework that brings together social semiotic theory (notably the concepts of motivated sign, affordances, mode and semiotic resources [see Chapter 4]) with ethnography. Ethnography is an interpretive approach that aims to produce accounts of cultural and social practices through prolonged fieldwork in a particular setting.

Multimodal ethnography investigates how meanings are produced and understood in social and cultural contexts. It evolved from a group of researchers who drew on a social semiotic approach and new literacy studies to study children's meaning making in and outside schools. Key scholars using this approach include Rosie Flewitt, Charmian Kenner, Lesley Lancaster and Kate Pahl. They are concerned with understanding children's communicative and literacy practices and contexts. They argue that, while offering important theoretical tools, social semiotics does not provide all the concepts and methods needed to understand how multiple social factors shape children's production of artefacts:

> A focus on semiosis could show what choices children made, and what
> modes were made available to them through diverse traditional and 'new'

literacy texts in diverse media, but this constituted 'thin' descriptions which situated the production and reception of meanings within physical and material social settings, but did not make accessible more holistic insights into their literacy learning. . . . For this deeper level of understanding, the study was dependent on ethnographic data, which constituted a rich backstory of how networks of cultural and social values permeated the children's homes and nursery. While multimodal analysis captured something of the communicative complexity of the studied field, ethnographic approaches to data collection and interpretation helped to situate that complexity in particular social, cultural and historical contexts.

(Flewitt, 2011: 302)

In this approach, social semiotics is used to produce a micro analytical account of artefacts (texts and objects), their multimodal design and the social and cultural norms and discourses they materialize, using the concepts outlined earlier in this book (see Chapter 4). Alongside this, an ethnographic approach is used that insists on engagement with the social contexts that artefacts are produced in and through. In other words:

[A]n ethnographic lens gives multimodal analysis a social map.

(Street, Pahl and Rowsell, 2014: 230)

The research questions addressed by multimodal ethnography are concerned with the role of everyday processes, practices and contexts in meaning making. This approach has been used to investigate children's meaning making in a variety of settings, including playgrounds, online environments, nursery and primary school classrooms. For example, Pahl (1999) used multimodal ethnography in her study of young children's artefacts and how these were drawn into play across the home and school. The combination of ethnographic observation and social semiotic analysis of textual artefacts enabled Pahl to explore the link between home and school activities, genres and content topics. Questions she addressed included, 'Where do children develop their meanings? How do they represent meanings anew? How do they transform meaning? What differences are there in children's meaning making at home and at school?'

Materials for a study using multimodal ethnography are usually collected using observations. The ethnographer documents practices in field notes and video recordings. In addition, unstructured and semi-structured interviews are held with members of the community under study, and the artefacts they use are also documented or collected. Drawing on the methodological concepts of *openness*, *situatedness* and *reflexivity*, these materials are then used to gain insight into participants' lived experiences in the social and cultural context of study.

- *Openness to materials:* This involves taking an 'open' approach to the development of the ethnographic account, allowing the pursuit of unanticipated avenues for further analysis. Initial research questions are used as guiding directions along which to explore the materials in the analysis, but they are not fixed.
- *Situatedness:* This is used to gain insight into concrete instances of meaning making situated in time and space. This complements the semiotic reading and interpretation of artefacts without reference to documentations of their context of production. Connections with the participants' history, local policies and so forth are then also explored.
- *Reflexivity:* In ethnography, the role of the researcher in the production of 'data' and analysis is acknowledged and investigated. The researcher and the research are seen as being intimately connected. It is the researcher's job to make those connections explicit, rather than trying to separate the two.

Although social semiotics and ethnography have different starting points, their shared view of 'culture-as-text' and ' "text" as semiotic instantiations of lived practices' enables them to be brought together in productive ways (Flewitt, 2011: 307). According to Flewitt, multimodal ethnography can help a study to stay 'faithful' to the insider account of the phenomena under investigation:

> by taking into account participant perspectives . . . and safeguard against the 'webs of significance' identified through the research process being spun from an entirely 'outsider' perspective.
>
> (Flewitt, 2011: 307)

Thus emphasis is placed on getting the researcher's account 'validated' by the people whose practices have been studied. To this some will say that such validation is often sought in verbal statements, which offer very limited potential to explicate how meaning was made.

In multimodal ethnography, the temporal unfolding of social processes is examined to bring the complexity of interconnected elements into view: the person, the situated encounter and the communities of practice in institutions and their networks. The analytical focus moves iteratively between the textual artefacts in use and the practices and social framings that the text is embedded within. Sometimes the researcher starts with the text in action and moves out to explore the broader context, and sometimes the broader context is the starting point.

A semiotic account of material artefacts and objects is built up with attention to how these shape and are shaped by socially situated norms and practices, while their relationship to meaning making practices, identity and community is explored using an ethnographic approach (video and 'thick description,' a term used in ethnography to refer to description that provides a contextual description – e.g. of a behaviour and the behaviour context – such that it is meaningful to a reader who was not present). These are used to produce transcripts of key moments in the interaction.

In an early study on children reading non-fiction in the classroom, Moss (2001: 110) argues that this combination enables:

> closer attention to the design of non-fiction and differences in its presentation . . . as a material object, the affordances and resistances of the stuff from which it is made, the particular combination of a written text and image it synthesizes and co-ordinates on the given space of the page . . . as well as the need to consider the text in its context of use. For the context of use can work with or against the grain of the text and what it offers.

It is this iterative tension between the context of use and the 'grain of the text' – in other words, its meaning potentials – that is the crux of this combined approach.

> [This] can lead to the production of grounded, theorized, detailed and holistic insights into literacy as social practice, revealing how micro-moments of multimodal meaning making unfold in a complex network of socially-situated norms and practices.
>
> (Flewitt, 2011: 297)

In summary, a multimodal ethnographic approach contributes to theorizing multimodality by foregrounding the situatedness of meaning making. It makes a methodological contribution by highlighting the role of field work and prolonged engagement in a setting such as a school, so as to become familiar with the range of contexts in which meaning is made in situ.

## Corpus-based multimodal analysis

Corpus-based multimodal analysis sets out to empirically evaluate, critique and validate multimodal hypotheses and theories of meaning making through the analysis of multimodal artefacts and interaction. It is a response to multi-modal studies that focuses on analysing a small number of texts, offering a limited empirical ground to generalize. In short, corpus-based multimodal analysis calls for systematic analysis of larger corpora of texts to provide a stronger empirical grounding for multimodal theory. John Bateman, a leading proponent of such an approach, put it as follows:

> As studies of multimodality progress, it is increasingly important to evaluate hypotheses and theories concerning multimodal meaning-making against data, i.e., actual artefacts and performances involving the deployment of semiotic resources drawn from and combining modalities of various kinds. Discussions of single illustrative cases play an important role in the initial stages of research and theory development, but as theories mature we need to establish the degree to which they can cover and explain uses of multimodality more generally. We need to be able to explore potential boundaries within which the theories might operate and locate gaps or inaccuracies in those theories' predictions. Until this is done, accounts remain 'working hypotheses' which may or may not be applicable in any particular case.
>
> (Bateman, 2014c: 238)

Thus Bateman treats many of the concepts that are being used in multimodal research as proposals or 'hypotheses' that need to be tested against a large corpus of artefacts. Bateman has adopted this approach to analyse websites and films (Bateman, 2008; Bateman, Delin and Henschel, 2004). Antony Baldry, Paul Thibault and Kay O'Halloran have also contributed to the development of corpus-based multimodal analysis.

The approach has developed hand in hand with technological advances that have made both large quantities of digital data readily available and provided the tools that make it possible to search that data for patterns:

> Both aspects need to be present for corpus analysis to be effective: insufficient quantities of data raise the danger that the patterns found are accidental and do not generalise, while a lack of facilities for searching larger scale bodies of data means that researchers cannot get at the patterns, even if they are there.
>
> (Bateman, 2014c: 239)

Bateman (2014c: 243–246) makes a distinction between multimodal corpora that consist of linear and non-linear data.

- *Linear data* is used to refer to material that is essentially organized to unfold along a single dimension of actualization (e.g. space, as in traditional written-text data, or in time, as in recordings of spoken language)
- *Non-linear data* is used to refer to material where there is no single organizing dimension that can be used for providing access (e.g. spatially distributed information and visual representations – pages of documents, printed advertisements, paintings, websites etc.)

Different approaches and tools are used to build, annotate and analyse these two categories of data: in the case of linear data, *ELAN* (discussed in Chapter 5), the Multimodal Corpus Authoring (MCA) system (Baldry and Thibault, 2006) and Multimodal Analysis Video (O'Halloran and Lim, 2014; O'Halloran, Tan and E, 2015) (discussed in Chapter 3); for non-linear data (i.e. static artefacts), Bateman's GeM framework (discussed later in this section) and Multimodal Analysis Image (O'Halloran, Tan and E, 2015) (discussed in Chapter 3).

Corpora have been built to research a wide range of everyday printed and digital artefacts such as websites, brochures, newspapers and magazines. The GeM study (Bateman, 2008), for example, used bird field guides, print and online newspapers, and technical manuals.

Corpus-based multimodal analysis has been used to address a range of questions related to the factors that affect the multimodal structure of artefacts, what kinds of patterns can be identified in their multimodal structure, 'semiotic values' and their realization in artefacts, and how multimodal structures of artefacts change over time. The longitudinal potential of this approach can be particularly useful in exploring the historical process of the development of structures. For instance, GeM set out to:

[D]evelop a framework that would let us account for consistencies in visual style (including layout and typographical decisions) in terms of an extended notion of multimodal genre . . . exercise constraints on selections within layout structures . . . and rhetorical organization.

(Bateman, 2014c: 32)

Corpus-based multimodal analysis has been used to test and explore many multimodal concepts. Bateman and colleagues have, for instance, used this framework to examine Kress and van Leeuwen's claims in *Reading Images* (1996) (see Chapter 4). They examined to what extent Kress and van Leeuwen's notion of information value (in which different information value is attributed to elements on the left 'given' and the right 'new') can be supported (Bateman, 2014c).

Here we briefly discuss the concepts and stages of this approach. First, a multimodal corpus ('data set') is constructed. This is a collection of 'instances of phenomena or patterns of concern' (Bateman, Delin and Henschel, 2004: 6).

Second, this set of 'bare' or 'raw' data is annotated ('tagged') in ways that are directly supportive of further questioning:

> Once the target data have been fixed, they must then be prepared for corpus use. Bare data are generally insufficient for effective empirical research because it is difficult, or even impossible, to interact with the data in ways that are appropriate for framing and exploring research questions.
>
> (Bateman, 2014c: 241)

This raises the challenging question of, 'What kinds of data annotation might be useful?' This leads to selection of an existing annotation schema (*definitely* recommended for those starting out) or, potentially, the development of a new model. The GeM model (Bateman, 2008; Bateman, Delin and Henschel, 2004) provides a standardized annotation schema for non-linear artefacts, which is summarized in the following list. It attends to five levels of description of the artefact:

1  *Content structure:* The 'raw' data out of which documents are constructed
2  *Rhetorical structure:* The rhetorical relationships between content elements; how the content is 'argued'
3  *Layout structure:* The nature, appearance and position of communicative elements on the page
4  *Navigation structure:* The ways in which the intended mode(s) of consumption of the document is/are supported
5  *Linguistic structure:* The structure of the language and the layout elements

GeM also provides standardized annotation features to account for how a document genre is constituted in terms of the constraints that operate during its production:

■ *Canvas constraints:* Constraints arising out of the physical nature of the object being produced (e.g. paper or screen size)
■ *Production constraints:* Constraints arising out of the production technology (e.g. limit on page numbers, colours, cost)
■ *Consumption constraints:* Constraints arising out of the time, place and manner of acquiring and consuming the document (e.g. readability)

The third step in the process is one of measurement and identifying patterns using the annotated corpus.

Annotated data may then support the search for generalizations by allowing examination of potential correlations across the various levels of descriptions that corpora provide. Establishing such dependencies represents a crucial step towards understanding how multimodal meaning making operates. Moreover, for larger-scale corpus work, an increasing reliance on automatic analysis and visualization methods in appropriate combination with manual approaches will be essential (Bateman, 2014c: 252).

A multimodal corpus provides the basis for both quantitative and qualitative computational analyses. For instance, Hiippala used the GeM model in a corpus-based multimodal analysis of tourist brochures about Helsinki, published between 1967 and 2008, to explore a range of theoretical hypothesis (Hiippala, 2015). For example, he measured the proportion of writing and image in the corpus of tourist brochures and noted that the average amount of layout space taken up by images was 50 per cent for each year. He also found that the discourse structure of the brochures had changed significantly after 1985 with the introduction of desktop publishing software. Analysis of the structural patterns found in the corpus showed a statistically significant move from 'linear-interrupted written language towards a fragmented non-linear design' (Hiippala, 2015).

Other approaches have involved developing purpose-built multimodal analysis software. For example, Kay O'Halloran and colleagues developed Multimodal Analysis Image and Multimodal Analysis Video software (O'Halloran, Tan and E, 2015) (see Chapter 3). The software applications have facilities for importing media files (i.e. image and video files, respectively), developing multimodal frameworks, creating projects and annotating media files using the theoretical frameworks entered into the software. The results of the multimodal analysis are stored in a database for exportation to Excel for further data processing and visualization. In the case of Multimodal Analysis Video, there is a visualization facility built into the software so that combinations of semiotic choices (e.g. language, image, film techniques and sound) can be viewed as states (i.e. combinations of semiotic choices) that unfold over time. It is then possible to see various patterns and phases in the video, revealing how it achieves it communicative purpose through repeated and contrasting combinations of multimodal choices. The software is designed to handle the complexity of multimodal analysis, with a view to developing new techniques for modeling and visualizing multimodal data. The software applications come with default systems for language, image and video analysis, based on Michael Halliday, Michael O'Toole and Theo van Leeuwen's social semiotic approach (see Chapters 3 and 5).

The fourth step is to feed the analytical results back into the development of multimodal theory. Hiippala (2015) used his findings to interrogate the concept of the visual turn. He used his findings to show that while the rhetorical structure of the brochures and the visual/written proportions remained the same regardless of the medium, the changes in technology in 1985 shifted the central design principle from written text ('text-flow') to the entire layout space ('page-flow') (Hiippala, 2014: 116). In other words, his analysis critiqued the 'so-called visual turn' at the same time as providing precision on how it was realized in a particular set of artefacts (tourist brochures), concluding that 'The visual turn in the tourist brochures affected structure, not appearance'.

In another initiative, Kay O'Halloran and her interdisciplinary team used automated computational techniques for multimodal analysis of large cultural data sets. For example, social patterns and trends were derived from analysis of photographs of Japanese street fashion (Podlasov and O'Halloran, 2014), social media texts in the form of geo-located Tweets and Instagram images in Singapore (O'Halloran, Chua and Podlasov, 2014) and Flickr images (Cao and O'Halloran, 2014). Following on from this, Kay O'Halloran, John Bateman and colleagues are working towards integrating rich, close multimodal analysis with data mining and visualization techniques for big data analytics (see Chapter 3).

The potential for developing interactive digital platforms for corpus-based multimodal analysis is at an early stage: mapping, analysing and retrieving the patterns of inter-semiotic relations in the dynamic environment of digital technology require further exploration. Corpus-based multimodal analysis has made a significant contribution to multimodality through its use of large corpora to critique and empirically validate multimodal concepts and to establish the degree to which they can explain uses of multimodality more generally (e.g. Kong, 2013; O'Halloran, 2015c).

## Multimodal reception analysis

Multimodal reception analysis examines the cognitive processes that underlie recipients' interaction with complex materials. It sets out to undertake empirical research that shows how multimodal messages are perceived and comprehended by their users (as opposed to what was intended by the 'messenger'). By tracking eye movements in real-time contexts of use, it explores how people interact with a text design. Multimodal eye-tracking has been used to test social semiotic concepts and theories of design. Holsanova (2014b) has led this area of work with the Cognitive Science Department and Eye Tracking Group at Lund, Sweden. It brings together:

■ *Social semiotic theory*, related to the composition of multimodal artefacts and its potential for meaning making
■ *Cognitive theory*, related to perception and attention
■ Methods of tracking and analysing eye movements

Holsanova puts it as follows:

> Whereas the social semiotic approach emphasizes the way meaning potentials are selected and orchestrated to make meaning in particular contexts, the interest of the cognitive research lies in how the selected meaning potentials and their orchestration have been perceived and interpreted by the recipients. Furthermore, whereas a text represents a window on its maker in the social semiotic approach, eye movement data serve as a window on the mind of the user, revealing perceptual and cognitive processes underlying users' interaction with the multimodal messages.
>
> (Holsanova, 2014b: 293)

Eye tracking generates empirical data that can be used to explore the ways in which individual readers engage with a text and respond to the reading paths, salience, composition and framing created by the maker of the text. The concepts of *attention*, *fixations* and *saccades* are central to this approach.

- *(Selective) attention* is understood as being borne out of limited human cognitive capacity to actively read and process information in multiple places simultaneously. Reading requires focusing attention (which is reflected in the gaze) to relevant 'signifiers' – letters, words, parts of the image – so that they fall onto a high-resolution area of the eye (Holsanova, 2014b: 289).
- *Fixations* are stops or periods of time when the point of attention is relatively still/static, allowing for information to be acquired/processed. The length of a fixation, or fixation duration, is a measure of how much cognitive effort is put into engaging with that which the eyes are fixated on.
- *Saccade* is a term used to refer to a rapid eye movement allowing the 'reader' to reorient the point of attention from one spatial position to another.

Research questions raised by this approach might include, What reading paths do newspaper pages have? Are the intended reading paths the same as those that the readers actually choose? How do readers navigate texts, choose entry points and reading paths? How do readers create coherence? How do they integrate information from different sources and modes in the process of meaning making? How do readers interact with complex multimodal artefacts in real time? How does the design of educational artefacts support problem solving? How do readers mentally animate and visualize problems? Eye tracking's empirical focus is on everyday textual artefacts, including both printed and digital materials (e.g. newspapers, teaching and learning resources, textbooks, diagrams), including both static and dynamic graphics (e.g. graphs, maps, video clips, animations).

The analytical process consists of a detailed analysis of eye movements in the reading and scanning process.

A textual artefact or a series of them is selected for the study. These may be 'authentic' artefacts or ones that have been designed for the study. For instance, a realistic-looking newspaper double spread may be designed in which the placement of advertisements, diagrams or images is changed to enable comparisons in how textual artefacts are attended to via gaze behaviour, the amount of time spent, the order of reading, the aspects of the artefact that attract attention, and so on.

The participant wears an eye-tracking device (static or mobile) that records eye movements with the artefact as a set of measurements. Other methods might be used alongside eye-tracking. For instance, participants could be asked to simultaneously describe their interaction with the artefact ('talk-aloud' protocols), or they might be interviewed or asked to complete comprehension tests and/or questionnaires.

The eye movement data is analysed to identify fixations and saccades to show which objects and areas of the artefact the reader has fixated on, in what order and for how long. This data is synchronized and compared with the talk-aloud data to identify what stands out to the reader, as well as what ideas and thoughts correspond to points of fixation (Holsanova, 2008).

This approach takes multimodality into a new direction by examining and theorizing cognitive processes involved in meaning making. It provides a method for testing claims made on the basis of an analysis of the text alone. By accumulating eye-tracking data from a large number of respondents in experimental settings, general patterns in the reception of multimodal artefacts can be explored, as well as the factors that affect the perception and interpretation process (e.g. prior knowledge, experience) (Holsanova, 2014b).

Eye-tracking methods can also be used to support analysis of multimodal interaction, i.e. by establishing the gaze direction of participants (e.g. the reading of food labels in a supermarket).

## Concluding comments

In this chapter we have discussed five more multimodal approaches. We have shown how they take multimodality in new directions, foregrounding the role of space and place, interaction and insider perspectives and providing means to test theories of multimodal design and reception. It is significant that these approaches have emerged from specific empirical and theoretical concerns. In part they are responses to perceived limitations of a particular method or concept in the field of multimodality.

While we have focused on just five approaches that combine multimodality in different ways, we are certain that other possibilities and directions will emerge to contribute to the field of multimodality.

# CHAPTER 7

# Designing a multimodal study

We have made the case for multimodality and mapped its methodological terrain and scope in the previous chapters. In this chapter, we shift gears and show how to design a multimodal study. We outline eight key elements that you will need to consider when designing a multimodal study:

1   Choosing an approach
2   Deciding on a research area/focus
3   Formulating research questions
4   Selecting an empirical focus
5   Collecting research materials
6   Managing your research materials
7   Transcribing research materials
8   Considering the ethical dimensions of multimodal research

## Choosing an approach

One of the first challenges of designing a multimodal study is how to navigate the diverse field of multimodality and where to position yourself within it.

Whatever your route to multimodality, being clear on your theory of meaning making will provide a solid grounding for the design of your study. You need to ensure that your methods and questions are aligned with, and do not become disconnected from, the theoretical beliefs in which they are embedded.

Throughout this book, we have been clear that there is no 'right' or 'best' approach to multimodality, and we have instead pointed to the need to consider the *aptness* and coherence of an approach for a study. The different approaches that we have discussed in this book provide a particular lens on the world. We have discussed how their different principles and key concepts bring different aspects of multimodality into focus. Each shapes multimodal research in a particular direction with implications for your research focus – aim and topic, the type of questions that can be addressed, the type of materials that need to be collected, as well as the research outcomes.

Your choice of approach will be shaped by your history, academic training, life circumstances, experiences, passions and interests; the history, origin and disciplinary home of the approach; the specific history of where you are studying or working, as well as your supervisor or mentor's history and research area. In other words there is an interconnection between a researcher's disposition, their concerns and context and their choice of an approach. Research is a complex process that involves our becoming aware of and understanding our stance to knowledge, to the world, to others and to ourselves. That is, choosing an approach goes beyond a purely technical process: it is about finding and taking a theoretical position on meaning. Engaging reflexively with your fundamental interest and questions, what *you* think is important and possible to know and understand, and considering and comparing the aims and theories of meaning of the approaches set out in this book (summarized Table 7.1) will support you in designing your study.

Table 7.1 Summary of the aims and theory of meaning of multimodal approaches

| | *Aim and theory of meaning* |
|---|---|
| **SF-MDA** | **Aim:** To understand the ways in which meaning systems are organized and used to fulfil a range of social functions.<br>**Theory of meaning**: Meaning systems are conceptualized social semiotic resources for creating meaning. The meaning potential of a system is reflected in its underlying organization that is modelled as interrelated systems of meaning. The systems are 'networks of interlocking options' (i.e. choice between different forms), and 'text' is a process and product of the selection (and materialization) from that potential (e.g. Halliday, 2008). |
| **Social semiotics** | **Aim:** To recognize the agency of social actors and social/power relations between them.<br>**Theory of meaning**: Based on the notion of the *motivated sign*, which holds that the relation between 'signifier' and 'signified' is always motivated (and never 'arbitrary'). |

*(Continued)*

Table 7.1     (Continued)

| | Aim and theory of meaning |
|---|---|
| **CA** | **Aim:** To recognize social 'order' in the ways in which people *organize* themselves in and through interaction.<br>**Theory of meaning**: Based on the notion of *sequential action*: action unfolds in time, one action after another. Each social action is understood in relation to the action that preceded and followed. That principle provides a basis for making claims about the meanings that people make. |
| ***Geo-semiotics*** | **Aim:** To provide an account of the semiotic landscape by revealing the power of discourses in place.<br>**Theory of meaning**: The meaning of artefacts is realized through their physical and social context – through attention to emplacement and indexicality. |
| ***Multimodal (inter)action analysis*** | **Aim:** To explore how a variety of semiotic resources are brought into and are constitutive of social interaction, identities and relations.<br>**Theory of meaning**: The work of the actor is central because it is through interaction, as well as how space and artefacts mediate interaction, that social occasions are instantiated. |
| ***Multimodal ethnography*** | **Aim:** To make visible the cultural and social practices of a particular community.<br>**Theory of meaning**: The person, the situated encounter, and the communities of practice in institutions and their networks instantiate meaning. |
| ***Multimodal corpus analysis*** | **Aim:** To empirically evaluate, critique and validate multimodal hypotheses and theories of meaning making.<br>**Theory of meaning**: This approach draws on SF-MDA and social semiotic theories of meaning. |
| ***Multimodal reception analysis*** | **Aim:** To examine how multimodal messages are perceived and comprehended by their users.<br>**Theory of meaning**: Cognitive theories of perception and attention and SF-MDA and social semiotic theories of textual meaning making. |

## How to decide on a research area, topic and questions

A second challenge you will encounter when you design a multimodal study is the need to clarify your research focus, that is what it is that you want to know more about, what you wish to understand, explain, explicate or infer about. This challenge will differ depending on whether you are *doing* multimodality or *adopting multimodal concepts*.

If you are *doing* multimodal research, the methodological potentials and historical uses of the particular approach that you use will frame the area and topic of your study. The requirements of the approach will guide the questions that your study will focus on. Of course, you will still need to make choices and decisions within this frame. Alternatively, if you are *adopting multimodal concepts* for your study, you will need to bring a research area, topic or question from another theoretical context. In both cases, you will need to specify an area, topic and questions in your study design.

Within the bounds of the frame of your approach, you can generate ideas to identify a *research area* in different ways. You could review and engage with the research literature on multimodality within a given approach. You could consider the character of the multimodal artefacts and/or interactions that you encounter or observe through your experiences or in a locale of particular interest to you. The choice of research area needs to be shaped through an engagement with multimodality. If you are interested in, say, linguistic landscapes, you would need to be willing to move beyond the 'linguistic' and consider the semiotic landscape to warrant being labelled multimodal. As discussed in Chapter 2, multimodality challenges the assumption that language is the most resourceful and important of all modes and that it can be studied in isolation from other modes. To this end, a study of a public space would need to engage with all signs rather than extracting its linguistic elements and analyse them in isolation from the other signs. So if you were to do a multimodal analysis of a shop front, for instance, you'd look at the arrangement of objects on display as much as at the written text on the window. More generally, the examples discussed across the chapters of this book give an indication of the wide range of research concerns that multimodality connects with and the domains in which they have been explored, including health, education, family and home, work and so on.

Next you will need to formulate a set of research questions to focus your research. Research questions provide a useful guide and anchor for your study regardless of your approach. Multimodal studies balance the design work done prior to the collection of materials and in the field in different ways. A research topic and/or questions can be clearly established prior to the fieldwork and analysis. While it can be useful to enter the research field with some sense of a research topic and question, these can, in some approaches, unfold and be established as a part of the research process itself. Prior research topics and questions can be honed and refined throughout a study, iterating between phases of collecting materials and preliminary analysis. You will need to engage with the existing multimodal research literature to ensure your research questions connect with prior research.

The type of questions that you ask will vary depending on the approach you use in your study. Table 7.2 illustrates the type of research topic and questions typical of the approaches we set out in this book. If you adopt multimodal concepts, incorporating them into other approaches, you will need to ensure that

**Table 7.2**  Examples of research questions in multimodal approaches

| | *Examples of research questions* |
|---|---|
| **SF-MDA** | Unsworth (2007), building on Martinec and Salway (2005), explored the nature of text–image relations in school textbooks and other educational materials by developing a classification system that documents the types of logical relations established between the text and images. In this SFL approach, the questions that are asked include, 'What is the nature of the text–image relations? Are these compatible with the communicative purpose of the educational materials? What, if any, challenges do they represent for young learners?' |
| **Social semiotics** | Mavers (2011) looked at a teacher's instructions and the drawings that children made subsequently in a science classroom. As in any social semiotic study, questions she addressed included, 'How did the sign makers use the modes available to them (in this case drawing and writing) to re-present the world? What did they attend to? What did they highlight? What was gained and lost in the process of "translating" from one mode to another?' |
| **CA** | Goodwin and Tulbert (2011) looked at toothbrushing in family houses. In 'plain English', their question can be formulated as, *'How do parents get their children to brush their teeth?'* In a CA framework, such formulations get translated into questions, such as, 'How do members of a community (in this case, families) organize their routine activities? How do they use their bodies, objects and the built environment as resources for the accomplishment of these activities? How do they achieve a joint focus of attention? How do they jointly "build up" the activity? How are the activities related?' |
| **Geo-semiotics** | 'How is power structured through situated everyday "public discourse signs"? How do people produce discourses in place through their interpretation of signs in place? What "work" do signs allow us or require us to do in a social situation? How do people negotiate the meanings of an artefact through interaction?' |
| **Multimodal (inter)action analysis** | 'How *do* people produce their identities through interaction across a range of sites and contexts? What kinds of higher- and lower-level actions feature?' |
| **Multimodal ethnography** | 'What is the role of everyday processes, practices and contexts in meaning making? For example, how are artefacts drawn into play across the home and school? Where do actors develop their meanings? How do they represent meanings anew? How do they transform meaning? What differences are there in an actor's meaning making across spaces?' |

|  | *Examples of research questions* |
|---|---|
| **Multimodal corpus analysis** | 'What factors affect the multimodal structure of artefacts? What kinds of patterns can be identified in their multimodal structure, "semiotic values" and their realization in artefacts? How do the multimodal structures of artefacts change over time?' |
| **Multimodal reception analysis** | 'How do readers navigate texts, choose entry points and reading paths? How do readers integrate information from different sources and modes in the process of meaning making? How do readers interact with complex multimodal artefacts in real time? How does the design of educational artefacts support problem solving? How do readers mentally animate and visualize problems? |

these are compatible with your research questions. You will need to rework your questions to align them with the approach to multimodality that you use.

As with any study, when deciding on a research topic it is important to ensure that it is researchable and feasible to undertake within the limits of the time and resources that are available to you.

## Empirical focus

Once you have clarified your research area, topic and questions, you can turn to the next stage of research design: deciding on what kind of materials, or 'data', you need to address your questions.

Throughout this book, we have distinguished between two broad types of empirical focus: artefacts and interaction:

- Research with an empirical focus on *artefacts* produced by the people whose meaning-making practices are being studied; these can take the form of advertisements, leaflets, videos, maps, diagrams, as well as three-dimensional objects, such as cars, buildings. This usually involves analysis of image, writing, colour, layout and composition and so on.
- Research with an empirical focus on '*interaction*' recorded by the researcher. This usually involves analysis of how people use gesture and gaze, how they use their body posture, how they speak – their use of voice, rhythm and pace – the ways they manipulate objects ('artefacts') with their hands and so on.

Note that recordings of interaction are, of course, artefacts themselves; they bear traces of meanings made by the researcher, and it is possible to focus on artefacts in interaction. Nonetheless, the distinction between these two empirical foci is useful because, in practice, many researchers focus on either one or the other.

As discussed in other chapters in this book, different approaches to multimodal research typically use particular research materials. Before discussing the differences in the kind of materials that you may need to collect for your particular multimodal study, we must make three general points regarding the essential qualities of materials for multimodal analysis in relation to the three main approaches that we focus on in this book:

1    The aim is usually to collect multimodal materials in the 'natural' settings of the people under study, instead of in laboratories, where the conditions of interaction or production and reception of artefacts can be controlled (but see Multimodal Reception Analysis in Chapter 6). This does not mean that research materials are being treated as being entirely 'untouched' (Silverman, 2011: 274); they are always shaped, in some way, by the involvement of the researcher, for instance, in choosing how and what is recorded.

2    Multimodal materials need to allow for fine-grained analysis to support an account of all the modes that are in use. They need to be collected at the granularity necessary for you to explore modes and their relationship to one another and to meaning. The collection methods that you use need to be attuned to the environment that you are researching to ensure that the holistic multimodal character of the artefacts and/or interaction is captured. If you are researching digital texts, for example, you will need to use data collection methods with the potential to collect moving images.

3    In the approaches discussed in this book, materials for multimodal analysis, whether recordings of artefacts or interaction, need to document the socially and culturally situated construction of meaning.

The possibilities for collecting materials vary significantly across different research settings. Some settings are relatively calm and stable, while others are rapidly changing and unpredictable. As you collect materials, you may need to balance these three considerations in order to ensure that you get the best-quality data possible with which to address your research questions.

The empirical focus of the approaches outlined in this book differs with respect to the kinds of questions and emphasis they place on different aspects of representation, communication and interaction. These are summarized in Table 7.3.

**Table 7.3** Summary of the empirical focus of multimodal approaches

| | *Empirical focus* |
|---|---|
| **SF-MDA** | Readily available 'artefacts', often from popular media, including print and digital texts, videos and three-dimensional objects and sites (e.g. advertisements, TV programmes, websites, social media), educational media (e.g. textbooks and other education materials) and art and crafts (e.g. sculptures, buildings). |
| **Social semiotics** | Initially focused on 'artefacts' (especially print media, film and games), both 'professional' (e.g. an advert in a magazine) and 'vernacular' (e.g. a child's drawing), then also began to account for embodied interactions recorded on video through fieldwork. |
| **CA** | Researcher-generated video recordings of interaction: Video recordings of 'naturally occurring' social encounters (i.e. encounters that were not initiated by the researcher), obtained through fieldwork, showing all participants involved in an activity. Activities include those in which speech is used only occasionally, such as when two people assemble a piece of furniture. |
| **Geo-semiotics** | Researcher-generated photographs, video recordings and observational materials on people's 'naturally occurring' social encounters with public signs (e.g. people engaged with signs, notices, logos, advertisements, graffiti, as well as monuments and the built environment). |
| **Multimodal (inter)action analysis** | Researcher-generated video recordings of people's interaction focused on 'naturally occurring' social encounters. |
| **Multimodal ethnography** | Researcher-generated video recordings of people's interaction focused on 'naturally occurring' social encounters. Materials include observations, documents such as field notes and video recordings. Unstructured and semi-structured interviews are conducted, and the artefacts they use are also documented or collected. |
| **Multimodal corpus analysis** | Corpora built from a wide range of everyday printed and digital artefacts (e.g. websites, brochures, print and online newspapers and magazines, bird field guides, and technical manuals). |
| **Multimodal reception analysis** | A text or a series of texts is selected for a study. These may be 'authentic' texts or ones that have been designed for the study. Materials are collected via participants wearing an eye-tracking device (static or mobile) that records their eye movements with an artefact as a set of measurements. |

## Collecting materials for multimodal analysis

The processes of collecting materials for multimodal analysis are different for each approach. They are summarized in Table 7.4.

Table 7.4   Summary of the methodology of multimodal approaches

|  | *Methodology* |
| --- | --- |
| **SF-MDA** | Detailed transcription and analysis of selected fragments of the texts, as well as the analysis of larger corpora and 'multimodal analytics'. |
| **Social semiotics** | Typically involves detailed analysis of texts (e.g. drawings), sometimes a few, sometimes a larger collection, and sometimes involving historical comparisons. |
| **CA** | Typically involves detailed transcription and analysis of (collections of) small fragments or strips of interaction (say up to 30 seconds) illustrating a phenomenon of interest. |
| **Geo-semiotics** | Descriptive analysis of the semiotics of signs, their emplacement and the participants' embodied interaction in the space being investigated. |
| **Multimodal (inter)action analysis** | A detailed analysis of selected short episodes of video data; the (hierarchical) structures of the interaction, modal shifts, intensity and complexity of the higher-level actions throughout the interaction sequence. |
| **Multimodal ethnography** | A detailed semiotic account of material artefacts is built up with attention to socially situated norms and practices, identity and community using an ethnographic approach (using thick description) to produce transcripts of key moments in the interaction. |
| **Multimodal corpus analysis** | A range of quantitative tools are used to annotate and analyse a large corpora of texts, including longitudinal analysis of texts. |
| **Multimodal reception analysis** | The participants' eye movement data is analysed to identify fixations and saccades to show which objects and areas of the artefact the reader has fixated on, in what order and for how long. |

Collecting, documenting and recording artefacts

Ideally, you will be able to collect and work with original artefacts because this will give you unmediated, direct access to all its semiotic features, including its size, colour and texture. While leaflets and adverts and other documents can easily be collected, it is not always possible to collect the original multimodal artefact for your research. The owner may not be prepared to give you the artefact, such as something a student made in a lesson that is needed by a teacher. It may be too big – for example a billboard, sign or building – to physically 'collect' or cannot be removed. In such cases, you will need to use photography or digital scanning to make a copy of the text. These copies are not replicas of the original artefact. For instance, they smooth over and erase materiality and texture. Textual descriptions can be used to compensate for the changes involved in digitization/recording processes (see e.g. Ormerod and Ivanič, 2002).

Collecting dynamic multimodal artefacts, such as blog posts, websites, YouTube videos, raises some particular challenges. The dynamic, interactive, layered structure of such artefacts, combined with their changing character, places new demands on methods of collection. One way to overcome these challenges is to create an offline stable database using screen capture applications. Static screen capture tools can be used to make a still digital record of a screen (including mobile phone screens). Dynamic screen capture applications can be used to record dynamic artefacts (e.g. animations and embedded video). This can also be used to record how people use/interact with screen-based applications, e.g. how they navigate an online site. For example, in a multimodal study that compared digital finger-painting with finger-painting in a paper environment (Crescenzi, Jewitt and Price, 2014), a dynamic screen capture application was used to capture the digital finger-painting on a tablet as it unfolded in time. Online games include a similar built-in facility to record game activity (this produced the genre Machinima, a recording facility that has been used by game researchers). However, these solutions are not viable for all digital data. For example, Adami (2009) studied video interaction on YouTube, yet she was unable to download the video materials she was researching because this is prohibited by the site's copyright policy and terms of use. In such instances, you will need to access your research materials online through the streaming functionality of a site, which means that you cannot play and transcribe the video in an application such as ELAN.

Deciding on the boundary of an artefact is another challenge when collecting artefacts as research materials. For instance, if you were studying gender in advertisements in magazines, would you collect the advertisement only? Would you collect the page of the magazine on which the advertisement appears? Would the double page spread be needed? Would you collect the whole magazine? The answer to these questions will depend on the requirements of the approach that you choose to use and your research questions. For example if you isolate an advertisement by removing it from the wider context of the page and the magazine, you would be able to analyse the multimodal features of the advert but not the page layout, page position and the placing of the advert in the context of the magazine. To ensure that you collect the materials that you need for your study, you will need to think through these questions and decide on the boundary you want to place around your materials before you start to collect your materials.

This question links to another challenge to consider in the design of your study when working with artefacts: how much and what kind of contextual information do you need to analyse your materials? Again this will be shaped by the requirements of the approach you use and your research questions. Returning to our example of gender in advertisements in magazines, would you want to collect materials on their design and production? How is their placement in the magazine decided, and by whom? Perhaps you would want to know about the aim and focus of the magazine? Would you want to collect information on who the typical reader of the magazine is or on its circulation figures? Maybe you would want to understand how and when the magazine's readers engage with the advertisements? You will need to consider how much and what type of contextual information you need when you design your study.

## Documenting and recording interaction

If your multimodal study is interaction orientated, your main materials will be collected using observation and video-recording. Three features underpin the distinctive potential of video recorded materials for multimodal research. First, video recording can preserve 'the temporal and sequential structure which is so characteristic of interaction' (Knoblauch et al., 2009: 19), enabling us to explore the interactional synchrony between modes. Second, video recording can provide a fine-grained sequential record of an event detailing gaze, facial expression, body posture, gesture and so on. This enables the researcher to rigorously and systematically examine resources and practices through which participants in interaction build their social activities and how the semiotic resources they use mutually elaborate one another. This kind of record cannot be made using any other technology. Third, video provides a durable, malleable, shareable record that can be repeatedly viewed and manipulated to be viewed in slow or fast motion, freeze-frame, with or without sound or image. These three qualities enable different levels of analytical gaze, multiple passes across research materials and multiple viewpoints, including those of participants, to be brought into the analysis.

Despite its power to capture events, video recordings are, like all research materials, partial, providing a restricted view of events (e.g. no peripheral vision, limited mobility, narrow angle view) in that it includes some and excludes other elements of interaction. The video recordings that you make will need to be sufficiently detailed to capture the particular interaction event that you are interested in as a chronological account that is 'in sync with the meaning of events' (Goldman, 2007: 30–32). It also needs to be a 'truth-like' account that makes clear the perspective of the video camera and brings the viewer 'inside' it through a sense of 'Being there/Being with' the researcher (Goldman, 2007: 30–32). Whenever possible, it is useful to gain an understanding of the setting through observational fieldwork before you video-record. This can help you to mitigate the partiality of video as a research tool through your decisions concerning camera position.

You can choose from a range of video cameras to collect your data (e.g. small flip cameras, larger cameras and, depending on your research site, 'embedded' cameras, that is cameras that are used by or available to the people you study). Once you have decided on the type of camera to use, you will need to consider another set of questions. Where to position a camera is significant because it marks the relationship to the event being established and frames what is being recorded. (When working with archive or online video materials, examining where the camera was placed can be a useful dimension of the analysis in that it can highlight what the maker of a video considered central to the interaction.) While there is no standard 'right position' for a camera, you will need to locate it as unobtrusively as is possible and minimize the need for reframing and disruption. At the same time, you need to ensure that the camera is able to record the pertinent action. This requires a sound knowledge of the context you are studying, what interactions need to be video-recorded, their scale and the space of activity that needs to be covered by the video camera. Observation of the environment prior to video-recording will help you to decide where best to position a video camera and whether a fixed camera is adequate and/or a roaming mobile camera is required.

You will need to decide whether to hold the camera or to fix it on a tripod or to do both. A fixed camera tends to be used to video-record relatively stable interactions between people within a designated field of vision over a long period of time (e.g. two people sitting on a bench having a conversation). Such interactions are best captured using a consistent long shot with a wide-angle camera without movement, panning and zooming (Erickson, 2007). Fixing a camera also means that the researcher can observe the event at some distance: a tripod is less obtrusive than a human camera holder. However, in dynamic contexts where people move around, a mobile roaming camera may be necessary to take account of the detail of the interaction.

You will also need to decide how many video cameras to use. Again, your theoretical approach and research context will help you to make this choice. Some research contexts might require more than one camera, for example where there are many local scenes of activity running in parallel, with periodic joint, plenary activity. For instance, if your study is focused on classrooms, you may choose to use two or more cameras to weave together local and whole-class activity. It would, however, be misleading to think that, when taken together, a certain number of cameras can capture 'everything'. Indeed, some commentators have argued that a single camera is the preferred option as it preserves a more holistic account of interaction and maintains the integrity of sequences of interaction, reduces the data collected, does not add multiple perspectives to the data and does not 'fracture' sequences of interaction (Heath, Hindmarsh and Luff, 2010). Others disagree and in principle think the use of multiple cameras is better, arguing that not all the data needs to be used. Ultimately, the number of cameras you use will be set by consideration of matters of obtrusiveness, human and technical resources (e.g. the number of people available to control the cameras).

The choices and the decisions that you make are part of your research design and *always* come back to the question of what the video recordings are going to be used for – your research topic and questions – and the multimodal approach that you will use to analyse them. Careful consideration of each of these choices in tandem with your approach, as well as, if possible, some trials and experiments, will support you in achieving the most appropriate design of video recording for your study.

## How much material do you need?

Whatever materials your study is focused on, there is no universal 'right amount' of research materials to collect. The amount of materials required is guided by your research approach, study topic, aim and questions, alongside more pragmatic questions such as how much time and resource are available to you. For instance, in the case of the three main approaches discussed in Chapters 3 to 5:

An *SF-MDA* approach usually sets out to work with a larger corpus of texts, as discussed in Chapter 3. For example, Bell and Milic (2002) analysed advertisements from a representative sample of magazines in terms of the semiotic resources that are the basis for gender stereotypes. They collected a total of 827 one- and two-page display advertisements from eight popular Australian 'men's' and 'women's' magazines, as well as magazines aimed at a general readership. All of the magazines were published during 1997–1998. Every second issue of the magazines was collected over a 12-month period. All advertisements depicting one male or one female model, a group (two or more) of males or of females or an isolated part of the body (leg, hand, lips etc.) were analysed to explore gender stereotypes.

A *social semiotic* approach, as discussed in Chapter 4, tends to work with small collections of artefacts; some studies have worked with just one, yet others have worked with larger collections. For example, Jewitt explored notions of masculinity in sexual health leaflets by analysing a data set of 32 leaflets and posters produced between 1986 and 1996. The corpus was compiled using criteria drawn from the relevant research literature (1997). The leaflets and posters were gathered from a range of organizations with a sexual health remit using four selection criteria: topic, the producer, the medium, and the intended audience. These criteria were informed by evidence in the literature that the range of modes in leaflets and posters may be influenced by the topic of the material, that the producer of materials influences the way in which events are modally constructed and that the medium used (e.g. cartoon, photograph, drawing) may portray particular dimensions and states of an event. The selection criteria included the intended audience – young heterosexual men aged 13 to 19 years of age – as this was shown to affect the imagery in leaflets and posters. The sample enabled the representational differences between the leaflets to be analysed.

The appreciation of 'smallness' in a *conversation analysis* approach, discussed in Chapter 5, limits the potential for analysing large amounts of video recordings. Typically short episodes are transcribed and analysed, and over time, collections are built up of examples supporting or invalidating working hypotheses about the social organization of action. Sometimes the selection of clips is informed by a preliminary analysis of the entire video corpus aimed at identifying what the main 'themes' and 'categories' are (and what their frequency of occurrence is). Instances of each of these themes and categories are then selected for more detailed, interactional analysis.

Data collection and sampling is an essential part of research design. Whatever approach and type of research materials you are going to use in your study, you will need to make clear and justify the choices that you make concerning the amount of materials you collect. As the preceding examples suggest, it is important to work out how much material you need for your study. Too little and you will be unable to answer your research questions or fulfil your research aim adequately. Too much and you will waste valuable research time collecting materials that you will not have the time to analyse or hit problems in your analytical stage as you drown in the materials trying to make sense of them all. Doing in-depth analysis might mean that you cannot always analyse all of your data. For this reason, we sample the data to select instances (fragments or episodes) for detailed analysis. Again, how many texts or episodes of interaction are analysed will depend on your approach.

## How can you manage your research materials?

The management and storage of research materials are important aspects of empirical research, whatever kind of materials you are working with. Whatever approach you use in your study and whatever your materials, you can do a number of things to help manage them effectively:

- Create a labelling code to ensure that you have a systematic record of your materials: recording, for example, the date/time it was collected, as well as the participant and/or site where it was collected.
- Review your materials soon after collecting them to ensure you have documented all the details that you need. Check that the image/video/sound recording has been successfully captured. Keeping track of what you already have can inform and improve your future collection of materials (e.g. by alerting you to a 'gap' – such as a set of text types you have failed to collect or an activity you have observed but not yet recorded.
- Compile a 'data-log' of each set of materials as you review them. This could include a short descriptive account of the artefacts or, in the case of video, a synopsis of what occurred during the session. If your study is artefact based, the logging process might include 'thumbnail' depictions of particular excerpts. In the case of video, you might include a note of timings of key shifts

in activity and any significant (off-camera) observations and conversations. You might also want to include some short descriptions and/or sketches of the layout of the setting where you collected your materials.

Data-labelling codes and data logs provide you with an overview of your materials and an efficient way to search them. Alongside but separate from your log, you might want to note any initial analytical thoughts or questions that came up as you were reviewing the materials. When you start your analysis, such logs, narrative summaries, vignettes, diagrams and maps can be helpful in identifying possible inroads into your data or even patterns of interaction and condensing the complexity of your data.

## Do you need to transcribe your materials?

Although we have discussed transcription in relation to specific approaches in earlier chapters, in this chapter we draw attention to how transcription can support and shape multimodal analysis and raise some more general considerations. The practice of transcription is usually associated with language and linguistic conventions for 'translating' speech into writing. Transcription conventions are used to graphically represent features of speech, such as intonation, hesitations or pauses, that are not normally expressed in writing. Nonetheless:

> [E]ven [with] the most sophisticated set of conventions, the transcriber has to accept that there are details which are lost; the letters merely suggest the phonemic interpretation of sounds, not the actual sounds; 'accents' and voice quality are lost, and so forth. At the same time, what is gained from the transcript is the potential to rearrange speech units to enable certain aspects to come to the fore, such as the synchrony or asynchrony of speakers, their turn-taking patterns, or their repeated use of certain lexical items.
>
> (Flewitt et al., 2014: 45)

The use of video recording in multimodal research raises many questions for transcription inasmuch as interaction is not limited to speech. This raises the question, 'How to transcribe gesture, and gaze, for instance?' One response to this is to use not just writing but also other resources to represent interaction, such as image, layout and colour, that is to create a *multimodal* transcript. According to Mavers, a transcript is multimodal:

> [W]hen it contains more than one mode. Including image as well as writing as a means of transcription forces the transcriber to decide which meanings will reside where and how these modes relate.
>
> (Mavers, 2012: 4)

In the process of (multimodal) transcription, some of the features of interaction are sustained, while others are lost and added. You will need to be aware of and address these gains and losses.

Despite its limitations, making a transcript can be a useful analytical exercise because it requires you to attend to the details of a text or a video recording of a sequence of interaction and:

> [It] . . . can enable you to gain a wealth of insights into the situated construction of social reality, including insights in the collaborative achievements of people, their formation of identities and power relations, and the socially and culturally shaped categories through which they see the world.
>
> (Bezemer, 2014: 158)

There are no fully settled conventions for multimodal transcription. The multimodal transcripts presented throughout this book show that there is significant variation in transcription practices. Your choice of transcription method will need to be informed by the methodological and theoretical framework that you choose. (See Example 7.1.)

*Example 7.1*   The methodological and theoretical implications of multimodal transcription.

Bezemer and Mavers (2011) examined the process of transcription as 'semiotic work' (193) and transcripts as 'artefacts that mediate social interaction 'between the 'makers', the represented materials and the (imagined) 'readers'' (120). They used a social semiotic approach to compare and analyse a small number of 'multimodal' transcripts made by researchers undertaking video-based social research to reflect on the methodological and theoretical implications of choices around transcription. Their discussion is summarized here with attention to the common principles, the process of transduction, and the methodological differences that they identified.

Three common principles involved in transcription were discussed:

1  *Principles of framing:* 'Transcripts never operate in isolation; they are part of academic practice, such as the writing of a journal article, a paper presentation at a conference, a data session or a course on teaching methods. These contexts of use – particular social environments – "frame" . . . the transcript' (193).

2  *Principles of selecting:* 'Transcripts, like any representation, are partial . . . Of central methodological concern are the principles of selection and omission that are in play as the researcher transcribes the selected strip of interaction' (194).

3  *Principles of highlighting:* 'Salience refers to what is highlighted in the transcript, or which of the re-made features are given prominence . . . for instance through size and positioning . . . foregrounding certain features, which may even have appeared in the background of the original interaction' (194). For example, the transcript in Figure 4.1 (page 76) omits the teacher's gaze, facial expression, position and so on – as well as the 29 children in the class and the environment of the classroom – because the current rhetorical focus is the framing of the task.

Transcription was explored as a process of *transduction*, or shifting between modes. In the representation of social interaction, 'translations' are constantly made between (ensembles of) modes (e.g. writing, image and layout):

> Video data which are turned into multimodal transcripts are not merely descriptive, nor are they mere 'translations'. They are transducted and edited representations through which analytical insights can be gained and certain details are lost (195).

Through a comparison of multimodal transcripts, they exemplified the types of transduction that transcribers engage in when transcribing:

■ *Writing in transcripts:* The lexis of writing provides a range of choices for transducting – 'describing', 'annotating' – modes of communication other than speech (e.g. gaze becomes 'looks at . . . '). Punctuation can also be used to transcribe gaze. For instance, underlining parts of a transcribed utterance to indicate that the participant is looking at the co-participant, or a series of dots ('. . . . . ') that one party is turning towards another (Heath, Hindmarsh and Luff, 2010: 71). In addition, different conventions are used that make use of the affordances of alphabetic script for showing the cadences and turn taking of speech, capitalizing on such resources as typography (e.g. emphasis, underlining), punctuation and layout. For example, Norris (see page 117 of this book) expresses the rising and falling of intonation patterns in curves, vocal stress is expressed in the size and boldness of letters, and participants are allocated distinctive assorted shades of font colour.

- *Image in transcripts:* Different types of images are used in transcripts, including drawings (e.g. Mavers) and video stills (e.g. Norris) to depict the visual characteristics of people, objects and places, and relationships between them, as well as sequences of action. In some transcripts, modes such as gesture and speech are separated out, while image leaves the reader to discern different modes or to refer to a written commentary. Irrespective of participation in the interaction, whoever is physically co-present and within shot of the camcorder is included. These stills have the potential to bring out visual characteristics and appearance (e.g. skin colour, hairstyle, clothing, facial expression, posture, gesture and spatial proximity), supplying a certain specificity that must be described or omitted in writing. However, image-in-transcription involves processes of selection, and the recording is itself a selection. Image, like writing, can be used to suggest how 'real' the representation of a statement is through the use of a range of resources to indicate its 'modality' including its spatial and pictorial detail, depth, colour or background (Kress and van Leeuwen, 2006).

- *Layout in transcripts:* Transcription involves making decisions about how writing and image are set out on the page or screen. Spatial organization can be used to construct separation and cohesion and to suggest how an activity unfolded in time. Single video stills can be used as snapshots to show posture, expression and gaze as they were at that split second. A sequence of stills can be shown to mark the moment-by-moment shifts in unfolding interaction, and different moments in time can be joined together in one image.

Comparing three transcripts discussed in this book, we can make the following observations about layout in transcripts:

- In Heath, Hindmarsh and Luff's transcript (Figure 5.3, page 99), time is represented by a horizontal line, whilst the participants and modes are separated out on a vertical axis.
- Maver's transcript (Figure 4.1, page 76) shows an alternative common layout for transcription: the tabular format. This constructs temporality on a vertical axis and modal separation horizontally.
- Norris's transcript (Figure 6.1, page 117) highlights the moments in an unfolding activity to which she wishes to draw attention, such as the onset of a new 'higher-level action' (2004: 101) (e.g. when one of the participants starts a phone conversation while engaged in another social encounter).

Bezemer and Mavers (2011: 120) concluded by arguing that 'transcripts should be judged in terms of the "gains and losses" involved in re-making video data' rather than through a focus on 'representational 'accuracy':

It is crucial to make those gains and losses transparent, for example, which modes of communication used in the observed activity have been excluded from the transcript and why, and what the effect is of that exclusion on the analysis and subsequent reader interpretation? It also promotes reflection on the effects of transduction: how use of the mode of transcription shapes what is re-presented. Transcription conventions accommodate such transparency and consistency, but are currently utilized only in transcribing speech to writing. Contemporary practices in multimodal transcription may require information, for example, on how images were constructed. Such conventions cannot and need not be standardized beyond the study/project/publication for which they are used, but they need to be made transparent to readers.

(Bezemer and Mavers, 2011: 120)

One way to understand the potentialities and limitations of different ways of transcribing is to simply try them out on your data.

General points to consider when you are considering the transcription of your materials include:

■    What is the purpose of the transcript?
■    What is the focus or frame of the transcript?
■    What does your transcript select?
■    How does your transcript highlight?
■    What modes will you transcribe, and why?
■    What modes will your transcript use?
■    How will you lay out your transcript?
■    What conventions are you drawing on?
■    What is the time scale of your transcript?
■    What is your unit of analysis?
■    How will you use the transcript in your analysis?

## What ethical issues do you need to consider when designing a multimodal study?

In this section, we discuss some of the ethical issues in doing multimodal research; we do not discuss more general ethical considerations because these are covered well elsewhere (e.g. Hammersley and Traianou, 2012; Israel, 2015).

There are no specific ethical benchmarks or guidelines for doing multimodal research. While the general ethical principles of respect, protection, minimizing harm and maximizing benefits can be applied to all research, it is important to note that you may be seeking ethical approval from ethics committees who are not familiar with multimodal research. You will need to explain why you need to video-record in, say, a classroom or why you need to take photographs in public spaces, instead of taking notes, for instance.

As a rule, you need to obtain informed consent from participants to collect and use materials for research. There is some debate over whether informed consent should be sought to collect materials that circulate in the public domain, such as blog posts, tweets or YouTube videos. The British Association of Applied Linguistics (BAAL) state that:

> [In] the case of an open-access site, where contributions are publicly archived, and informants might reasonably be expected to regard their contributions as public, individual consent may not be required.
>
> (BAAL, 2006: 7)

Some scholars have, however, challenged this approach and suggest that even where material is readily available in the public domain, the content may be considered private by those who made it. Various strategies have been suggested for contacting the makers of such artefacts to gain consent, including notifying users of your study via a communal bulletin board (Davis, 2010) and contacting potential participants directly via their profiles (Goodings, 2012).

If your study involves taking photographs or video recordings in a public space (e.g. a street) featuring people the question of whether you need to obtain their consent is again contested. While some are of the opinion that consent should always be sought and obtained, others have argued that under certain conditions it may be acceptable not to do so.

When collecting materials in a semi-public environment (e.g. a museum), it is possible and generally expected by ethics committees that you obtain informed consent. It may not be possible to seek permission in advance. For example, in a study of family visitor interaction with a digital installation in a museum, Price, Sakr and Jewitt (2015) obtained informed consent as follows:

- Placed signs at the entrance to the gallery informing visitors that video recording was taking place for research purposes.
- On exiting the exhibit, a researcher gave the parent(s) an information sheet to read and explained the project, addressing any questions.
- While it is preferable to obtain informed consent prior to recording, in this case we requested consent as visitors exited the installation to reduce the interference of the research on their interaction.
- We obtained participants' written consent.
- To enable us to use the materials that we collected on the project website and in future publications and presentations, we requested separate consent for the following:
  - ☐ Use of the video recordings for research purposes
  - ☐ Use of the video recordings for teaching purposes (i.e. in seminars and conferences)
  - ☐ Use of the video recordings for the project website
  - ☐ The use of still photographs from the video for research publications, teaching, in seminars and conferences and the project website
- Where informed consent was granted, we took a photograph of each child and numbered the photograph and the form, so as to be able to identify them in the video recordings.

- Where informed consent was not given, the materials (being collected by cameras fixed within the installation) were destroyed.
- Visitors were also given research contact information and the project URL and asked whether they would like to provide their name and contact details to receive information on the research findings.

In studies where you will be undertaking your research in a more private domain, for instance a school, you will need to obtain informed consent in advance of entering the site. You will need to follow your own institutional ethics procedures as well as those of the site you wish to work in (e.g. if your study is in a health care context). This may involve attending meetings with key stakeholders to inform them about the project and to respond to their concerns. It is advisable to bring an information sheet to such an exploratory meeting.

When designing your consent form, we recommend that you give different options on how the materials can be used and by whom. For example, some participants may be happy to be photographed but may not want to have images of themselves or their children on a publically available website.

To sum up, we suggest that you consider the following:

- Is your research site public or private?
- Do you need to obtain informed consent to use the materials you need?
- What information do you need to provide your potential participants?
- How will you use the research materials – what different types of use (e.g. teaching, research, publications) do you need to request consent for?
- Are you in an environment where you need to make the general public aware that you are conducting research?

You will also need to consider participant anonymity and confidentiality. Again, there is some debate on the need for anonymity if you are working with materials in the public domain because anonymity is related to our understanding of the research object. BAAL guidelines (2006: 7) state:

> While anonymity is the default position for research participants even on public sites, in the case of certain texts – e.g. home pages, blogs, literary or artful texts – writers may see themselves as authors who should be formally acknowledged by the name used online.

Ensuring anonymity can raise challenges in multimodal research. For instance, if you write up a detailed analysis of a photograph, it would be difficult for readers to follow your interpretation if you cannot include the photograph – in which case you cannot guarantee that readers will not recognize who features in the photograph. Such challenges may be mitigated using a number of strategies:

- You may use video-recording or photographic strategies that focus on a particular activity and avoid the identifying features of the participants, although this may not suit your research (e.g. if you need to analyse gaze and facial expression).
- If you are working with still images or textual artefacts, you may be able to select or crop them to provide anonymity.
- The materials could be used for analytical purposes only; that is publications would not include any visual representations.
- When video recordings feature people who have given permission for their image to be used, these can be used alongside pseudonyms.
- If using online materials (e.g. blog posts), you could remove URLs and personal details that identify the location and identity of the material to reduce searchability.
- The names from drawings, contextual information such as logos or visual aspects that identify a building/street, or the visual identity of your research participants can be removed, blurred or obscured using digital applications. However, it has been argued that this process can dehumanize participants by invoking criminal associations, skew data and significantly reduce its meaning and power (Prosser, Clark and Wiles, 2008).
- You may choose to tackle anonymity by reproducing your data in a new form, for example turning a text or a still from a video into a line drawing or a video-recorded sequence of interactions into a cartoon.

As this albeit brief discussion suggests, it is important to think through the specifics of obtaining informed consent and anonymity and confidentiality to anticipate any potential problems that you may encounter during and after data collection and how you might deal with these. If you do this at the design stage, you may be able to avoid complications at the analytical, publication and dissemination stage.

In this chapter. we have walked you through the stages in designing a multimodal study, from choosing an apt approach through to the ethical dimensions. We have discussed the challenges, choices and decisions that designing a multimodal study involves and provided you with suggestions and guidance in tackling these.

# Glossary

**Adjacency pair** is a term used in *conversation analysis* to describe a two-part interactional structure, in which the first part is an invitation to the other to respond (e.g. a greeting followed by a greeting response). This structure was first identified in talk. Recent multimodal studies have shown that often only one or none of the two parts are realized in talk (e.g. an exchange of gestural greetings between two acquaintances who are not within earshot).

**Affordance** is a *social semiotic* term used to refer to the idea that different modes offer different potentials for making meaning. Modal affordances affect the kinds of semiotic work a mode can be used for, the ease with which it can be done and the different ways in which modes can be used to achieve broadly similar semiotic work. Modal affordances are connected to both a mode's material and its social histories, that is, the social purposes that it has been used for in a specific context.

**Artefact** refers to anything that bears the traces of semiotic work: a building, an inscription, a video recording or film, a landscape and so forth. In this book, we use the term specifically to refer to artefacts produced by the people whose practices we want to study and to make a methodological distinction between using such artefacts as an empirical ground for multimodal analysis (e.g. of 'text', which is common in *systemic functional grammar* and *social semiotics*) from using artefacts made by a researcher (such as a video recording of 'interactions') as an empirical ground for multimodal analysis (which is common in *conversation analysis*).

**Communication**, see *meaning making*.

**Conversation Analysis** (CA) is an approach to the study of social interaction. In its early days, the focus was on analysing 'talk' and 'conversations' (hence its name). The analytical scope has since been expanded to include attention to a much broader range of semiotic resources used in interaction. Central to a CA approach is the systematic and in-depth analysis of video recordings of multi-modal interaction, with a focus on the *sequential organization of action* and the *coordination of action.*

**Coordination of action** is a term used in *conversation analysis* to describe an analytical concern with the ways in which people who are engaged in 'collaborative work' coordinate their actions with the actions of others and accomplish their work through 'concerted action'.

**Critical Discourse Analysis (CDA)** is a branch of linguistics that investigates how linguistic choices connote broader discourses. It asks what kind of world, social values, ideas and identities are being represented in language. The aim is to reveal the social and power relations that are realized linguistically and to show what kinds of inequalities and interests they seek to create or perpetuate.

**Design** is a *social semiotic* term used to refer to the situated process in which a sign maker chooses and arranges semiotic resources to realize a particular social function or purpose. Design is conceived of as a starting point for making meaning, and both the original producer of a sign and its interpreter are understood as making meaning. It is always socially located and regulated, for example by the types of resources that are made available and to whom, as well as the regimes that regulate and shape how these resources are used to create various norms and expectations.

**Genre** is a term used in *systemic functional linguistics (SFL)* to describe how social processes unfold in a given culture. The concept, which is related to *register* theory, is conceived as the system of staged goal-oriented social processes through which social subjects in a given culture live their lives.

**Geo-semiotics** is a research framework that combines concepts and methods from linguistic anthropology, place semiotics and *social semiotics* in order to foreground the emplacement of semiotic artefacts and interaction.

**Interest** is a term used in a *social semiotic* approach to refer to a momentary condensation of all the social experiences that have shaped an individual's subjectivity – a condensation prompted by the social environment (of which the available *modes* are a significant element) that a sign is made within. A person's interest connects their choice of one resource over another with the social context of sign production.

**Meaning making** is a general term used in this book to recognize that meaning always involves a social actor. 'Expressing' and 'interpreting' or 'understanding' is an act of *making* meaning. Meaning making is a more generic term than *communication*, which is usually defined as involving 'expression' by one actor and 'interpretation' by another. When there is 'expression' and/or 'interpretation' by only one person (say, when someone makes a sketch or some notes of what she/he observes for her-/himself), we can still speak of meaning making, but not of communication.

**Metafunction** is the term that Michael Halliday developed to describe the functions of language in *systemic functional linguistics*: experiential meaning (to construct our experience of the world), logical meaning (to make logical connections in that world), interpersonal meaning (to enact social relations and create a stance to the world) and textual meaning (to organize messages). The metafunctional principle is adopted in *systemic functional multimodal discourse analysis (SF-MDA)* to understand the functionalities and underlying organization of semiotic resources and to investigate the ways in which semiotic choices interact to create meaning in multimodal texts and processes.

**Mode** is a term that is used within *systemic functional linguistics* and *social semiotics* to refer to a socially organized set of *semiotic resources* for making meaning. Examples of modes include image, writing, layout and speech, among others. For something to count as a mode, it needs to have a set of semiotic resources and organizing principles that are recognized within a community as realizing meaning. For example, the resources of gesture have been semiotically shaped into communicative modes to serve a diverse range of communities (e.g. hearing-impaired communities, visually and hearing-impaired people, ballet dancers).

**Motivated sign** is a *social semiotic* term used to reference that meaning ('signified') and form ('signifier') are brought together in a relation motivated by the *aptness of fit* between the *interest* of the sign maker and the *affordances* of a *semiotic resource*.

**Multimodal**, see *multimodality*; *multimodal approach.*

**Multimodal approach** refers to a distinct theoretical and methodological framework for the study of multimodality. (See also *multimodality*.)

**Multimodal corpus analysis** is a research framework that combines corpus analysis methods with SFL and social semiotics. It is used to empirically test/validate the hypotheses and advance concepts and theories of multimodal meaning making through the systematic analysis of a corpus of artefacts.

**Multimodal ethnography** is a research framework that uses social semiotic theory in ethnographic research to produce accounts of situated artefacts and interactions and the relations between them. These ethnographic accounts are also based on interviews with the members of the community of practice under study and on the ethnographer's field notes, documenting insights obtained through prolonged observation within the community.

**Multimodal (inter)action analysis** is a research framework that combines interactional sociolinguistics and a social semiotic approach to foreground identity formation through interaction.

**Multimodality**, in a broad definition, highlights that people draw on distinctly different sets of resources for meaning making (e.g. gaze, speech, gesture). The narrower definition adopted in this book also stresses that in actual instances of meaning making, these resources are used in conjunction to form multimodal wholes. (See also *mutual elaboration* and *affordance*.)

**Multimodal reception analysis** describes a research framework that uses psychological concepts and methods to investigate the cognitive processes involved in the 'perception' of textual artefacts and to 'test' semiotic principles proposed in *systemic functional linguistics* and *social semiotics*.

**Multisemiotic**, see *multimodality*.

**Mutual elaboration** (of semiotic resources) is a term used in *conversation analysis* to recognize that sets of semiotic resources (e.g. gesture) are partial and incomplete and that, when joined together, diverse semiotic resources mutually elaborate each other. The analyst's task is to account for the meaning of the 'sum' of which they are a part, not for the meaning of a verbal utterance, or a gesture, in isolation. This notion resonates with the *social semiotic* notion of *affordance*.

**Register** is a term used in *systemic functional linguistics* to describe the configurations of meaning across three key dimensions: the nature of the activity (field), the social relations in terms of the dimensions of power and solidarity (tenor), and the composition and information flow of the message (mode). These register variables are realized through the ideational (experiential and logical meanings), interpersonal and textual meanings in *systemic functional theory (SFT)*.

**Resemiotisation** is the re-construal of semiotic choices within and across multimodal processes and texts. Resemiotisation provides means for understanding how semiotic systems are called into play as social processes unfold. This is a key concept in *systemic functional multimodal discourse analysis (SF-MDA)*. (See also *transduction*.)

**Semiotic principle** is a term that is used to refer to principles for and features of meaning making that apply across modes. For instance, all modes have resources for producing *intensity*. In the mode of *speech*, that is realized by the intensity of sound – 'loudness'; it is also realized lexically, e.g. as 'very'. In the mode of *gesture*, intensity might be realized by the *speed of movement* of the hand or by the *extent* of the movement. In the mode of *colour*, it might be done through degrees of saturation, and so on.

**Semiotic resource** is a term used to refer to the meaning potential of material resources, which developed and accumulated over time through their use in a particular community and in response to certain social requirements of that community.

**Sequential organization of action** is a term used in *conversation analysis* to describe the principle that interaction unfolds in time, one action after another. Actions (which can be realized using different semiotic resources) are 'context-shaped' in that they serve as a response to the preceding action, and at the same time they are 'context-renewing', in that they shape and raise expectations about what is to happen next. The key to understanding the interlocutor's understanding of an action lies in their response to that action.

**Social semiotics** is an approach concerned with how the processes of meaning making (signification and interpretation or 'semiosis') shape and are shaped by individuals and societies to realize power and ideologies. It stresses the relationship between *modes* and their *affordances* and the social needs they are used to serve, the agency of the sign maker and the context of meaning making. It is related to three main strands of influence: *systemic functional linguistics*, semiotics and *critical linguistics/critical discourse analysis (CDA)*.

**System** is used in *systemic functional linguistics* to explain how semiotic resources are organized to create meaning. The systems are described in terms of systemic choices (the paradigm) that are mapped onto the structure of language (the syntagm, or chain). The notion of system is adopted in *systemic functional multimodal discourse analysis (SF-MDA)* to describe the meaning potential of semiotic resources and their interactions.

**Systemic Functional Grammar (SFG)** is the grammatical descriptions of language developed by Michael Halliday and colleagues to explain how language is organized to make meaning. The grammatical descriptions are organized as systems of meaning, which are formulated in terms of systemic choices (the paradigm), which are mapped onto the structure of language (the syntagm, or chain). These dimensions of language are called the paradigmatic and syntagmatic axes, respectively, following Ferdinand de Saussure.

**Systemic Functional Linguistics (SFL)** is the theory of language developed by Michael Halliday and extended by colleagues. Language is viewed as a social semiotic system: that is a resource for making meaning. The functions that language has evolved to serve in society are reflected in its underlying organization. From this perspective, a major goal of SFL is to develop a *systemic functional grammar (SFG)* to account for the meaning-making potential of language and to apply that model to understand actual language use. SFL is thus concerned with 'language as system' and 'language as text'. These same two dimensions are used in *systemic functional multimodal discourse analysis (SF-MDA)*.

**Systemic Functional Multimodal Discourse Analysis (SF-MDA)** is the systemic functional approach to multimodality based on Michael Halliday's *systemic functional theory (SFT)*. The approach aims to understand and describe the functions of different semiotic resources as systems of meaning and to analyse the meanings that arise when semiotic choices combine in multimodal phenomena over space and time.

**Systemic Functional Theory (SFT)** is theory of meaning developed by Michael Halliday for the study of language, which resulted in *systemic functional linguistics (SFL)*. The higher-order principles of SFT provide the foundations for *systemic functional multimodal discourse analysis (SF-MDA)*, where social semiotic resources are seen to be tools for creating meaning.

**System network** is used to refer to a taxonomic representation of the systematic, semiotic options that are possible within a semiotic or lexicogrammatical system or subsystem, e.g. the system of gaze. The options are usually of the either/or type (usually indicated by square brackets), although some semiotic relations are better described as scaled, marked by double-edged dotted arrows (e.g. that between high involvement potential with, or detachment from, a person or an object).

**Transduction** is a *social semiotic* term used to refer to the remaking of meaning *across* modes – a process in which 'meaning material' is moved from one mode to another. For example, something written might be remade as a diagram, or something said might be remade as an action. This compares with the remaking of meaning by changes *within* the same mode, referred to as *transformation*. A shift across modes demands a choice of fresh semiotic resources in an endeavor to retain constancy of meaning; however, this is complex because specific resources are often not modally shared (e.g. words, spelling, letter case and punctuation do not exist in image). Transduction has profound implications for meaning as it changes the resources that are available for making meaning.

**Transformation**, see *transduction*.

# Self-study guide

## Introduction

A self-study guide is provided to support your understanding of multimodality and to help you to design your own multimodal study.

## Self-study guide learning objectives

The overall learning objectives of the self-study guide are to support you in:

- Engaging critically with the notion of multimodality
- Recognizing the similarities and differences in theoretical and methodological positions
- Identifying and describing how multimodality has been taken up in systemic functional linguistics, social semiotics and conversation analysis
- Reflecting on the potentialities and challenges of frameworks that adopt multimodal concepts in combination with other methods
- Assessing the quality of multimodal research, notably aptness of fit between research questions, theories and methods in multimodality
- Engage critically with the process of designing a multimodal study

## Learning objectives

The self-study guide is designed to help you to:

- Familiarize and critically engage with the key topics of the book
- Make connections between the topics and ideas in this book and the field
- Apply the ideas in each chapter to your own work
- Design your own multimodal study

Study guide units

The self-study guide consists of seven units. Each unit is a study companion to its corresponding chapter in this book:

*Unit 1.* Accompanies Chapter 1, '*Navigating a diverse field*', and is designed to help you to engage critically with the notion of multimodality, to assess the centrality of multimodality in a study and to position yourself in the diverse field of multimodality.

*Unit 2.* Accompanies Chapter 2, '*Why engage with multimodality?*', and is designed to help you to interrogate the notion of multimodality and to make a case for engaging with multimodality.

*Unit 3.* Accompanies Chapter 3, '*Systemic functional linguistics*', and is designed to help you to get to grips with how multimodality has been taken up in systemic functional linguistics (SFL), to familiarize yourself with its key principles and concepts and to try out some basic SFL methods of analysis.

*Unit 4.* Accompanies Chapter 4, '*Social semiotics*', and is designed to help you to explore with a social semiotic approach to multimodality, to familiarize with its key principles and concepts and to try out some basic social semiotic analytical methods.

*Unit 5.* Accompanies Chapter 5, '*Conversation analysis*', and is designed to help you to understand how multimodality has been taken into conversational analysis (CA), to familiarize yourself with the key principles and concepts of CA and to try out some basic CA methods of transcription and analysis.

*Unit 6.* Accompanies Chapter 6, '*Five more approaches to multimodality*', and is designed to help you to engage with the possibilities for combining multimodal approaches with other methods, to consider the potentials and limitations of doing so and to familiarize yourself with five such approaches.

*Unit 7.* Accompanies Chapter 7, '*Designing a multimodal study*', and is designed to help you design a multimodal study and to walk you through the key aspects of that process: from reflecting on the most apt approach for your study, clarifying your research focus and questions, collecting research materials and assessing methods of transcription to the ethical considerations of multimodal research.

## How to use this self-study guide

Each unit sets out a clear learning objective and what it will help you to do. All units include:

- A chapter overview, with chapter *topics* and *summary*
- A set of study questions
- Exercises
- Tips
- Suggested resources

We recommend that you work through the self-study guide units in the order that they are presented. We also suggest that you reread the accompanying chapter as you tackle each unit.

## Unit 1. Navigating a diverse field

### Learning objectives

Study Unit 1 will help you to:

- Engage critically with the notion of multimodality
- Assess the centrality of multimodality in a study
- Position yourself in the diverse field of multimodality

### Overview of Chapter 1

#### Topics

- What is multimodality?
- What makes a study 'multimodal'?
- Three approaches to multimodal research

#### Summary

We started Chapter 1 by asking, 'What is multimodality?' We explored how the term 'multimodality' is used in the academic world. We showed that exactly how it is articulated and operationalized varies across and within the different disciplines and research traditions.

This led us to explore the question, 'What makes a multimodal study?' We suggested the need to assess the centrality of multimodality in a study through consideration of its aims, theory and method. We distinguished between two types of multimodal study:

■ *Doing multimodality:* Designing a study in which multimodality is central to aims/research questions, theory and method
■ *Adopting multimodal concepts:* Designing a study in which multimodality concepts (such as 'mode', 'semiotic resource') are used selectively

We made the case that it is difficult and potentially problematic to talk of multimodality without making explicit the theoretical and methodological position being taken. Three approaches to *doing* multimodal research were introduced: systemic functional linguistics, social semiotics and conversation analysis. We discussed the shared features of these three approaches. The distinctive features of each approach were summarized to show how each is grounded in a distinct discipline, with a distinct theoretical and methodological outlook.

## Study questions

Read Chapter 1, and think about how you would answer the following questions. Make notes of your responses, and review them when you have completed the self-study guide.

1   What does the term 'multimodality' mean to you?
2   In your view, what would make a study *not* count as 'multimodal'?
3   What would *doing* multimodality or *adopting* multimodal concepts mean for a study in your area of research?
4   Reflecting on the three summary descriptions of multimodal approaches (pages 8–11), which one connects best with your interests?

## Exercises

### Exercise 1.1: Defining multimodality

The term 'multimodality' is widely used and articulated and is operationalized differently across different disciplines and traditions.

a   Compare the definition of multimodality given in Chapter 1 (page 3) with the definition given or implied in one of the key readings for this book.
b   What differences and similarities are there between these definitions?
c   How would you define multimodality?

*Tip: When you design your multimodal study, you will need to have a clear (working) definition of multimodality.*

Exercise 1.2: Evaluating the centrality of multimodality to a study

Review the discussion of what makes a study multimodal in Chapter 1 (see page 5).

a   Identify some recent publications that have 'multimodal' or 'multimodality' in the title.
b   Read the paper and use the following questions to summarize its aims, research questions, theoretical framework, methodology and findings:

- Does it address research questions about meaning, communication, discourse or interaction?
- Does the study aim to contribute to the development of a theory of multimodality?
- What is the place of multimodality in the theoretical framework of the study?
- Is multimodality a central concept or is it referenced but not expanded on?
- Do the collected materials include documentation of artefacts and/or interactions?
- Do the researchers attend to a number of means of meaning making?
- Do they give equally systematic attention to all?
- What can you say about the centrality of multimodality in each part of the paper?

c   Would you assess the paper as *'doing multimodality'* or *'adopting multimodal concepts'*?

*Tip: You will need to be clear about the place of multimodality in your study, that is whether you are 'doing' multimodality or 'adopting' multimodal concepts.*

Exercise 1.3: Compare how different multimodal
approaches frame a study

In Chapter 1 we discussed the features of three approaches to multimodality
and their implications for the kind of research questions a study can address,
the materials that need to be collected and the analysis that can be undertaken.

a   Read Emma Tarlo's (2007) study on the hijab as a visible indicator of differ-
    ence in multicultural London.
b   Address the following question: which approach(es) outlined in this book
    could you adopt for a study on dress in public spaces and why?
c   With attention to each of the possible approaches you have identified, formu-
    late research questions and detail what materials you would be analysing in
    the respective frameworks.
d   Which approach would *you* choose as the most apt for such a study and why?

   *Tip: You will need to choose the most apt approach for your study. You will
need to give a rationale for that choice, explaining why that approach is more apt
than another.*

## Unit 2. Why engage with multimodality?

### Learning objectives

Study Unit 2 will help you to:

■   Engage critically with the notion of multimodality
■   Make a case for engaging with multimodality

### Overview of Chapter 2

#### Topics

■   The rationale for multimodality
■   The claim that language is the most important of all modes
■   The claim that language can be studied in isolation

#### Summary

In Chapter 2 we engaged with and challenged assumptions about language
widely held among those studying language and the general public. We countered

the notion that language is the most resourceful, important and widely used of all modes, using three arguments:

- The *status of language varies across communities and contexts of use.* It is not possible to make general claims about what people do with language. Rather we suggested the need to ask, 'For *whom* is language the most resourceful, widely used and important mode of all, and in what *contexts of use*?' We demonstrated how a multimodal frame puts the significance of individual modes, including language, in perspective.
- *Many 'linguistic' principles are actually general semiotic principles.* We presented examples showing that many of the principles and social structures described by those studying language can be realized in a variety of different ways. These principles and structures are common semiotic principles.
- *Each mode offers distinct possibilities and limitations.* We pointed out some of the limitations of language and possibilities of other modes not shared with language, and proposed that a mode always offers distinct yet always limited potentialities.

We concluded that a multimodal perspective enables you to differentiate between the *general* and *particular* in language and to recognize both what language has in common with other modes and how it is distinctly different.

We went on to problematize the notion that *language can be studied in isolation* by showing that the meaningful wholes that people produce are almost always multimodal. The elements in a multimodal whole are mutually modifying, making it problematic to attend to language alone.

## Study questions

Read Chapter 2, and think about how you would answer the following questions. Make notes of your responses and review them when you have completed the self-study guide.

1. What does it mean to consider general semiotic principles? Or what is the difference between a 'linguistic' and a 'semiotic' principle/feature?
2. Watch a 'tutorial' on YouTube. What can you say about the status of language in these videos relative to other modes?
3. What would attention to language alone fail to capture when analysing an interview?
4. Why is it important to take account of the distinct possibilities and limitations of each mode in a multimodal account?

## Exercises

### Exercise 2.1: Why look beyond natural language?

a    Read the following statement by American linguist Jerrold Katz:

> I take it as some empirical evidence for the claim that natural languages are effable that speakers almost always find appropriate sentences to express their thoughts, that difficulties in thinking of a sentence are invariably regarded as a failing on the part of the speaker rather than the language, and that there is nothing to indicate that there is any type of information that cannot be communicated by the sentences of a natural language.
>
> (Katz, 1972: 19)

b    The *Oxford Dictionary* defines 'effable', from the Latin for 'utter', as 'able to be described in words'. How would you respond to the principle he called effability? Can you think of anything that is not effable?

*Tip: Being clear as to what is not effable will help to strengthen your rationale for doing a multimodal study.*

### Exercise 2.2: Evaluating the place of language

a    Select a multimodal artefact or an everyday context where you can observe people interacting (e.g. a café or a rail station ticket office)
b    Use the following questions to reflect on the status of language in that particular context or use:

- *For whom* is language the most resourceful?
- In what *context is it used*?
- What do other modes feature?
- What is the status of language relative to the other modes in use?
- What does understanding language as only one part of an 'ensemble' reveal?

*Tip: Being able to state clearly what a multimodal approach offers in comparison to a solely linguistic one will help to strengthen the rationale for doing a multimodal study.*

Exercise 2.3: Critique the rationale for multimodality in a published paper

a   Search online for some recent publications that have 'multimodal' or 'multi-modality' in the title and that relate to your area of study.
b   Identify a research paper that represents one of the multimodal approaches discussed in this book.
c   Read the paper, and review the case that is made for the use of a multimodal approach. Highlight all elements of the paper that contribute to the rationale.
d   Address the following questions:

   ■   What is the main argument made in the paper to support the use of a multimodal approach?
   ■   What criticisms would you make of the arguments presented?
   ■   How could the paper's rationale for a multimodal approach be strengthened?

Exercise 2.4: Make a case for your multimodal study

a   Imagine that you need to convince someone – maybe a sceptical supervisor, colleague or journal editor – of the need to engage with multimodality in your study. Reflect on the following statements:

   ■   The status of language varies across communities and contexts of use.
   ■   Many 'linguistic' principles are actually general semiotic principles.
   ■   Each mode offers distinct possibilities and limitations.
   ■   Language cannot be studied in isolation from other modes.

b   Use your responses to these statements to build your case.
c   Try your argument out on a few colleagues. Listen to their responses, and use their questions, criticisms, and counterarguments to refine and strengthen your case.

## Unit 2 suggested resources

### Further reading

Kress, G. R., & van Leeuwen, T. (2001). *Multimodal Discourse. The Modes and Media of Contemporary Communication.* London; New York: Arnold; Oxford University Press (especially chapter 1).

Online resources

Interview with Gunther Kress: Why adopt a multimodal approach? https://youtu.be/rZ4rMVCWkQs

## Unit 3. Systemic functional linguistics

### Learning objectives

Study Unit 3 will help you to:

- Engage critically with a systemic functional approach to multimodality
- Familiarize yourself with the key principles and concepts of systemic functional theory (SFT)
- Try out some basic systemic functional multimodal discourse analysis (SF-MDA)

### Overview of Chapter 3

#### Topics

- The origins and early development of systemic functional linguistics (SFL) and how it has been adapted for the study of multimodality
- Key principles and concepts in systemic functional theory (SFT)
- Methods and analysis in systemic functional multimodal discourse analysis (SF-MDA)
- Fields of application, limitations, potentialities and challenges

#### Summary

In Chapter 3, we discussed the background and origins of systemic functional linguistics (SFL), developed by Michael Halliday and extended by Ruqaiya Hasan, Christian Matthiessen, Jim Martin and others. We explained how language is viewed as a resource for making meaning in SFL. We discussed how the functions that language serves in society are reflected in its underlying organization. From this perspective, we explained that a major aim of SFL is to provide a functional grammar to account for the meaning making potential of language. We explained that systemic functional theory is a theory of meaning, and, as such, the fundamental principles of the approach apply to the study of other semiotic resources. We used the term 'systemic functional theory (SFT)' to refer to the higher-order principles that apply to systemic functional multimodal discourse analysis (SF-MDA), and we used SFL to refer to the application of SFT for the study of language. We discussed how SF-MDA is a subfield of social semiotics, which is concerned with the systematic organization of semiotic resources as tools for creating meaning in society.

We explained that each semiotic resource has its own systems of meaning, units of analysis and structure and that meaning arises as result of semiotic combinations, where the whole is other than the sum of the parts. We introduced the following concepts as part of this discussion:

- **Function** refers to the four strands of meaning, called metafunctions, which semiotic resources realize: (1) experiential meaning: to construct our experience of the world; (2) logical meaning: to logically connect happenings in that world; (3) interpersonal meaning: to enact social relations and create a stance to the world; (4) textual meaning: to organize messages. The metafunctional principle plays an important role for understanding the functionalities and underlying organization of semiotic resources and investigating the ways in which semiotic choices combine and interact to create meaning in multimodal phenomena.
- **System** refers to the systems of meaning through which semiotic resources fulfil the four metafunctions. Each semiotic resource has its own functionalities and systems of meaning. The systems are represented as system networks of options.
- **Register and genre** are two key concepts in SF-MDA. Register is used to interpret the meaning of multimodal texts and processes in relation to the context of the situation: the nature of the activity (the field), the social relations in terms of the dimensions of power and solidarity (the tenor), and the composition and information flow of the message (the mode). Genre is derived from the configurations of tenor, field and mode, which unfold as social processes in a given culture. Multimodal patterns are built up culturally over time, so that any instance of multimodal semiosis is conditioned by previous configurations of choices, and these need to be taken into account in SF-MDA.
- **Multimodal systems, processes and texts** are the important dimensions of SF-MDA, where the principles of system and text encapsulate the two major aims of the approach: (1) to model the meaning potential of semiotic resources as sets of systems and (2) to analyse the meaning arising from the semiotic interactions in multimodal processes and texts according to context.

■ **Intersemiosis and resemiotisation** are two major processes for SF-MDA. Intersemiosis refers to the interaction of semiotic choices through which meaning is derived. Resemiotisation refers to the re-construal of semiotic choices within and across multimodal phenomena. These two processes explain how meaning expansions occur multimodally and why different resources are accessed at different times.

The chapter then described the key methods, explaining how the SF-MDA approach involves developing metafunctionally organized systems, analysing the text according to the system choices that are selected and interpreting combinations of choices according to register and genre. We gave examples of systems for language and images and demonstrated sample analyses of texts, images and videos using multimodal analysis software. We discussed the fields of application and noted the limitations of the approach and directions for future research.

## Study questions

Read Chapter 3, and answer the following questions. Make notes of your responses, and review them when you have completed the self-study guide.

1   How are the concepts of function and system used in SF-MDA?
2   In your view, what is the difference between the meanings made by language, images and music?
3   Reflecting on Example 3.3, how does mathematics make meaning, and why do you think it is difficult for people to learn?
4   A video analysis is presented in Example 3.4. How would you analyse a video?

## Exercises

### Exercise 3.1: Working with key concepts

a   Select a paper from one of the suggested readings for Chapter 3.
b   Which of the theoretical concepts discussed in Chapter 3 are used in this paper (e.g. system, metafunction, register and genre, intersemiosis and resemiotisation)?
c   How are these theoretical concepts used in the analysis?
d   In your view, are the analytical claims justified?
e   Would you have come to a different conclusion? How and why?

Exercise 3.2: Exploring visual semiosis

Analyse a famous painting (e.g. *Mona Lisa*, *The Last Supper*, *Starry Night*, *The Scream* etc.) using the systems for images listed in Table 3.1.

a    Construct a list of possible system choices for each system.
b    Analyse the painting using this framework.
c    How does the painting create meaning?
d    Can you explain why the painting is famous, based on your analysis?

*Read chapter 1 of Michael O'Toole's (2011)* The Language of Displayed Art.

Exercise 3.3: Exploring multimodal semiosis

Select any instance of a multimodal process or text (e.g. print text, video, website) and:

a    List the semiotic resources that are used to create meaning.
b    Describe the functions of each resource; that is, which resources are used for what purposes?
c    How would you describe the capabilities of the different semiotic resources in this case?
d    Which semiotic combinations seem critical?

*Tip: The metafunctions can be useful to help describe the uses of the semiotic resources.*

## Unit 3 suggested resources

### Key reading

O'Halloran, K. L. (2011). Multimodal discourse analysis. In K. Hyland & B. Paltridge (Eds.), *Companion to Discourse Analysis* (pp. 120–137). London: Continuum.
O'Halloran, K. L., & Lim, F. V. (2014). Systemic functional multimodal discourse analysis. In S. Norris & C. Maier (Eds.), *Texts, Images and Interactions: A Reader in Multimodality* (pp. 137–154). Berlin: Mouton de Gruyter.

### Further reading

O'Halloran, K. L. (2015). The language of learning mathematics: A multimodal perspective. *The Journal of Mathematical Behaviour*. http://www.science direct.com/science/article/pii/S0732312314000534
O'Toole, M. (2011). *The Language of Displayed Art* (2nd ed.). London & New York: Routledge.

## Unit 4. Social semiotics

Study Unit 4 will help you to:

- Engage critically with a social semiotic approach to multimodality
- Familiarize yourself with the key principles and concepts of social semiotics
- Try out some basic social semiotic analytical methods

## Overview of Chapter 4

Topics

- The origins and early development of social semiotics and how it has been developed to account for multimodality
- Key social semiotic principles and concepts
- Methods and analysis
- Fields of application, limitations, potentialities and challenges

Summary

In Chapter 4, we discussed the origins of social semiotics in three main strands of influence: systemic functional linguistics, semiotics and critical discourse analysis (CDA).

We showed how these three strands came together through the work of the Newtown Semiotic Circle and the collaborations of Kress with Hodge and then van Leeuwen. In the 1980s, the focus was on the visual; in the late 1990s, attention was broadened to include a range of modes, and the notion of multimodality was introduced.

We showed how a social semiotic approach highlights the social dimensions of meaning, its production, interpretation and circulation, and its implications. It sets out to reveal how processes of meaning making (i.e. signification and interpretation, or what is called semiosis) shape individuals and societies. The focus of social semiotics is on understanding the affordances of modes, the semiotic choices available to a person in a specific context, how people choose from these to make meaning and what motivates their choices, as well as the social effects of these choices. We also noted the interest of social semiotics in how modes change over time. We introduced the following social semiotic concepts:

- **Semiotic resource** refers to the meaning potential of material resources, which developed and accumulated over time through their use in a particular community and in response to certain social requirements of that community.
- **Mode** refers to a socially organized set of semiotic resources for making meaning. Examples of modes include image, writing, layout and speech, among others. For something to count as a mode, it needs to have a set of semiotic resources and organizing principles that are recognized within a community as realizing meaning.
- **Modal affordance** refers to the idea that different modes offer different potentials for making meaning. Modal affordances affect the kinds of semiotic work a mode can be used for, the ease with which it can be done, and the different ways in which modes can be used to achieve broadly similar semiotic work. Modal affordances are connected both to a mode's material and social histories, that is, the social purposes that it has been used for in a specific context.
- **Motivated sign** is a term used to reference that meaning (the signified) and form (the signifier) are brought together in a relation motivated by the *aptness of fit* between the **interest** of the sign maker and the **affordances** of a **semiotic resource**.
- **Interest** is a term used to refer to a momentary condensation of all the social experiences that have shaped an individual's subjectivity – a condensation prompted by the social environment (of which the available **modes** are a significant element) that a sign is made within. A person's interest connects their choice of one resource over another with the social context of sign production.
- **Design** is used to refer to the situated process in which a sign maker chooses and arranges semiotic resources to realize a particular social function or purpose. Design is conceived of as a starting point for making meaning, and both the original producer of a sign and its interpreter are understood as making meaning. It is always socially located and regulated, for example, by the types of resources that are made available and to whom, as well as the regimes that regulate and shape how these resources are used to create various norms and expectations.

The chapter then described the methodology of a social semiotic approach, its focus on the motivated character of sign making and how it is highly responsive to and shaped by the artefacts and interaction that it works with. We showed how, in a social semiotic approach, the analyst shifts between processes of deduction and induction. We showed how observational methods are used to recognize and theorize the social meaning and effect of signs. We also outlined the typical research questions and applications that social semiotics is used to address and discussed the limitations of the approach.

## Study questions

Read Chapter 4, and think about how you would answer the following questions. Make notes of your responses, and review them when you have completed the self-study guide.

1   How is the multimodal concept 'mode' used within a social semiotic approach?
2   In your view, what does the concept of motivated sign mean for multimodality?
3   Reflecting on the two boxed examples presented in Chapter 4, why in your view would it be important to understand what modes and semiotic resources are made available, to whom, and the different ways these are brought together?
4   What can you say (and what not) about the 'interest' of a sign maker by analysing the artefacts that he or she makes?

## Exercises

### Exercise 4.1: Operationalizing social semiotic concepts

a   Select a paper from one of the suggested readings for Chapter 4.
b   Which of the theoretical concepts that we have discussed in Chapter 4 are used in the paper (i.e. semiotic resource, mode, modal affordance, motivated sign, interest, design)?
c   How does the author of the paper connect these theoretical concepts with the materials that they analyse?
d   How do they warrant their analytical claims?
e   In your view, is the analysis convincing? If yes, why; if not, why not?

*Tip: You will need to show whether and how the theoretical concepts that you use connect with the materials you use in your study.*

Exercise 4.2: Exploring the motivated sign

The concept of the *motivated sign* is intimately connected to the *interest of a sign maker* and the social-cultural *context of their sign making*. This exercise explores how these three interconnected concepts can shape a social semiotic analysis.

a   Select a context where you can observe someone making a multimodal arte-fact (such as, writing a text message on a phone, or in Word, or posting something on Facebook, or watching a child making a drawing).
b   If possible, video-record them while they are making the artefact.
c   Map the range of modes and semiotic resources that were *available* to them.
d   Describe the modes and resources that *they used* to make the artefact.
e   How did the social and cultural setting shape the sign maker's choice of resources and the artefact made?
f   How did their 'interest' (including their skills and abilities) shape the process of making the artefact?

Exercise 4.3: Exploring the layout of an artefact through commutation

In Chapter 4 we introduced commutation as an analytical process used in social semiotics to explore the design of multimodal texts, notably layout as a mode and the relationships between image and writing. In this exercise, we invite you to try it out:

a   Select a text that you are interested in analysing.
b   Identify the layout structure of the text. This might be in the form of boxed areas, columns, strips or grid-like structures on the page or screen. (You could use a pen or annotation tool to highlight these.)
c   Rearrange the elements of the text, using drawing software (e.g. Paint for Windows) to 'cut and paste' (or working manually with printouts and scis-sors), to create three variations of the artefact.
d   Explore how the reconfiguration of the modal relationships impacts on the relations between the modes and the meaning of the text.

*Tip: The commutation test is a way to explore the choices available to a sign maker by changing a signifier – e.g. substituting one lexical item for another or one spatial arrangement for another – and considering its effect on the signified meaning.*

## Unit 4 suggested resources

### Key reading

Kress, G. (2010). *Multimodality: A Social Semiotic Approach to Contemporary Communication*. London; New York: Routledge.

### Further reading

Adami, E. (2009). 'We/YouTube': Exploring sign-making in video-interaction. *Visual Communication* 8(4), 379–399.

Bezemer, J., & Kress, G. (2016). *Multimodality, Learning and Communication: A Social Semiotic Frame*. London: Routledge.

Kress, G., & van Leeuwen, T. (2006). *Reading Images: A Visual Grammar of Design* (2nd ed.). London: Routledge.

Mavers, D. (2011). *Children's Drawing and Writing: The Remarkable in the Unremarkable.* New York: Routledge.

van Leeuwen, T. (2005) *Introducing Social Semiotics*. London: Routledge.

### Online resources

Interview with Arlene Archer: Social semiotics, social justice and multimodal pedagogy. http://mode.ioe.ac.uk/interviews-with-6icom-keynote-speakers/

## Unit 5. Conversation analysis

### Learning objectives

Study Unit 5 will help you to:

- Engage critically with how multimodality has been taken up in conversation analysis (CA)
- Familiarize yourself with key principles and concepts of CA
- Try out some basic CA methods of transcription and analysis

### Overview of Chapter 5

### Topics

- The origins of CA and its connection with multimodality
- Key CA principles and concepts

- Methods of transcription and analysis
- Fields of application, limitations, potentialities and challenges of CA

## Summary

We opened Chapter 5 with a brief history of CA, sketching its development in the US in the early 1960s as an approach in sociology. We explained that CA is concerned with people's 'lived experiences', which it explores through detailed observation and analysis of social interaction. We outlined how in the 1970s Goodwin – and later Heath, Mondada and others – began to expand CA by analysing *video* recordings of everyday interactions, prompting interest in the role of gaze, gesture and other resources in what is now often called multimodal interaction.

We set out the key principles and processes of a CA approach. We discussed the CA principle of *staying close* to the selected video clip (i.e. avoiding high inferences, grounding claims in visible and audible features in the clip) and '*slowing down*' the analytical process to recognize 'order' in the ways in which people *organize* themselves in and through interaction. Each action is understood in relation to the action that preceded and followed it. That key principle provides a basis for making claims about the meanings that people make. We introduced the key concepts that have been used in accounts of multimodal interaction:

- **Mutual elaboration of semiotic resources** is the notion that people 'build action' using distinctly different, mutually elaborating 'semiotic resources';
- **Sequential organization of action** is the principle that action unfolds in time, one action after another;
- **Coordination of action** is the idea that the accomplishment of collaborative work demands coordinated, concerted action;
- **Multi-activity** is the phenomenon that different activities possibly involving different, sometimes partially overlapping participants, operate in conjunction in order to pursue concurrent courses of action.

We noted that in CA video, recordings of 'naturally occurring' social encounters are used as data, i.e. encounters that are not initiated by the researcher. Short clips are then selected for detailed transcription and analysis. We discussed CA transcription conventions, along with their central role in the analytical process, and discussed the process of producing a transcript. We also outlined the typical research questions and applications that CA is used to address and discussed the limitations of this approach.

## Study questions

Read Chapter 5, and think about how you would answer the following questions. Make notes of your responses, and review them when you have completed the self-study guide.

1   How is the term 'mode' used within a CA approach?
2   What does the concept of mutual elaboration mean to you?
3   Reflect on the models of transcription presented in Chapter 5 and their differences.
4   What kind of insights does a CA approach offer to the study of multimodality?

## Exercises

### Exercise 5.1: Warranting claims – staying close to the data and slowing down

In Chapter 5 we discussed the centrality of *staying close to the selected video clip* and *slowing down.* This means that when you adopt a CA approach, the claims that you make about what happens in the recorded interaction should always be grounded in observations in the clip. While it is important to know a good deal about the context in which the interaction occurred, the focus is always on what happens *in this clip.*

a   Select a paper from one of the suggested readings for this chapter.
b   Read it to see how the author makes claims about what happens in the inter-action that is presented.
c   How do the concepts just discussed feature in the account of the interaction?
d   Is the analysis plausible? If yes, why; if not, why not?

### Exercise 5.2: Analysing sequentiality

a   Reflect on Heritage's (1997) proposal that every action is 'context-shaped' in that it acts as a response to the previous action and that at the same time it is 'context-creating' in that it raises expectations about what is to happen next.

b   Make a short video recording of an everyday interaction (e.g. use your phone to make a 2- to 3-minute video recording of family or friends cooking a meal, dining or playing a game).

c   View the clip or a part of it, and describe the setting, and the participants and the social roles they enact. The aim of these viewing sessions is to collect 'noticings' from different perspectives.

- What kind of activity/activities are they engaged in?
- How are they using gaze, gesture, objects (e.g. kitchen tool, cookbook), body placement and talk?
- Are people doing what's expected of them, or are they doing something different? What are they orienting to?
- How is the activity built up? How does it unfold in time? Why did it unfold in the way it did?
- How did the actions of each person shape what another person did and said next? How did they take turns?

*Tip. It is important to suspend judgements about what you see. Move from description to interpretation. Look for evidence in the clip for all claims made about what happens. Whenever you make an observation, ask yourself, 'How do I know?'*

## Exercise 5.3: Analysing coordination of action

a   Video-record instances of object passings, e.g. of food at the dinner table or at a market stall. (You might also find examples on YouTube.)

b   View the clip repeatedly. What can you say about how the passing is achieved? What resources do the participants draw on, and how are they mutually modifying?

c   Make a transcript of one object passing. Visualize on a timeline the direction of gaze and the movement of the hands of the various participants, and transcribe what they say. What can you say now about the accomplishment of the passing? Has the transcript validated or challenged your initial noticings?

*Tip: Use ELAN to systematically re-present the sequential unfolding of simultaneously produced actions. ELAN a professional tool for the creation of complex annotations on video and audio resources (https://tla.mpi.nl/tools/tla-tools/elan/). In this way, you can render visible the degree of alignment between different participants and their actions.*

## Unit 5 suggested resources

### Key reading

Heath, C., Hindmarsh, J., & Luff, P. (2010). *Video in Qualitative Research.* London: Sage.

Streeck, J., Goodwin, C., & LeBaron, C. (2011). Embodied interaction in the material world: An introduction. In J. Streeck, C. Goodwin & C. LeBaron (Eds.), *Embodied Interaction. Language and Body in the Material World* (pp. 1–26). Cambridge: Cambridge University Press.

### Further reading

Goodwin, C. (2000). Action and embodiment within situated human interaction. *Journal of Pragmatics* 32, 1489–1522.

Streeck, J., Goodwin, C. & LeBaron, C. (Eds.). (2011). *Embodied Interaction. Language and Body in the Material World.* Cambridge: Cambridge University Press.

### Online resources

Charles Goodwin's website: http://www.sscnet.ucla.edu/clic/cgoodwin/

Interview with Lorenza Mondada: Multimodal methods for researching social interaction. https://youtu.be/PwR6jQy7sQg

## Unit 6. Five more approaches to multimodality

### Learning objectives

Study Unit 6 will help you to:

■ Engage critically with the possibilities for mixing multimodal with other methods
■ Familiarize yourself with approaches that have mixed multimodality with other methods and theories
■ Consider the potentials and limitations of these combined approaches

### Overview of Chapter 6

### Topics

■ Research frameworks combining multimodality with other theories and methods
■ The potentialities and challenges of these frameworks and their contribution to multimodal research

## Summary

In Chapter 6, we explored the analytical potential of bringing approaches to multimodality into contact with other methodological or theoretical frameworks. We presented five approaches that have combined multimodal concepts with other approaches, that have some settled conventions and practices and an (emergent) research community and that have made a distinct contribution to extending the scope of multimodality. The five frameworks were:

1   **Geo-semiotics** (or discourses in place) combines linguistic anthropology and place semiotics with a social semiotic approach to foreground the placement of semiotic artefacts and interactions in the wider spatial environment.
2   **Multimodal (inter)action analysis** combines interactional social-linguistics and a social semiotic approach to foreground identity formation through interaction.
3   **Multimodal ethnography** uses social semiotic theory in ethnographic research to produce accounts of situated artefacts and interactions and the relations between them.
4   **Corpus-based multimodal analysis** combines corpus analysis methods with SFL and social semiotic approaches to empirically evaluate, critique and validate the hypotheses and theories of multimodal meaning making through the analysis of artefacts.
5   **Multimodal reception analysis** combines psychological concepts and methods to investigate the cognitive processes involved in the 'perception' of textual artefacts and to 'test' semiotic principles proposed in systemic functional linguistics and social semiotics.

We outlined the scope, aims and research questions of each approach, as well as their theory of meaning, concepts and methods, and highlighted their contribution to multimodality. We illustrated the potential of connecting multimodality with other theories and taking it in new directions, specifically to foreground space and place, identity, insider perspectives, and to test theories of meaning. We also discussed the need to ensure that such combinations achieve an internal coherence and the challenges of doing so.

## Study questions

1   When might it be necessary to combine multimodality with another approach?
2   Do these five combined approaches change the multimodal concepts that they use? If yes, how?

3    What do you think are the main benefits and challenges of *incorporating* multimodal concepts into another research framework?

4    In your view, are any methods or theories 'incompatible' with multimodality? If not, why not? If so, which ones would be incompatible?

## Exercises

Exercise 6.1: Assessing the benefits and challenges of combining multimodality with other methods

a    In Chapter 6 we quoted the following statement by Rosie Flewitt:

> A focus on semiosis could show what choices children made, and what modes were made available to them through diverse traditional and 'new' literacy texts in diverse media, but this constituted 'thin' descriptions which situated the production and reception of meanings within physical and material social settings, but did not make accessible more holistic insights into their literacy learning . . . . For this deeper level of understanding, the study was dependent on ethnographic data, which constituted a rich backstory of how networks of cultural and social values permeated the children's homes and nursery. While multimodal analysis captured something of the communicative complexity of the studied field, ethnographic approaches to data collection and interpretation helped to situate that complexity in particular social, cultural and historical contexts. (Flewitt, 2011: 302)

b    What tensions can you see in combining a social semiotic and ethnographic approach? How does Flewitt resolve these tensions?

(You may want to engage with the full paper [see further readings] to help you with this exercise.)

*Tip: If you combine multimodality with other theories and methods, you will need to be explicit about the benefits and challenges of doing so.*

Exercise 6.2: Evaluating the contribution to multimodal research

a    Select one of the five approaches presented in Chapter 6.

b    Choose a paper written by the named scholar who has led its development from the further reading for this unit or the references at the end of this book.

c    Read the paper and address the following questions:

- ■ Is it clear how the authors have used multimodal concepts in their research framework?
- ■ In your view, does the approach extend the multimodal approach that it draws on? If so, how? If not, why not?

*Tip: It might be useful to be explicit about what contribution is made to methods by using multimodality in a research framework with other methods in your study.*

## Exercise 6.3: To mix or not to mix?

a    Select one of the multimodal artefacts or short video clips of interaction that you engaged with to undertake the exercises in Units 3 to 5.

b    Choose a research framework that you think is the most apt for your materials from those we discussed in Chapter 6.

c    How would the selected framework change the scope of materials that you would need to collect?

d    In your view, would there be any benefits in doing so? If yes, what are they? If no, why not?

e    What new tensions and challenges might this framework give rise to?

## Unit 6 suggested resources

### Further reading

Bateman, J. A. (2008). *Multimodality and Genre: A Foundation for the Systematic Analysis of Multimodal Documents.* Basingstoke [England]; New York: Palgrave Macmillan.

Dicks, B., Flewitt, R., Lancaster, L., & Pahl, K. (Eds.). (2011). Special issue: Multimodality and ethnography: Working at the intersection. *Qualitative Research* 11(3).

Flewitt, R. (2011). Bringing ethnography to a multimodal investigation of early literacy in a digital age. *Qualitative Research* 11, 293–310.

Holsanova, J. (2014). Reception of multimodality: Applying eye tracking methodology in multimodal research. In C. Jewitt (Ed.), *The Routledge Handbook of Multimodal Analysis* (2nd ed., pp. 287–298). Milton Park, Abingdon, Oxon: Routledge.

Norris, S. (2004). *Analyzing Multimodal Interaction: A Methodological Framework.* New York: Routledge.

Scollon, R., & Wong Scollon, S. (2003). *Discourses in Place: Language in the Material World.* London: Routledge.

Online resources

John Bateman's website on Multimodal Documents and Film. http://www.fb10.
    uni-bremen.de/anglistik/langpro/webspace/jb/info-pages/multi-root.htm
Sigrid Norris's website on Multimodality. http://www.sigridnorris.com/index.htm

## Unit 7. Designing a multimodal study

### Learning objectives

Study Unit 7 will help you to:

- Engage with the process of designing a multimodal study
- Reflect on which approach is most apt approach for your study
- Identify a research focus and questions for your study
- Identify your empirical focus
- Explore and assess methods for transcribing and managing your research materials
- Engage with the ethical dimensions of multimodal research

### Overview of Chapter 7

#### Topics

- Choosing an apt research approach
- Formulating a research focus and questions
- Selecting an empirical focus
- Collecting research materials
- Transcribing and managing your research materials
- Ethical dimensions of multimodal research

#### Summary

In Chapter 7 we discussed how to design a multimodal study. We started the chapter by discussing the two routes into multimodality, *doing multimodality* or *adopting multimodal concepts*, and pointed to the need to assess how central multimodality is to your study and the need to choose an approach accordingly.

- If you are *doing multimodality*, your first design decision will be to choose an apt approach for your study (e.g. CA, SFL or social semiotics and the frameworks in Chapter 6). Each of these approaches will provide you with a framework to guide your study, formulate research questions and choose an empirical focus.

■ If you are *adopting multimodal concepts*, your starting point will be different. You will likely be coming to multimodality with a clear research interest or question formulated from a different theoretical position. You will need to select a research framework and reframe your research interest and questions to account for a multimodal perspective.

We then presented and discussed the key elements that need to be considered when designing a multimodal study (see the list of Chapter 7 topics).

## Study questions

1   How does the route to multimodality, *doing* multimodality or *adopting* multimodal concepts affect the process of designing a multimodal study?
2   How does the choice of an approach shape the design of a study more generally?
3   In your view, what are the challenges of focusing on either artefacts or interaction or both in a multimodal study?
4   What benefits and challenges can transcribing research materials present for a multimodal study?
5   How do you know when you have collected enough research materials?
6   What are examples of ethical issues that need to be addressed in a multimodal study?

## Exercises

### Exercise 7.1: Justifying an approach

a   Select a paper that uses a multimodal approach in an area of interest to you.
b   Do you think it the most apt approach for their study?

*Tip: Whatever your route to multimodality, you need to be clear on your theoretical orientation to provide a solid grounding for the design of your study.*

### Exercise 7.2: Focusing your research

A second challenge you will encounter when you design a multimodal study is the need to clarify your research focus. As discussed in Chapter 7, this challenge will vary depending on whether you are *doing* multimodality or *adopting multi-modal concepts*.

If you are *doing* multimodal research, the requirements of the particular approach that you select will frame the area and guide the questions of your study.

Alternatively, if you are *adopting multimodal concepts* for your study, you will need to bring a research area, topic or question from another theoretical context.

In both cases, you will need to make some significant choices and decisions within this frame regarding research area, topic and questions for your study design.

a   Use the following ways to generate, refine and focus your research area and questions:

- Collect some artefacts similar to those that you will research, and spend time exploring them.
- Read papers in your area of interest that use the multimodal approach you have chosen for your study. Do they suggest new directions for research? Do they reveal a gap your study could address?
- Talk to other students.
- Brainstorm ideas.

b   Ask yourself what your overarching research questions and subquestions are. Are they:

- Orientated to multimodality?
- Related to previous research on the topic that you are studying?
- Clear and answerable?
- Significant? That is, does the question matter to anyone, and to whom?
- Feasible to undertake within the limits of time and other resources that are available to you?

*Tip: A clear and answerable question that connects your study to multimodality and a body of previous research and that is interesting and significant, as well as feasible, will provide a useful anchor for your study.*

Exercise 7.3: Collecting artefacts as research materials

In Chapter 7 we made a distinction between two broad categories of research materials: artefacts produced by the people you want to study and recordings of their interaction produced by a researcher. We noted the qualities of the materials used across the different approaches discussed in this book (i.e. naturalistic, fine-grained and socially situated).

We discussed the specific requirements of different approaches and how these steer the type of materials needed for a study and their collection. The collection of artefacts as research materials was explored in Chapters 4 through 6 and Units 4 through 6 of this self-study guide.

The following exercise is a general one that needs to be considered in conjunction with your approach.

a   Identify the type(s) of artefact that you might need to collect for your study (e.g. children's drawings, leaflets, advertisements, building or street environment).

- Can you collect the original artefact, or do you need to reproduce it (e.g. in a photograph or a scan)?
- Will any aspects of the artefact be lost during the process of collecting it (e.g. its scale, textual qualities, dynamic elements)? How could you compensate for that loss?
- Are there any ethical or copyright concerns? How can you respond to these?

b   How will you set the boundary of the artefact (e.g. a section, a page, a book)?
c   How much and what kind of contextual information will you need to analyse your materials? Do you need to collect materials on how they were made, on where they are circulated, on how people engage with them?
d   How many artefacts will you need to address your research question?
e   Do you need to collect a range of artefacts or not?

*Tip: You will need to consider the losses involved in recording artefacts and how that might affect your analysis.*

*Tip: You will need to consider what type and how much contextual information you need about the artefacts you collect for your study.*

## Exercise 7.4: Recording materials to study interaction

The same caveats outlined for Exercise 7.3 apply to the recording of material to study interaction, discussed in Chapters 3, 5 and 6. The following exercise is a general one that needs to be considered in conjunction with your approach.

As discussed elsewhere in this book (Chapters 3 and 7), video is a medium for representing the world in sound and moving image, offering distinct potentialities and challenges for recording interaction. However, the use of video to collect materials for multimodal materials often involves trade-offs between detail and the bigger picture or context. How you set up your video to collect data will shape the data you collect, which in turn will shape your analysis.

a   Imagine you want to video-record a whole-class activity, involving some 20 students and a teacher in a classroom. How would the recordings of their interaction be shaped by each of the following five set-ups:

- A fixed video camera with a wide lens recording the whole class
- A fixed video camera focused on small groups of students, changing the group every 15 minutes
- A fixed camera zooming and panning
- A roaming video camera focused on (and moving with) with the teacher;
- Two video cameras, one focused on the teacher, the other on the students

b   What might be the challenges of the video recordings produced using a fixed camera, a roaming camera or multiple cameras?
c   What other materials might you collect to supplement the video recordings (e.g. field notes, [recordings of] artefacts such as documents)?
d   What are your (provisional) guiding questions? What subject, type of activity or phenomenon are you interested in? This will shape your filming decisions.
e   How many hours of footage will you need?

*Tip: You will need to have a clear idea of the kind of video recordings that you need to produce for your study. Do you need 'minimally edited' video, with minimal zooming and panning, giving a relatively fixed view of participants interacting (gathered using a wide-frame and long-shot)? Do you need video to capture facial expressions, hand movements etc. (which requires a tight-frame close-up camera)? Or do you need to capture both detail and the bigger picture by changing the camera position during video recording, using a roaming camera or more than one camera?*

Exercise 7.5: Transcribing research materials

The same caveats outlined for Exercise 7.4 apply to the transcription of material, which is also discussed in Chapters 3, 5 and 6 and Units 3, 5 and 6 of this self-study guide. The following exercise is a general one that needs to be considered in conjunction with your approach.

a    Look at the following three transcripts (each of these is discussed in more detail elsewhere in this book; see pages 76, 99 and 117).

| Visualizer | | Speech |
|---|---|---|
| (a) | places the bar magnets on a small board | okay (.) |
| (b) | touches each bar magnet and adjusts them slightly | two bar magnets (..) |
| (c) | | now looking back to what our aim for today was (.) Tom (..) okay (..) we will learn that forces act between two magnets (..) |
| (d) | touches each bar magnet and adjusts them slightly | so there are our two magnets okay (..) |
| (e) | | what do you think (.) think about this (.) don't put your hands up for now (.) |
| (f) | touches each bar magnet and adjusts them slightly | if I (..) move them |
| (g) | brings fingers together above the magnets | closer together (..) |
| (h) | | then let go (..) what do you think would happen to the magnets? |

Reprinted with permission from SAGE Publications and the author (Mavers, 2009: 146).

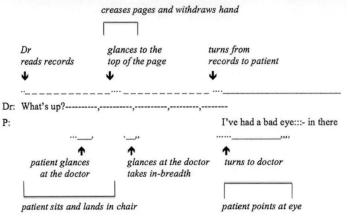

From Heath, Luff and Hindmarsh, 2010.

Reprinted from Norris, 2004: 102.

b Compare the three transcripts using the dimensions outline in Chapter 7 (Example 7.1, pages 146–149):

- ■ Principles of framing, selecting and highlighting
- ■ Types of transduction and use of modes: writing, image, layout, time
- ■ Time scale
- ■ Unit of analysis

c What aspects of interaction does each transcript foreground or background?

d Which aspects of interaction will be important to foreground in the transcripts for your study, and why?

e What model of transcription and conventions will you draw on in your study?

*Tip: You will need to select a model of transcription that aligns with your approach and the questions you want to address.*

## Exercise 7.6: Considering ethical dimensions

As discussed in Chapter 7, the planning of a study of multimodal interaction will usually involve gaining access to a site where you can video-record and obtain ethical approval. The question is whether the use of materials for multimodal analysis, especially video materials, throws up any specific challenges in this regard. Some highly experienced video researchers commented:

> One reason that is often raised for not using video in qualitative research is that it will be impossible to gain permission to make recordings from participants, or more generally, an organisation. Surprisingly perhaps, gaining access to undertake video recording rarely proves a major difficulty, as long as you are sensitive to the demands of the setting and address the concerns of the participants themselves. In recent years, video-based studies have been undertaken in such diverse settings and activities as medical consultations, management consultancy, counselling interviews, banking and financial management, surgical operations, air traffic control, hairdressing, surveillance, nursing, television and radio production, home life, shops and business meetings. Each of these settings poses different challenges for data collection and demands different techniques for securing consent.
>
> Heath, Hindmarsh and Luff (2010: 15)

a Imagine you want to do video-ethnographic fieldwork in a workplace.

b In your view, what, if any, unique ethical issues does the collection and use of video recordings in such a context throw up?

Note: We can make a distinction between **anonymity** and **confidentiality** (Derry et al., 2010). Anonymity cannot be ensured, unless you edit the video such that people's faces and voices can no longer be recognized (software such as Windows Movie Maker allows you to do that). In doing so, the video also loses some of its potential for making visible the phenomenon of interest. However, confidentiality can be protected by omitting personal information and information about the research site.

c   With reference to the strategies discussed in Chapter 7 (pages 150–153), how might you be able to manage those ethical issues?
d   What ethical issues might the use of video recording in your intended study site raise? What measures could you take to deal with them?

*Study design tip: Before you approach your participants, think through the concerns that your use of photography and/or video for the study might raise for them and how you can respond to their concerns.*

*Study design tip: When you design your consent form, give participants different options to opt in and out of (e.g. the use anonymized clips and transcripts and/or unanonymized clips and transcripts for research, training or publication purposes).*

## Unit 7 suggested resources

### Further reading

Reading the publications of the many multimodal studies cited in the different chapters of this book provides you with a good starting point for designing your multimodal study.

### Transcription

Bezemer, J., & Mavers, D. (2011). Multimodal transcription as academic practice: A social semiotic perspective. *International Journal of Social Research Methodology* 14, 191–206.

Mavers, D. (2012). *Transcribing Video*. NCRM Working Paper. Unpublished Paper. http://eprints.ncrm.ac.uk/2877/4/NCRM_working_paper0512.pdf. Mavers discusses examples illustrating different ways of making relatively detailed transcripts of a small strip of interaction, accounting for bodily conduct alongside speech.

### Working with video

Derry, S. J., Pea, R. D., Barron, B., Engle, R. A., Erickson, F., Goldman, R., Hall, R., Koschmann, T., Lemke, J. L., Sherin, M. G., & Sherin, B. L. (2010). Conducting video research in the learning sciences: Guidance on selection, analysis, technology, and ethics. *Journal of the Learning Sciences* 19(1), 3–53.

Heath, C., Hindmarsh, J., & Luff, P. (2010). *Video in Qualitative Research*. London: Sage.

Jewitt, C. (2012). An Introduction to Using Video for Research. NCRM working paper. http://eprints.ncrm.ac.uk/2259/4/NCRM_workingpaper_0312.pdf

## Online resources

CAQDAS Networking Project offers practical support, training and information in the use of a range of software programs designed to assist qualitative data analysis, including multimodal data. http://www.surrey.ac.uk/sociology/research/researchcentres/caqdas/

Derry, S. J. (2007). *Guidelines for Conducting Video Research in Education*. Chicago: Data Research and Development Center, NORC at University of Chicago. http://drdc.uchicago.edu/what/video-research-guidelines.pdf

ELAN Transcription software is a professional tool for the creation of complex annotations on video and audio resources. https://tla.mpi.nl/tools/tla-tools/elan/

Mode: Multimodal Methodologies: The online MODE transcription bank is a collection of reflections on transcripts made from video recordings. Authors present transcripts they used in their research and provide accounts of why and how they made them. http://mode.ioe.ac.uk/category/transcription-bank/

## Checklist

This 'checklist' is designed to help you think through the design of your own study. Their relevance will vary depending on the approach that you use and the materials your study will analyse.

- Do you have a clear working definition of multimodality for your study?
- Are you clear about the place of multimodality in your study? Are you doing multimodality or adopting multimodal concepts?
- Have you chosen the most apt approach for your study? What is your rationale for that choice? Why is it more apt than the other approaches discussed in this book?
- Are you clear as to what aspects of your research are ineffable (that is cannot be expressed in words)? You can use this to help strengthen your rationale for doing a multimodal study.

- Have you stated clearly what a multimodal approach offers your study that a solely linguistic one does not? You can use this to help strengthen your rationale for taking a multimodal approach.
- Have you explained how you connect the theoretical concepts that you use to the analysis of your research materials?
- Have you considered what processes you will use to immerse yourself in your research materials (e.g. 'breaking and taking it apart' using commutation)?
- Can you show how you ground your claims in the recorded interaction?
- Have you considered how you will move from description to interpretation?
- If you are combining multimodal concepts into a framework that combines them with other theories and methods, have you been explicit about the benefits and challenges of doing so?
- Have you explained how you will combine multimodal concepts into a research framework with other methods in your study in order to make a methodological contribution?
- Whatever your route to multimodality, have you provided a clear, solid grounding for the design of your study?
- Have you established clear and answerable overarching and subresearch questions? Do these connect your study to multimodality and a body of previous research? Are they interesting, significant and feasible questions?
- Have you considered how your data collection process might lose aspects of the artefacts you want to collect and how to manage that in your study?
- Are you clear about the type and amount of contextual information that you need about any materials that you will collect for your study?
- Do you have a clear sense of the kind of video recordings that you need to produce for your study – and how you need to position and use your video cameras to achieve that?
- Have you selected a model of transcription for your study that aligns with your approach and the interactional features that you want to investigate?
- Have you thought through the ethical concerns of your study design and how you can respond to your participants' concerns in a way that will ameliorate these?
- Have you designed a consent form and project information leaflet for participants that set out different consent options for the use of video research materials?

# References

Adami, E. (2009). 'We/YouTube': Exploring sign-making in video-interaction. *Visual Communication* 8(4), 379–399.

Andersen, T. H., Boeriis, M., Maagerø, E., & Tønnessen, E. S. (2015). *Social Semiotics: Key Figures, New Directions*. London; New York: Routledge/Taylor & Francis Group.

Antaki, C. (Ed.). (2011). *Applied Conversation Analysis: Intervention and Change in Institutional Talk*. Basingstoke, Hampshire: Palgrave Macmillan.

Archer, A. (2014). Power, social justice, and multimodal pedagogies. In C. Jewitt (Ed.), *The Routledge Handbook of Multimodal Analysis* (pp. 189–198). Abingdon, Oxon; Milton Park, Oxfordshire: Routledge.

Avital, S., & Streeck, J. (2011). Terra incognita: Social interaction among blind children. In J. Streeck, C. Goodwin and C. LeBaron (Eds.), *Embodied Interaction, Language and Body in the Material World* (pp. 169–181). Cambridge: Cambridge University Press.

BAAL. (2006). BAAL recommendations on good practice in applied linguistics. *BAAL Newsletter* 41, 20–25.

Baldry, A., & Thibault, P. (2006). *Multimodal Transcription and Text Analysis*. London: Equinox.

Barthes, R. (1977 [1964]). Rhetoric of the image. In R. Barthes (Ed.) and S. Heath (Trans.), *Image Music Text* (pp. 32–51). London: Fontana.

Bateman, J. (2008). *Multimodality and Genre: A Foundation for the Systematic Analysis of Multimodal Documents*. Basingstoke, Hampshire; New York: Palgrave Macmillan.

Bateman, J. (2014a). Looking for what counts in film analysis: A programme of empirical research. In D. Machin (Ed.), *Visual Communication* (pp. 301–329). Berlin: De Gruyter Mouton.

Bateman, J. (2014b). *Text and Image: A Critical Introduction to the Visual/Verbal Divide*. London; New York: Routledge.

Bateman, J. (2014c). Using multimodal corpora for multimodal research. In C. Jewitt (Ed.), *The Routledge Handbook of Multimodal Analysis* (pp. 238–252). Abingdon, Oxon; Milton Park, Oxfordshire: Routledge.

Bateman, J., Delin, J., & Henschel, R. (2004). Multimodality and empiricism: Preparing for a corpus-based approach to the study of multimodal meaning-making. In E. Ventola, C. Charles & M. Kaltenbacher (Eds.), *Perspectives on Multimodality* (pp. 65–87). Amsterdam: John Benjamins.

Bateman, J., & O'Donnell, M. (2015). Computational linguistics: The Halliday connection. In J. J. Webster (Ed.), *The Bloomsbury Companion to M. A. K. Halliday* (pp. 453–466). New York: Bloomsbury Academic.

Bateman, J., & Schmidt, K.-H. (2012). *Multimodal Film Analysis: How Films Mean*. London; New York: Routledge.

Bell, P., & Milic, M. (2002). Goffman's gender advertisements revisited: Combining content analysis with semiotic analysis. *Visual Communication* 1, 203–222.

Bezemer, J. (2014). Multimodal transcription: A case study. In S. Norris & C. D. Maier (Eds.), *Interactions, Images and Texts: A Reader in Multimodality* (pp. 155–170). Berlin: De Gruyter Mouton.

Bezemer, J., Cope, A., Faiz, O. & Kneebone, R. (2012). Participation of surgical residents in operations: challenging a common classification. *World Journal of Surgery* 36(9), 2011–2014.

Bezemer, J., Cope, A., Kress, G., & Kneebone, R. (2014). Holding the scalpel: Achieving surgical care in a learning environment. *Journal of Contemporary Ethnography* 43(1), 38–63.

Bezemer, J., & Kress, G. (2008). Writing in multimodal texts: A social semiotic account of designs for learning. *Written Communication* 25(2), 166–195.

Bezemer, J., & Kress, G. (2014). Touch: A resource for meaning making. *Australian Journal of Language and Literacy* 37, 77–85.

Bezemer, J., & Kress, G. (2016). *Multimodality, Learning and Communication. A Social Semiotic Frame*. London: Routledge.

Bezemer, J., & Mavers, D. (2011). Multimodal transcription as academic practice: A social semiotic perspective. *International Journal of Social Research Methodology* 14, 191–206.

Bezemer, J., Murtagh, G., Cope, A., & Kneebone, R. (in press). Surgical decision making in a teaching hospital: A linguistic analysis. *ANZ Journal of Surgery*.

Bezemer, J., Murtagh, G., Cope, A., Kress, G., & Kneebone, R. (2011). "Scissors, Please" The practical accomplishment of surgical work in the operating theatre. *Symbolic Interaction* 34(3), 398–414.

Blommaert, J. (2005). *Discourse.* Cambridge: Cambridge University Press.

Bloor, T., & Bloor, M. (2013). *The Functional Analysis of English: A Hallidayan Approach* (3rd ed.). New York: Routledge.

Broth, M., Laurier, E., & Mondada, L. (Eds.). (2014). *Studies of Video Practices: Video at Work.* New York: Routledge.

Broth, M., & Mondada, L. (2013). Walking away: The embodied achievement of activity closings in mobile interaction. *Journal of Pragmatics* 47(1), 41–58.

Burawoy, M. (2009). *The Extended Case Method: Four Countries, Four Decades, Four Great Transformations, and One Theoretical Tradition.* Berkeley, CA: University of California Press.

Butler, C. (2003a). *Structure and Function: A Guide to Three Major Structural-Functional Theories, Part 1: Approaches to the Simplex Clause.* Amsterdam; Philadelphia: John Benjamins.

Butler, C. (2003b). *Structure and Function: A Guide to Three Major Structural-Functional Theories, Part 2: From Clause to Discourse and Beyond.* Amsterdam; Philadelphia: John Benjamins.

Campbell, S., & Roberts, C. (2007). Migration, ethnicity and competing discourses in the job interview: Synthesising the institutional and personal. *Discourse and Society* 18(3), 243–271.

Cao, Y., & O'Halloran, K. L. (2014). Learning human photo shooting patterns from large-scale community photo collections. *Multimedia Tools and Applications.* doi:10.1007/s11042–11014–12247–11040

Chandler, D. (2007). *Semiotics* (2nd ed.). Abingdon, Oxon: Routledge.

Cook, G. (2003). *Applied Linguistics.* Cambridge: Cambridge University Press.

Crescenzi, L., Jewitt, C., & Price, S. (2014). The role of touch in pre-school children's learning using iPad versus paper interaction. *Australian Journal of Language and Literacy* 37, 86–95.

Davis, J. (2010). Architecture of the personal interactive homepage: Constructing the self through MySpace. *New Media & Society* 12(7), 1103–1119.

Deppermann, A., & Schmidt, R. (2007). Koordination. Zur Begründung eines neuen Forschungsgegenstandes. In R. Schmitt (Ed.), *Koordination. Studien zur multimodalen Interaktion* (pp. 15–54). Tübingen: Gunter Narr.

Derry, S. J. (2007). *Guidelines for Conducting Video Research in Education.* Chicago: Data Research and Development Center, NORC at University of Chicago. http://drdc.uchicago.edu/what/video-research-guidelines.pdf

Derry, S. J., Pea, R. D., Barron, B., Engle, R. A., Erickson, F., Goldman, R., Hall, R., Koschmann, T., Lemke, J. L., Sherin, M. G., & Sherin, B. L. (2010). Conducting video research in the learning sciences: Guidance on selection, analysis, technology, and ethics. *Journal of the Learning Sciences* 19(1), 3–53.

Dicks, B., Flewitt, R., Lancaster, L., & Pahl, K. (Eds.). (2011). Special issue: Multimodality and ethnography: Working at the intersection. *Qualitative Research* 11(3).

Dowling, P. (2004). Mythologising and organising. Online paper. http://www.pauldowling.me/publications/mo/index.htm

Dreyfus, S., Hood, S., & Stenglin, M. (Eds.). (2011). *Semiotic Margins: Meaning in Multimodalities*. London; New York: Continuum.

Eggins, S. (2005). *An Introduction to Systemic Functional Linguistics* (2nd ed.). London: Continuum.

Erickson, F. (2004). *Talk and Social Theory. Ecologies of Speaking and Listening in Everyday Life*. Cambridge: Polity.

Erickson, F. (2007). Ways of seeing video: Toward a phenomenology of viewing minimally edited footage. In R. Goldman (Ed.), *Video Research in the Learning Sciences* (pp. 145–158). Mahwah, NJ: Lawrence Erlbaum Associates.

Flewitt, R. (2011). Bringing ethnography to a multimodal investigation of early literacy in a digital age. *Qualitative Research* 11, 293–310.

Flewitt, R., Hampel, R., Hauck, M., & Lancaster, L. (2014). What are multimodal data and transcriptions. In C. Jewitt (Ed.), *The Routledge Handbook of Multimodal Analysis* (pp. 44–59). Abingdon, Oxon; Milton Park, Oxfordshire: Routledge.

Flewitt, R., Kucirkova, N., & Messer, D. (2014). Touching the virtual, touching the real: iPads and enabling literacy. *Australian Journal of Language and Literacy* 37, 107–116.

Fowler, R., Hodge, R., Kress, G., & Trew, T. (1979). *Language and Control*. London: Routledge and Kegan Paul.

Garfinkel, H. (1967). *Studies in Ethnomethodology*. Cambridge: Polity.

Gibson, W. (2009). Intercultural communication online: Conversation analysis and the investigation of asynchronous written discourse. *Forum: Qualitative Social Research* 10(1), Art. 49.

Goffman, E. (1961). *Asylums: Essays on the Social Situation of Mental Patients and Other Inmates*. New York: Doubleday.

Goffman, E. (1981). *Forms of Talk*. Oxford: Blackwell.

Goffman, E. (1983). The interaction order: American Sociological Association, 1982 presidential address. *Americal Sociological Review* 48(1), 1–17.

Goldman, R. (Ed.). (2007). *Video Research in the Learning Sciences*. Mahwah, NJ: Lawrence Erlbaum Associates.

Goodings, L. (2012). Understanding social network sites: Lessons from MySpace. *Visual Communication* 11, 485–510.

Goodwin, C. (1979). The interactive construction of a sentence in natural conversation. In G. Psathas (Ed.), *Everyday Language: Studies in Ethnomethodology* (pp. 97–121). New York: Irvington.

Goodwin, C. (1981). *Conversational Organization: Interaction Between Speakers and Hearers*. New York: Academic Press.

Goodwin, C. (1994). Professional vision. *American Anthropologist* 96(3), 606–633.

Goodwin, C. (2000). Action and embodiment within situated human interaction. *Journal of Pragmatics* 32, 1489–1522.

Goodwin, C. (2001). Practices of seeing, visual analysis: An ethnomethodological approach. In T. van Leeuwen & C. Jewitt (Eds.), *The Handbook of Visual Analysis* (pp. 157–182). London: Sage.

Goodwin, C., Goodwin, M. H., & Olsher, D. (2009). Producing sense with nonsense syllables: Turn and sequence in conversations with a man with severe aphasia. In P. Griffiths, A. J. Merrison & A. Bloomer (Eds.), *Language in Use: A Reader* (pp. 272–285). London: Routledge.

Goodwin, M. H., Goodwin, C., & Yaeger-Dror, M. (2002). Multi-modality in girls' game disputes. *Journal of Pragmatics* 34, 1621–1649.

Goodwin, M., & Tulbert, E. (2011). Choreographies of attention: Multimodality in a routine family activity. In J. Streeck, C. Goodwin & C. D. LeBaron (Eds.), *Embodied Interaction: Language and Body in the Material World. Learning in Doing: Social, Cognitive and Computational Perspectives* (pp. 79–92). New York: Cambridge University Press.

Gumperz, J., & Hymes, D. (Eds.). (1964). The ethnography of communication. *American Anthropologist* 66(6), part 2.

Hak, T. (1999). 'Text' and 'con-text': Talk bias in studies of health care work. In S. Sarangi & C. Roberts (Eds.), *Talk, Work and Institutional Order: Discourse in Medical, Mediation and Management Settings* (pp. 427–452). Berlin: Mouton de Gruyter.

Hall, E. T. (1990). *The Silent Language*. New York: Anchor Books.

Halliday, M. A. K. (1976 [1956]). Grammatical categories in modern Chinese. *Transactions of the Philological Society 1956*, 180–202.

Halliday, M. A. K. (1978). *Language as Social Semiotic: The Social Interpretation of Language and Meaning*. London: Edward Arnold.

Halliday, M. A. K. (1985a). *An Introduction to Functional Grammar* (1st ed.). London: Edward Arnold.

Halliday, M. A. K. (1985b). *Spoken and Written Language*. Geelong, Victoria: Deakin University Press [republished by Oxford University Press 1989].

Halliday, M. A. K. (1994). *An Introduction to Functional Grammar* (2nd ed.). London: Edward Arnold.

Halliday, M. A. K. (2002). A personal perspective. In J. J. Webster (Ed.), *The Collected Works of M. A. K. Halliday. Volume 1. On Grammar* (pp. 1–29). New York: Bloomsbury Academic.

Halliday, M. A. K. (2003 [1977]). Ideas about language. In J. J. Webster (Ed.), *The Collected Works of M. A. K. Halliday. Volume 3. On Language and Linguistics* (pp. 92–115). New York: Bloomsbury Academic.

Halliday, M. A. K. (2004). Introduction: How big is a language? On the power of language. In J. Webster (Ed.), *The Language of Science: Collected Works of M. A. K. Halliday Volume 5* (pp. xi–xxiv). New York: Bloomsbury Academic.

Halliday, M. A. K. (2006). *The Collected Works of M. A. K. Halliday. Volume 5. The Language of Science* (Ed. by J. Webster). London; New York: Continuum.

Halliday, M. A. K. (2008). *Complementarities in Language*. Beijing: Commercial Press.

Halliday, M. A. K. (2015). The influence of Marxism. In J. J. Webster (Ed.), *The Bloomsbury Companion to M. A. K. Halliday* (pp. 94–100). New York: Bloomsbury Academic.

Halliday, M. A. K., & Fawcett, R. P. (1987). Introduction. In M. A. K. Halliday & R. P. Fawcett (Eds.), *New Developments in Systemic Linguistics, Vol. 1: Theory and Description* (pp. 1–13). London: Frances Pinter.

Halliday, M. A. K., & Hasan, R. (1985). *Language, Context, and Text: Aspects of Language in a Social-Semiotic Perspective*. Geelong, Victoria: Deakin University Press [republished by Oxford University Press 1989].

Halliday, M. A. K., & Matthiessen, C. M. I. M. (2014). *Halliday's Introduction to Functional Grammar* (4th ed., revised by C. M. I. M. Matthiessen, ed.). London; New York: Routledge.

Hammersley, M., & Traianou, A. (2012). *Ethics in Qualitative Research: Controversies and Contexts*. Thousand Oaks, CA: Sage.

Hasan, R. (2015). Systemic functional linguistics: Halliday and the evolution of a social semiotic. In J. J. Webster (Ed.), *The Bloomsbury Companion to M. A. K. Halliday* (pp. 101–134). New York: Bloomsbury Academic.

Haviland, J. (2011). Musical spaces. In J. Streeck, C. Goodwin & C. LeBaron (Eds.), *Embodied Interaction. Language and Body in the Material World* (pp. 289–304). Cambridge: Cambridge University Press.

Heath, C. (1986). *Body Movement and Speech in Medical Interaction*. Cambridge: Cambridge University Press.

Heath, C., Hindmarsh, J., & Luff, P. (2010). *Video in Qualitative Research*. London: Sage.

Heritage, J. (1997). Conversation analysis and institutional talk: Analyzing data. In David Silverman (Ed.), *Qualitative Research: Theory, Method and Practice* (pp. 161–182). London: Sage.

Herrlitz, W. (1994). Spitzen der Eisberge. Vorbemerkungen zu einer vergleichenden Analyse metonymischer Struktur in Unterricht der Standardsprache. *Osnabrücker Beiträge zur Sprachtheorie* 48, 13–52.

Hiippala, T. (2014). Multimodal genre analysis. In S. Norris & C. D. Maier (Eds.), *Interactions, Images and Texts: A Reader in Multimodality* (pp. 111–123). Berlin: De Gruyter Mouton.

Hiippala, T. (2015). *The Structure of Multimodal Documents: An Empirical Approach, Routledge Studies in Multimodality*. New York: Routledge.

Hindmarsh, J., & Heath, C. (2007). Video-based studies of work practice. *Sociology Compass* 1(1), 156–173.

Hindmarsh, J., & Pilnick, A. (2002). The tacit order of teamwork: Collaboration and embodied conduct in anesthesia. *The Sociological Quarterly* 43(2), 139–164.

Hindmarsh, J., & Pilnick, A. (2007). Knowing bodies at work: Embodiment and ephemeral teamwork in anaesthesia. *Organization Studies* 28(9), 1395–1416.

Holsanova, J. (2008). *Discourse, Vision and Cognition: Human Cognitive Processing*. Amsterdam, Philadelphia: John Benjamins.

Holsanova, J. (2012). New methods for studying visual communication and multimodal integration. *Visual Communication* 11, 251–257.

Holsanova, J. (2014a). In the mind of the beholder: Visual communication from a recipient perspective. In D. Machin (Ed.), *Visual Communication: Handbook of Communication Science* (pp. 331–354). Berlin; Boston: De Gruyter Mouton.

Holsanova, J. (2014b). Reception of multimodality: Applying eye tracking methodology in multimodal research. In C. Jewitt (Ed.), *The Routledge Handbook of Multimodal Analysis* (pp. 287–298). Abingdon, Oxon; Milton Park, Oxfordshire: Routledge.

Hutchins, E. (1995). *Cognition in the Wild*. Cambridge, MA: MIT.

Iedema, R. (2003). Multimodality, resemiotization: Extending the analysis of discourse as a multisemiotic practice. *Visual Communication* 2(1), 29–57.

Israel, M. (2015). *Research Ethics and Integrity for Social Scientists: Beyond Regulatory Compliance.* London; Thousand Oaks, CA: Sage.

Jakobson, R. (1968). *Selected Writings. Word and Language.* The Hague: Mouton and Co.

Jefferson, G. (2004). Glossary of transcript symbols with an introduction. In G. H. Lerner (Ed.). *Conversation Analysis: Studies from the First Generation* (pp: 13–31). Amsterdam: John Benjamins.

Jewitt, C. (1997). Images of men: Male sexuality in sexual health leaflets and posters for young people. *Sociological Research Online* 2(2).

Jewitt, C. (2002). Move from page to screen. *Visual Communication* 1(2), 171–196.

Jewitt, C. (2005a). Multimodal 'reading' and 'writing' on screen. *Discourse* 26(3), 315–332.

Jewitt, C. (2005b). Classrooms & the design of pedagogic discourse: A multimodal approach. *Culture & Psychology* 11(3), 309–320.

Jewitt, C. (2008a). *Technology, Literacy and Learning: A Multimodal Approach.* London: Routledge.

Jewitt, C. (2008b). Multimodal literacy in classrooms. *Review of Research in Education* 32, 241–267.

Jewitt, C. (2013). Multimodal methods for researching digital technologies. In S. Price (Ed.), *The Sage Handbook of Digital Technology Research* (pp. 250–265). London; Thousand Oaks, CA: Sage.

Jewitt, C. (Ed.). (2014). *The Routledge Handbook of Multimodal Analysis.* Abingdon, Oxon; Milton Park, Oxfordshire: Routledge.

Jewitt, C., Bezemer, J., Jones, K., & Kress, G. (2009). Changing English? The impact of technology and policy in the 21st century. *English Teaching: Practice and Critique* 8(3), 21–40.

Jewitt, C., & Kress, G. (2003). *Multimodal Literacy.* New York: Peter Lang.

Jewitt, C., Moss, G., & Cardini, A. (2007). Pace, interactivity and multimodality in teacher design of texts for IWBs. *Learning, Media and Technology* 32(3), 302–318.

Jones, C., & Ventola, E. (Eds.). (2008). *From Language to Multimodality: New Developments in the Study of Ideational Meaning.* London: Equinox.

Katz, J. J. (1972). *Semantic Theory.* New York: Harper & Row.

Kendon, A. (1990). *Conducting Interaction. Patterns of Behavior in Focused Encounters.* Cambridge: Cambridge University Press.

Kendon, A. (2004a). *Gesture: Visible Action as Utterance.* Cambridge: Cambridge University Press.

Kendon, A. (2004b). On pointing. In *Gesture: Visible Action as Utterance* (pp. 199–224). Cambridge: Cambridge University Press.

Kenner, C., & Kress, G. (2003). The multisemiotic resources of biliterate children. *Journal of Early Childhood Literacy* 3, 179–202.

Knoblauch, H., Schnettler, B., Raab, J., & Soeffner, H.-G. (Eds.). (2009). *Video Analysis: Methodology and Methods; Qualitative Audiovisual Data Analysis in Sociology* (2nd ed.). Frankfurt am Main: Peter Lang.

Koffka, K. (1935). *Principles of Gestalt Psychology*. London: Lund Humphries.

Kong, K. C. (2013). A corpus-based study in comparing the multimodality of Chinese- and English-language newspapers. *Visual Communication* 12, 173–196.

Kress, G. (2014). What is a Mode? In C. Jewitt (Ed.) *Routledge Handbook of Multi-modal Analysis* (pp. 60–75). London: Routledge.

Kress, G. R. (1993). Against arbitrariness: The social production of the sign as a foundational issue in critical discourse analysis. *Discourse & Society* 4, 169–191.

Kress, G. R. (1997). *Before Writing: Rethinking the Paths to Literacy*. London; New York: Routledge.

Kress, G. R. (2003). *Literacy in the New Media Age*. London: Routledge.

Kress, G. R. (2010). *Multimodality: A Social Semiotic Approach to Contemporary Communication*. London; New York: Routledge.

Kress, G. R., & Hodge, R. (1979). *Language as Ideology*. London; Boston: Rout-ledge/Kegan Paul.

Kress, G. R., & Hodge, R. I. V. (1988). *Social Semiotics*. Cambridge: Polity Press.

Kress, G. R., Jewitt, C., Jones, K., Franks, A., & Hardcastle, J. (2005). *English in Urban Classrooms: A Multimodal Perspective on Teaching and Learning*. London; New York: Routledge Falmer.

Kress, G. R., Jewitt, C., Ogborn, J., & Tsatsarelis, C. (2014). *Multimodal Teaching and Learning: The Rhetorics of the Science Classroom* (2nd ed.). New York: Bloomsbury Academic.

Kress, G. R., & van Leeuwen, T. (1996). *Reading Images: The Grammar of Visual Design*. London: Routledge.

Kress, G. R., & van Leeuwen, T. (2001). *Multimodal Discourse: The Modes and Media of Contemporary Communication*. London; New York: Edward Arnold/ Nottinghamshire; Oxford University Press.

Kress, G. R., & van Leeuwen, T. (2006). *Reading Images: The Grammar of Visual Design* (2nd ed.). London: Routledge.

LeBaron, C., & Streeck, J. (1997). Built space and the interactional framing of experience during a murder interrogation. *Human studies* 20(1), 1–25.

Lemke, J. (1998). Metamedia literacy: Transforming meanings and media. In D. Reinking, M. McKenna, L. Labbo & R. Kieffer (Eds.), *Handbook of Literacy and Technology: Transformations in a Post-typographic World* (pp. 283–302). Mahwah, NJ: Erlbaum.

Lemke, J. L. (2009). Multimodal genres and transmedia traversals: Social semiotics and the political economy of the sign. *Semiotica* 177(1–4), 1–27.

Levinson, S. (1983). *Pragmatics*. Cambridge: Cambridge University Press.

Liu, Y., & O'Halloran, K. L. (2009). Intersemiotic texture: Analyzing cohesive devices between language and images. *Social Semiotics* 19(4), 367–387.

Luff, P., Hindmarsh, J., & Heath, C. (2000). *Workplace Studies: Recovering Work Practice and Informing System Design*. Cambridge: Cambridge University Press.

Machin, D., & van Leeuwen, T. (2007). *Global Media Discourse: A Critical Introduction*. London; New York: Routledge.

Martin, J. R. (1992). *English Text: System and Structure*. Amsterdam: John Benjamins.

Martin, J. R. (2002). Meaning beyond the clause: SFL perspectives. *Annual Review of Applied Linguistics* 22, 52–74.

Martin, J. R., & Rose, D. (2007). *Working with Discourse: Meaning Beyond the Clause* (2nd ed.). London: Continuum.

Martin, J. R., & Rose, D. (2008). *Genre Relations: Mapping Culture*. London: Equinox.

Martinec, R., & Salway, A. (2005). A system for image–text relations in new (and old) media. *Visual Communication* 4, 337–371.

Matthiessen, C. M. I. M. (2015). Halliday on language. In J. J. Webster (Ed.), *The Bloomsbury Companion to M. A. K. Halliday* (pp. 137–202). New York: Bloomsbury Academic.

Mavers, D. (2009). Student text-making as semiotic work. *Journal of Early Childhood Literacy* 9, 141–155.

Mavers, D. (2011). *Children's Drawing and Writing: The Remarkable in the Unremarkable, Routledge Research in Education*. New York: Routledge.

Mavers, D. (2012). *Transcribing Video*. NCRM Working Paper. Unpublished Paper. http://eprints.ncrm.ac.uk/2877/4/NCRM_working_paper0512.pdf

Mehan, H. (1980). The competent student. *Anthropology & Education Quarterly* 11(3), 131–152.

Mehan, H. (1996). The construction of an LD student: A case study in the politics of representation. In M. Silverstein & G. Urban (Eds.), *Natural Histories of Discourse* (pp. 253–276). Chicago: University of Chicago Press.

Mondada, L. (2011). The organisation of concurrent courses of action surgical demonstrations. In J. Streeck, C. Goodwin & C. LeBaron (Eds.), *Embodied Interaction. Language and Body in the Material World* (pp. 207–226). Cambridge: Cambridge University Press.

Mondada, L. (2014). Instructions in the Operating Room: How the surgeon directs their assistant's hands. *Discourse Studies* 16(2), 131–161.

Moss, G. (2001). To work or play? Junior age non-fiction as objects of design. *Reading: Literacy and Language 35*, 106–110.

Newfield, D. (2014). Transformation, transduction and the transmodal moment. In C. Jewitt (Ed.), *The Routledge Handbook of Multimodal Analysis* (pp. 100–115). Abingdon, Oxon; Milton Park, Oxfordshire: Routledge.

Norris, S. (2004). *Analyzing Multimodal Interaction: A Methodological Framework*. New York: Routledge.

Norris, S. (2014). Modal density and modal configurations. In C. Jewitt (Ed.), *The Routledge Handbook of Multimodal Analysis* (pp. 86–99). Milton Park, Oxfordshire; Abingdon, Oxon: Routledge.

O'Donnell, M., & Bateman, J. (2005). SFL in computational contexts: A contemporary history. In R. Hasan, C. M. I. M. Matthiessen & J. Webster (Eds.), *Continuing Discourse on Language: Volume 1* (pp. 343–382). London: Equinox.

O'Halloran, K. L. (1999a). Interdependence, interaction and metaphor in multisemiotic texts. *Social Semiotics* 9(3), 317–354.

O'Halloran, K. L. (1999b). Towards a systemic functional analysis of multisemiotic mathematics texts. *Semiotica* 124(1/2), 1–29.

O'Halloran, K. L. (2000). Classroom discourse in mathematics: A multisemiotic analysis. *Linguistics and Education* 10(3), 359–388.

O'Halloran, K. L. (Ed.). (2004). *Multimodal Discourse Analysis*. London: Continuum.

O'Halloran, K. L. (2008). Inter-semiotic expansion of experiential meaning: Hierarchical scales and metaphor in mathematics discourse. In C. Jones & E. Ventola (Eds.), *New Developments in the Study of Ideational Meaning: From Language to Multimodality* (pp. 231–254). London: Equinox.

O'Halloran, K. L. (2011). Multimodal discourse analysis. In K. Hyland & B. Paltridge (Eds.), *Companion to Discourse Analysis* (pp. 120–137). London: Continuum.

O'Halloran, K. L. (2015a). The language of learning mathematics: A multimodal perspective. *The Journal of Mathematical Behaviour* 40, Part A, 63–74.

O'Halloran, K. L. (2015b). Mathematics as multimodal semiosis. In E. Davis & P. J. Davis (Eds.), *Mathematics, Substance, and Surmise* (pp. 287–303). Berlin: Springer.

O'Halloran, K. L. (2015c). Multimodal digital humanities. In P. Trifonas (Ed.), *International Handbook of Semiotics* (pp. 383–409). Dordrecht: Springer.

O'Halloran, K. L., Chua, A., & Podlasov, A. (2014). The role of images in social media analytics: A multimodal digital humanities approach. In D. Machin (Ed.), *Visual Communication* (pp. 565–588). Berlin: Mouton de Gruyter.

O'Halloran, K. L., E, M.K.L., Podlasov, A., & Tan, S. (2013). Multimodal digital semiotics: The interaction of language with other resources. *Text and Talk: Special Edition for Michael Halliday* (ed. by Geoff Thompson) 33(4–5), 665–690.

O'Halloran, K. L., E, M.K.L., & Tan, S. (2014). Multimodal analytics: Software and visualization techniques for analyzing and interpreting multimodal data. In C. Jewitt (Ed.), *The Routledge Handbook of Multimodal Analysis* (2nd ed., pp. 386–396). London: Routledge.

O'Halloran, K. L., & Lim, F. V. (2014). Systemic functional multimodal discourse analysis. In S. Norris & C. Maier (Eds.), *Texts, Images and Interactions: A Reader in Multimodality* (pp. 137–154). Berlin: Mouton de Gruyter.

O'Halloran, K. L., Tan, S., & E, M. K. L. (2013). 'Above all': The myth of 'dreams' as advertising tool. In B. Pennock-Speck & M. M. d. S. Rubio (Eds.), *The Multimodal Analysis of Television Commercials* (pp. 113–135). Valencia: Publicacions de la Universitat de València.

O'Halloran, K. L., Tan, S., & E, M. K. L. (2014). A multimodal approach to discourse, context and culture. In J. Flowerdew (Ed.), *Discourse in Context* (pp. 247–272). New York: Bloomsbury Academic.

O'Halloran, K. L., Tan, S., & E, M. K. L. (2015). Multimodal analysis for critical thinking. *Learning, Media and Technology.* doi: 10.1080/17439884.2016.1101003

O'Halloran, K. L., Tan, S., & Wignell, P. (in press). SFL and multimodal discourse analysis. In G. Thompson, W. L. Bowcher, L. Fontaine & J. Y. Liang (Eds.), *The Cambridge Handbook of Systemic Functional Linguistics.* Cambridge UK: Cambridge University Press.

Ormerod, F., & Ivanič, R. (2002). Materiality in children's meaning-making practices. *Visual Communication* 1, 65–91. doi:10.1177/147035720200100106

O'Toole, M. (1994). *The Language of Displayed Art.* London: Leicester University Press.

O'Toole, M. (2004). Opera ludentes: The Sydney Opera House at work and play. In K. O'Halloran (Ed.), *Multimodal Discourse Analysis: Systemic Functional Perspectives* (pp. 11–27). London: Continuum.

O'Toole, M. (2011). *The Language of Displayed Art* (2nd ed.). London; New York: Routledge.

Pahl, K. (1999). *Transformations – Meaning Making in Nursery Education*. Stoke-on-Trent, Staffordshire: Trentham Books.

Podlasov, A., & O'Halloran, K. L. (2014). Japanese street fashion for young people: A multimodal digital humanities approach for identifying socio-cultural patterns and trends. In E. Djonov & S. Zhao (Eds.), *Critical Multimodal Studies of Popular Culture* (pp. 71–90). New York: Routledge.

Price, S., Sakr, M., & Jewitt, C. (2015). Exploring whole-body interaction and design for museums. *Interacting with Computers*. doi:10.1093/iwc/iwv032

Prior, P. (2005). Moving multimodality beyond the binaries: A response to Gunther Kress' 'Gains and Losses'. *Computers and Composition* 22, 23–30.

Prosser, J., Clark, A., & Wiles, R. (2008). *Visual Research Ethics at the Crossroads*. Working Paper No. 10. ESRC National Centre for Research.

Rampton, B., Bezemer, J., Jewitt, C., & Lefstein, A. (2007). *Illustrations of Linguistic Ethnography in Action: Indicative Analyses of a Job Interview*. Unpublished manuscript. http://eprints.ncrm.ac.uk

Sacks, H., Schegloff, E., & Jefferson, G. (1974). A simplest systematics for the organization of turn-taking for conversation. *Language* 50, 696–735.

Saussure, F. de (1916/1983). *Course in General Linguistics* (Trans. by Roy Harris). London: Duckworth.

Schegloff, E. A. (2007). *Sequence Organization in Interaction: A Primer in Conversation Analysis, Vol. 1*. New York: Cambridge University Press.

Schegloff, E., & Sacks, H. (1973). Opening up closings. *Semiotica* 8, 289–327.

Scollon, R., & Wong Scollon, S. (2003). *Discourses in Place: Language in the Material World*. London: Routledge.

Silverman, D. (1999). Warriors or collaborators: Reworking methodological controversies in the study of institutional interaction. In S. Sarangi & C. Roberts (Eds.), *Talk, Work and Institutional Order* (pp. 401–425). Berlin: Mouton de Gruyter.

Silverman, D. (2011). *Interpreting Qualitative Data: A Guide to the Principles of Qualitative Research* (4th ed.). Thousand Oaks, CA: Sage.

Stein, P. (2012). *Multimodal Pedagogies in Diverse Classrooms: Representation, Rights and Resources*. London: Routledge.

Streeck, J., Goodwin, C., & LeBaron, C. (Eds.). (2011). *Embodied Interaction. Language and Body in the Material World*. Cambridge: Cambridge University Press.

Street, B. V., Pahl, K., & Rowsell, J. (2014). Multimodality and new literacy studies. In C. Jewitt (Ed.), *The Routledge Handbook of Multimodal Analysis* (pp. 227–237). Abingdon, Oxon; Milton Park/Oxfordshire: Routledge.

Suchman, L. (1987). *Plans and Situated Actions: The Problem of Human–Machine Communication*. Cambridge: Cambridge University Press.

Tarlo, E. (2007). Islamic cosmopolitanism: The sartorial biographies of three Muslim women in London. *Fashion Theory: The Journal of Dress, Body & Culture* 11(2–3), 143–172.

Thompson, G. (2004). *Introducing Functional Grammar*. London: Edward Arnold.

Thompson, G., Bowcher, W. L., Fontaine, L., & Liang, J. Y. (Eds.). (in press). *The Cambridge Handbook of Systemic Functional Linguistics*. Cambridge: Cambridge University Press.

Tuan, Y.-F. (1991). Language and the making of place. *Annals of the Association of American Geographers* 81, 684–696.

Unsworth, L. (2007). Image/text relations and intersemiosis: Towards multimodal text description for multiliteracies education. In L. Barbara & T. Sardinha (Eds.), *Proceedings of the 33rd International Systemic Functional Congress. Presented at the 33rd International Systemic Functional Congress* (pp. 1165–1205). Sao Paulo, Brazil: PUCSP.

Unsworth, L. (Ed.). (2008). *Multimodal Semiotics: Functional Analysis in Contexts of Education*. New York: Continuum.

Unsworth, L., & Cleirigh, C. (2009). Multimodality and reading: The construction of meaning through image–text interaction. In C. Jewitt (Ed.), *The Routledge Handbook of Multimodal Research* (pp. 151–163). London; New York: Routledge.

van Leeuwen, T. (1991). Conjunctive structure in documentary film and television. *Journal of Media and Cultural Studies* 5(1), 76–114.

van Leeuwen, T. (1999). *Speech, Music, Sound*. London: Macmillan.

van Leeuwen, T. (2005). *Introducing Social Semiotics*. London: Routledge.

van Leeuwen, T. (2008). *Discourse and Practice: New Tools for Critical Discourse Analysis*. Oxford: Oxford Univerity Press.

Ventola, E., Charles, C., & Kaltenbacher, M. (Eds.). (2004). *Perspectives on Multimodality*. Amsterdam: John Benjamins.

Ventola, E., & Moya, J. (Eds.). (2009). *The World Told and the World Shown: Multisemiotic Issues*. Basingstoke, Hampshire: Palgrave Macmillan.

Wittenburg, P., Brugman, H., Russel, A., Klassmann, A., & Sloetjes, H. (2006). ELAN: A professional framework for multimodality research. *In Proceedings of LREC 2006, Fifth International Conference on Language Resources and Evaluation* (pp. 1556–1559), May 22–28. Genoa, Italy.

Wodak, R. (2006). Critical linguistics and critical discourse analysis. In J. Verschueren & J.-O. Östman (Eds.), *Handbook of Pragmatics* [2006 installment] (pp. 1–24). Amsterdam; Philadelphia: John Benjamins.

# Index

Note: Tables and figures are indicated by italicized page numbers.